# CONCRETE, BULLETPROOF, INVISIBLE & FRIED

**Also by Chris Connelly**

*Confessions of the Highest Bidder*

*Ed Royal*

# CONCRETE, BULLETPROOF, INVISIBLE & FRIED

## MY LIFE AS A REVOLTING COCK

CHRIS CONNELLY

SHIPWRECKED INDUSTRIES

First edition published in 2007 and reprinted in 2010 by SAF Publishing in the UK.
Second edition published in 2014 by Shipwrecked Industries in the USA.

ISBN 978-0-9664065-5-9

*Also available in ebook and audiobook formats.*

www.chrisconnelly.com
www.shipwreckedindustries.com

*For*
*Jim, Tucker, Tracey & Raven.*

# FOREWORD

"And who might you be?"

It's late morning and I've just woken. I'm on the couch in the front of the Pigface bus rubbing the sleep out of my eyes. Chris Connelly stands before me, smiling, awaiting a response.

"I'm… Jolene."

What I didn't tell him is that I'd hitched a ride on the band's bus in Cleveland. I was offered to come along to Detroit when my friend—who was also my ride home—wanted some alone time with one of the roadies. That was fine by me. I always found the tour bus an exciting place to be. Not wanting to miss out on the general chatter amongst those still awake, I fought to keep my sleepy eyes open when one of the crew guys offered me a "bump". My eyes lit up as I assumed this was some sort of mysterious new slang word for a spongy, pink, marshmallow-covered chocolate cake, also known as the Hostess Sno Ball. Sadly, I was mistaken and therefore declined.

I was a shy sort of groupie. I would find my way backstage and be perfectly content to listen in on what my favorite musicians had to say. And I was always beyond thrilled when they had something to say to me in particular. I'd been a fan of Chris' ever since the summer of 1986, and when he spoke to me on that day in the early 90s, I was too shy to converse. How does one respond when asked by one of your favorite musicians who you are… and why you're on their tour bus? Thankfully, at that point, someone else came onto the bus and I happily returned to being the quiet observer.

Back in those days, bands like Pigface, RevCo, Ministry, and Skinny Puppy didn't perform in Toledo, Ohio, where I was from. Attending shows generally required taking day trips that were painstakingly difficult due the combined factors of "who would drive?", "would we have enough gas money?", "would the car break down?", or "should we take a Greyhound?" If we managed to arrive at the venue before the show started, we were victorious.

Discovering new music in the 80s and early 90s was not quite as easy as it is today. There was no Spotify, Pandora, or YouTube, and being from a midwestern town that embraced mainstream hair bands at the time, one couldn't count on the radio for anything more than Top 40 or classic rock. If you were lucky enough to have paid Cablevision, you could tune in on Sunday nights to watch *120 Minutes*, which featured more eclectic acts. Another fun way to discover new music was by way of the pen-pal scene, in which I was an active participant.

If you were absolutely compelled to try to converse with your favorite bands, it took a lot more effort than simply creating a Twitter or Facebook account. A dedicated fan had to be more creative back then. I reached out to many musicians through land mail and, to my surprise, heard back from several, including Kevin Ogilvie (Ogre) from Skinny Puppy and Ronny Moorings from Clan of Xymox. I've always been interested in the mind of the musician and their creative process—and I can't explain why—but I was always shocked when they showed their vulnerable sides; the side behind the stage persona. This is what makes Chris' book is such an enjoyable read. Each page induces hearty chuckles and takes me back to the Wax Trax! days, when a Walkman and a handful of mix tapes were essential.

A gifted storyteller, Chris writes as though he's speaking directly to you, just telling you how it was. Stories from the past, and the struggles to find success with an diverse mix of creative personalities in, what Chris refers to as, "Reagan's America". An articulate and candid account of what wasn't clearly visible from the outside, *Concrete, Bulletproof, Invisible and Fried* is definitely a trip down memory lane that you don't want to miss.

Jolene Siana
Author, *Go Ask Ogre: Letters from a Deathrock Cutter*
Brooklyn, New York 2014

# PREFACE

The inspiration to write a book came from my reaction to the very public and grossly fabricated stories that Al Jourgensen decided to start telling about his former partner, Paul Barker, in the press.

Paul left Ministry. I have never pressed him for his reasons, perhaps because I know why; in my opinion, after decades of keeping the Ministry ship floating, being a devoted and faithful friend, and cleaning up Al's Herculean messes, maybe Paul got sick of it. I know there had to be a straw breaking a leather-clad camel's back in there at the end, but that's between Al and Paul.

Then, out of the stormy sky, appeared the Cocks back catalogue, re-mastered—with bonus tracks, no less—on the Rykodisc label. Someone—not me, Paul, Bill, or Luc—had either licensed or sold it without asking anyone. Someone—not me, Paul, Bill, or Luc—had redone the graphics so that there were a LOT of current pictures of AL sprawled all over the beige-tinted artwork, but there were very few images of Paul. Gosh, who would do that?

Times were hard—speaking for myself—so I wrote to Al's attorney, asking, politely but firmly, why the fuck no one was consulted.

I got a beautifully and artfully drafted missive back from the Jourgensen camp, letting me know, in no uncertain terms, that I was "cowardly", "a greedy parasite", "an asshole", "ungrateful" and "snotty"—"no WONDER Al used drugs for so long"!

I was also told that I was "welcome" for the bump in my royalties that these reissues would generate. I'm still waiting for that because, of course, nobody cared—nobody bought the crappy reissues.

Furthermore, if I told anyone about this letter, they said, I would be sued. I sent it to everyone I knew, to much hilarity.

I was single-handedly responsible for Al taking drugs. My God, the hunter gets captured by the game!!!!!

# PROLOGUE

## SAY IT WITH SATAN

December 1992. The post-Lollapalooza, post-*Psalm 69*-is-a-fucking-hit-album touring concern is packing up and leaving some stupid, ass-fuck sports arena in stupid, ass-fuck Seattle. I am on the bus being a stupid ass-fuck, a rolled up bill in my nose, with some of the rest of the band —and the singer from Sepultura, one of the opening bands, who is along for the ride. (Perhaps he had a tiff with the missus—who is also, maybe, Sepultura's tour manager?—I don't know.) But he is sitting, talking to me, Roland Barker, and maybe Louis Svitek. He is a soft-spoken Brazilian… a little shy, and very sweet. We are talking about music and he eventually starts talking about how much he loves Ministry.

"Thanks, man, that's very nice of you," we murmur. But he does not stop.

"You know, man, I mean that from the HEART," he says, with a little more emphasis, whilst thumping his chest softly with his right fist. He goes on like this for a little too long, making us all feel a bit uncomfortable.

"What do you think of my band?" he asks.

I think they're God-awful, but I like them as people. I feel terrible as I open my mouth up to lie. "Great, man, you guys are great."

Roland concurs. "Yeah, man, we watch your show every night…"

Suddenly all bets are off as the diminutive, soft-spoken Brazilian's eyes roll back in his head and his face turns from long-haired Labrador pup into dreadlocked tarantula.

"SAY SEPULTURA'S YOUR FAVOURITE BAND! SAY IT!!!" His voice has turned into the satanic death metal voice. "SAY-IT-FROM-THE-HEEEEART!" He points at me, then Roland.

"Urrrm… Sepultura's my favourite band!" we state shakily.

"NO!!!! SAY IT LIKE YOU MEAN IT!! Say Sepultura's your favourite band of all time!!!!"

Roland and I are backed into a corner with this demented metal warlord from South America. The bus is moving. There doesn't seem to be anyone else around except him and us. If we ran to the driver for help he's probably turn out to be Freddy Krueger. The death metal tarantula is advancing on us.

"SAAAAAAY IT!!!!!"

Then, all of a sudden, Al appears, swooping down like Superman brandishing a pharmacopeia in each fist. "Come on man, take some of these," he says, giving the Genghis Khan of crap speed metal some Valium.

He takes them. We all wait. He continues some kind of rant, a little more gingerly with his demands now that El Supreme is here. The "SAY IT!" becomes more polite. Like, "YOU SHOULD REALLY SAY SEPULTURA'S YOUR FAVOURITE BAND," then, "OH I DO WISH YOU'D SAY SEPULTURA'S YOUR FAVOURITE BAND." Slower, slower, softer, softer-and then, "BAAAAAAAAAAAAAAAAAAH WE ARE GOING TO TAKE OVER THE WORLD! SEPULTURA SEPULTURAAAA!"

Fuck! Are you sure these were Valiums and not Ritalin or some other terrifying stimulant they give to Berserker warriors prior to battle? He is ROARING through the bus—everyone is awake. He is spinning around in a Jesus Christ pose, "BAAAAAAAAAAAAAAAAH HA HA HA HA!!" until, finally, spectators face a mask of heavy metal HORROR. He pukes his weight in vomit and collapses, either asleep or dead.

Okay… question: How did a nice wee boy from Edinburgh end up careening down Interstate 5 in the middle of the night with a puking, demented, Brazilian death metal singer?

*WELL?????*

**Above:** My UK passport with US visa, secured just in time for these adventures.

# 1

# BEGINNING TIMES

That's me! Dramatically conspicuous amongst the blandly grazing travellers moving around the international gate of Manchester Airport, uncomfortable in my sorry attempt at "smart but casual": blue-checked Marks & Spencer shirt tucked into my jeans, Doctor Martens as shiny as I can get them, everything a bit too wide for my emaciated frame, but, let's face it, as smart as I am going to get, given my wardrobe of army fatigues and cigarette smoke and my diet of speed and cigarette smoke.

I was boarding an American Airlines flight to Chicago; it was my first time. Everyone had told me that given my history and general demeanour, they would turn me away at customs in the USA—but for now, each step of the pre-boarding procedure was a major victory for me, pulling a fast one on the scrubbed, flawless and mildly robotic American Airlines staff. There was probably something encrypted into the fabric of my passport saying "known drug abuser", "unemployed and unemployable", "Goddamn anarcho-communo-lefty sheep-shagging cross-dressin' son of a bitch!"—but they can't have caught the encryption, because they let me board the plane without any fuss. For better or for worse, I was on my way to Reagan's America.

For me 1987, and 1986 for that matter, were bad years in music. It seemed like all the exciting underground bands had either split, or peaked and levelled off, tired of not selling records, wanting a bit of the chart action and major label pampering that people like the Zodiac Mindwarp, The Cult and… um… Curiosity Killed the Cat were having. Bands that had once been at the vanguard of extreme sounds like Test Department, Cabaret Voltaire, SPK, the Virgin Prunes, etc., were no longer threatening and dangerous, and had become either wilfully bland and dancey in a kind of off-brand-New Order way, or they had become victims of their own hype, or—worse still—Arts Council grant whores. The Smiths were over, Public Image was a sing-a-long Christmas panto tragedy, and everything else had just ceased to be interesting. The Beastie Boys were huge, *License to Ill* having hit big, but I personally always disliked their shtick—I hate people who talk too much, and they never seemed to shut up.

The early 80s had shown such promise, with the dual escalation of noisy, atonal, industrial music coupled with a strong DIY mentality. Throw a rock in any direction in 1981 and you'd hit someone's homemade cassette album or LP with a Xeroxed, pasted-on cover. Out of this had risen labels like Some Bizarre, ultra-hip purveyors of very strange records. They managed—albeit only for a short while—to license these records to major labels on the strength of their very own synth-pop cash cow, Soft Cell. However, this short-lived victory by such subversives put paid to much of DIY's success—the populous does not put really weird records into the charts, and really weird records cannot scrub up like Jon Bon Jovi or Terence Trent D'Arby, sneaking into the charts without anyone noticing. It was kind of like Peter Sutcliffe or John Wayne Gacy showing up at your party wearing Dolce & Gabbana and trying to charm the pants off the ladies.

In late 1986, I had just turned twenty-two, my band the Fini Tribe had reached somewhat of an impasse, and I was bored out of my mind. I was a craver. I craved things all the time. I was very rarely satisfied: fame, drugs, drink, records, and women—maybe in that order, but not necessarily, depending on how much of the second two I'd had. I wanted them, as well as adventure, but at that time in Thatcher's Britain I was completely penniless, like so many, which kind of negated everything on my list except the women and adventure—there was no charge for these.

A series of semi-related events led me to the Revolting Cocks: I had been working part time for an independent distributor called Fast Forward—we supplied record shops north of the border with all indie releases from Depeche Mode to Crass, and everything in between. There was not really any pay, but my boss and co-workers were refreshingly nihilistic, and there was a constant flow of speed and hash, as well as free records. One week I picked up *Big Sexy Land* by the Revolting Cocks. I was drawn to it because it had an enchanting image on the cover of a topless girl kissing a doc. I listened to it, and something clicked. It was something new, noisy—I loved my noise!—yet kind of danceable. It was different sonically to the Fini Tribe—we were more organic, where the Cocks were synthetic—but still, this was the closest to what we were doing I had ever heard, and we needed some kindred spirits. More than that, I intended to be a Revolting Cock. The record had a label and a London telephone number. I called and spoke to a very friendly American woman called Allison. I told her I loved the record and I would tell every record shop in Scotland how great it was, and could I come to London and play her a tape of my band? Any time, she told me.

Every few months for the previous seven years, a delegation from my band had gone down to London on the overnight coach, clutching a new demo and no money. Trawling around the record companies was just soul destroying. Absolutely no one cared about the Fini Tribe, to the point where we started arranging meetings with the real biggies like Arista and CBS, invading their offices with cassettes of shrill feedback experiments just to try and coax a little notoriety, if not a recording budget.

It was with this very much in mind that I boarded the overnight bus at St. Andrews' bus station in Edinburgh's East End one cold November night in 1986. I had with me a cassette of the latest Fini Tribe effort, a tin of tobacco and some Rizla papers, about five quid, and the address of someone who apparently knew someone and was happy to let me crash for a night of two—there was, luckily, an extended network of friends, old school friends, and ex-lovers/partners (people didn't really have boyfriends or girlfriends in the role-defying 80s) who had drifted south for various reasons, ranging from the artistic to the political via the Collegiate (hello Angus Cameron, Mary Brown, Meriel Scott). Anyway, like I said, there was always floor space.

(Someone should really write a book about squats. I remember staying at one squat that was a whole street of semi-detached houses in north London all knocked together so you could walk the length of the street indoors via huge gaping holes in the walls. Just as well, because the only working toilet was at the end in the last house.)

The coach would pull up behind King's Cross at about 7 AM, your waking moments a churning blur of bad driving and various aches from sleeping upright all night. Now there were few hours to kill until your hosts may awaken, or the office doors of your possible future record company would swing open for you.

The friendly American woman, Allison, was even more friendly in person. Tall and big, definitely not fat, but easily six feet with a shock of spiky, blonde hair. She had one of these weird in-betweeny accents that was decidedly American—however, occasionally it would veer shockingly into cockney ("I'm ganna fix us a cup ah caffee, ROIGHT??"). She seemed to really like the tape I played her, and after showing me around Southern Studios (an unassuming, almost suburban house in N22) and introducing me to the staff, she asked me if I wanted to meet Al Jourgensen, who was working on a new Ministry album right now in the actual studio, which was housed in the garage outside across the back garden.

I was fully expecting him to look like an updated refugee from a Bosch or Bruegel painting, or Gerard Depardieu in a leather duster coat and acting like a giant, pompous intellectual Belgian (his name was spelled "Alain" on the record covers, and I knew that at least one other Revolting Cock was a Belgian), so I could not have been more shocked when I was introduced to a maniacally grinning American; short, with a bird's nest of dirty, bleach-blonde hair, shades, and a classic rock 'n' roll personality.

I can't express how thrown I was, because I expected something more nihilistic and misanthropic, sombre and humourless, whose manifesto I would have to endure. However, sombre and humourless he definitely was not, brooding he was not either.

He suggested that we "go out for pints" to the favoured pub in the neighbourhood. So, out for pints we went... at 11 AM. Me, Al and Allison—Al regaling me with incredible tales of debauchery, the likes of which would bring the entire culture of ancient Rome to its knees in awe, and all of which had taken place in THIS VERY SAME PUB! And but a few hours ago, apparently! He had been thrown out, crept back in, and got into a fistfight with the DJ over a wig, bought tons of speed ("fuckin' ass loads of Sulphate, man!"), snorted it all, and then fucked every woman in Wood Green. He told me stories about the studio, about Jah Wobble's legendary drunkenness, Lee Perry's legendary madness, Adrian Sherwood's legendary loudness, and the Jesus and Mary Chain's sulkiness.

A couple of pints into our "breakfast meeting", Al asked if I wanted to sing on something—like NOW, as in that morning. I enthusiastically accepted his offer, and immediately my brain started to browse around the leftover lyrics department for odds and ends I could concoct into something useable. I kind of wanted to sell myself, or rather, elbow myself into the gig either singing for Ministry or the Cocks or whatever other cockamamie ideas he had. So a few lagers later it was back to the studio where, within a few minutes, a taxi mysteriously appeared, its sole passengers a carton of cigarettes and a bottle of scotch. I wasn't about to question this heaven-sent delivery, just like I wasn't about to question the huge bag of speed that appeared like a paper rose in a magician's hand. All bases were covered, I suppose... these magic tricks and hedonistic gifts would continue to be a wonder for years to come.

Al played me the track he had in mind, at absolute ear-splitting volume, naturally. I would quickly learn that Al did everything at ear-splitting volume—just as well he wasn't a cat burglar. The track itself had a long introduction of brooding bass and metallic percussion before exploding into a veritable Dunkirk ambush of guitars at breakneck speed. It was hardcore punk played by machines, and it sounded pretty fresh, apart from owing a considerable debt to Foetus. (Jim Thirlwell, aka Scraping Foetus off the Wheel, You've got Foetus on your Breath, etc., etc. is the instigator when it comes to the marriage of machinery to hardcore punk.) It was not at all what I was expecting, but that didn't stop me from doing a series of inhuman lines of speed and improvising a cacophony of vocals over it. After a while it was mayhem, Al threw an extreme harmonizer effect on my voice that made it sound like a rabble of drunken Freddy Kreugers giving a motivational speech to the Third Reich. I was thrilled! Al seemed happy as well and started making noises about releasing it as a Revolting Cocks 12-inch (12-inch singles and EPs were almost more common than albums back then). The song would eventually come out as *I Will Refuse,* with different lyrics and vocals sung by Minor Threat/Fugazi singer Ian MacKaye, under the band name Pailhead. (This didn't bother me, it was an honour to be erased by Ian.)

Anyway, at the time I took this to be my formal *entrée* into the Cocks, and into Al's domain. I would learn that the Cocks' last singer, a gentleman named Richard 23, who actually WAS a nihilistic and rather pompous Belgian as well as being a self-professed "dance commando" with a daft haircut and a helicopter fetish, had left the band in a huff over an argument about the band's latest single, "You Often Forget". So, the post open, I giddily accepted the position in a haze of Al's exaggerated predictions for the band over the noise of the speakers. However, it was time for me to leave and get the overnight coach back to Edinburgh. It was mid-evening and I was completely fucked-up after a day of speed and scotch. I needed to make my way by Tube across London to King's Cross, jumping over turnstiles because I didn't have any money. Fortunately, because I was speeding my balls off, this proved to be a piece of cake… I made the coach with minutes to spare, found a seat and twitched, wide-eyed and legless, until dawn.

Al's whole world seemed like a punk-rock quantum leap. "You're loud? We're louder!" "You don't care? We care less!" The most attractive thing about it seemed to be Al's policy of upgrading his technology and immediately abusing it so all of his gear had a *Mad Max* quality in appearance. Bands like Sigue Sigue Sputnik had tried to do this techno-punk thing but had ended up being the butt end of everyone's jokes—they just weren't dangerous, they were simply a grim reminder of what happened if you gave an A&R executive coke and a big budget. They bombed, of course, just like their "Love Missile F-111" single. Kaboom! This was life in the post-Frankie music world when, thanks to Trevor Horn, the yuppie mentality had crept into the subculture. It was all contrived outrage to generate money. Nothing really new, but Horn had just taken Malcolm McLaren's concept, spliced it with prog rock, and let it loose on the dance floor scented with L'Oreal hair gel. I didn't hate it, but neither did I sport a "Frankie Says Relax" T-shirt.

Al was turning something loose on the dance floor as well, but it was more like the Lockerbie disaster. The music weeklies were grubbing around in the dirt in '86/'87, desperately looking for new punk, but it wasn't happening. Everything was being played out in Filofaxes, in wine bars, and anything remotely interesting had been sent scurrying into a subgenre as Mick Hucknall's banshee bleat carved up the airwaves. There was no way that punk was returning to the UK—but the summer of love was, house and rave culture being just around the corner. The UK did not want Al's assault of dance beats—but America did, in spades.

Up to this point, Edinburgh—actually the whole of the UK—had not been very nice to the Fini Tribe. We had been at it in one form or another for about seven years—but that whole saga is another book. We steadfastly stuck to our erratic path: dedicating ourselves wholly to the music we created, yet trying to encourage kinship with other bands, to little avail, although we certainly had our allies in the early days. At some point this turned sour, and we decided to just say "fuck off" back to the smarmy mid-80s, when such truly revolutionary acts such as the Visitors, the Associates, the Fire Engines, and Josef K had the run of the Scottish club scene. We were now in a netherworld of, on the one hand, high-budget bombast acts like the dreadful Wet Wet Wet, and on the other, the bed-wetting under achievers, such as the BMX Bandits and the Pastels—always out of tune and behind the beat, and always, always unfriendly. There was also a palpable delight and relief when anyone failed in their endeavours to achieve any kind of artistic success, coupled with a sickening disappointment when people became successful. This is a very common British trait, something to do with the class system and not rising above the level you were born into. It's all very ugly and boring. Anyway, the minute news leaked out that not only had the Fini's scored a deal with a "transatlantic" label with a pretty hip cache, as well as me becoming the Cocks' singer, the atmosphere of the anticipation of failure was electric amongst the gossiping hairdos in line at the DHSS. This, coupled with the fact that the very name Revolting Cocks was, in the eyes of the humourless short-haired Edinburgh University P.C. fascisti, completely sexist, meant that overnight the Fini Tribe, and especially me, went from barely tolerated to loathed. However, in Edinburgh, this would never manifest itself in confrontation—merely back-stabbing and innuendo.

Over the next few months, we kept ourselves busy recording and mixing, rehearsing, and finally going to London to hand over the new Fini Tribe EP entitled *The Sheer Action of Fini Tribe* to our new label. It was at that time that we met Paul Barker, who was going to remix our single for us. He named his price—twenty-four cans of lager (which he shared)—but we were a little in awe as he was in Ministry. His demeanour with us was of a zealously enthusiastic science teacher supervising an after-school club; a good-natured team player who knew when to reign us in. The rest of the Southern people took to us and rather enjoyed six excitable, shaven-headed Scots having run of the place.

After endearing ourselves to the staff of Southern, we packed up our hangovers and headed back to Scotland. A few days after returning, I tried to call Al in the States, standing in a telephone box (no phone in my flat) with a small stack of 50 pence pieces. (I have no idea how I came across this small fortune. I think I broke into our gas meter.) I managed to get Al on the line; he launched immediately into one of his "IT'S GONNA BE

FUCKIN' WICKED MAN, THIS ALBUM'S…"—when the phone booth door opened, two cops grabbed me and shoved me into the back of their car. I was more bewildered by the fact that we were probably fifty feet away from Gayfield Square Police Station, where they were clearly taking me. I really just happened to be the nearest warm body within proximity to the station. Anyway, one hour in a holding cell and then the two jokers drove me to a tenement block halfway down Leith Walk. Up the stairs and a knock on the door where a harassed-looking, forty year-old man opened and said immediately, "That's no' him. About a foot shorter, fat, wi' curly black hair!" I was free to go and, with a few embellishments, I could call back Al and tell him exactly about how thin a tightrope I walked through the mean streets of Edinburgh.

Touching down in Chicago for the first time and deplaning—Americans deplane, doesn't everyone else in the world simply disembark or get off?—even in the short space from the aircraft to the terminal, I could tell that everything was different: cleaner, blander, and more nasal than home. Twanging, preppy voices repeated themselves over and over again via tannoys, with the enthusiasm of a parent expounding to a reluctant child about the heroic properties of green beans. I was bracing myself for the inevitable herd of uniformed men who were just about to descend on me and whisk me off for some debriefing ending in violence, and me being jettisoned back from whence I came. I was almost glad that it would be over soon. I had presented my passport and been ushered through, suddenly there were glass doors and daylight and real yellow taxis. They must have found someone far more unemployed and drug hungry than I.

I had nothing tangible to really base a reality on. Where did Al live? In a skyscraper, I imagined. In America, one lives in a skyscraper, or in a shack on a plain somewhere, or maybe in a trailer like Jim Rockford.

"Was *Hill Street Blues* filmed here? I swear that's a guy from *Hill Street Blues*."

"Why does everything smell like caramel corn?"

Everything looked the way Bon Jovi sounds. Eventually I spotted Al when he ran up and gave me a hug and introduced Dannie Flesher, one of the partners of Wax Trax! Records, who was good enough to come and get me. Al thrust a Walkman into my hand and ordered me to listen. I put it on. The "play" button wouldn't depress. After a cursory inspection, lasting about five seconds, Al hammered the Walkman against a pillar in the baggage terminal. After slamming it hard about twenty times, it smashed into several pieces, so he left it where it was while I retrieved my suitcase.

Dannie's car turned out to be a huge, gold Jaguar. He relaxed behind the wheel with a menthol in his mouth, speaking with a soft southern accent. Nothing seemed to faze him; he would become one of my pillars of sanity in years to come. Al was a mile-a-minute as he spun stories on the way into the city. These fictions concerned two things: what he did last night, and what we would be doing tonight—and how shit-face fucked-up we would get doing whatever it was. Apparently, only a few hours ago, he'd been thrown out of every bar in Chicago, had fisticuffs with every DJ in Chicago, and, of course, he'd fucked the entire female population of Chicago. Dannie, aviator shades, one hand on the wheel, cig in mouth, punctuated all of this with a low, cool chuckle.

Eventually, we arrived at the Wax Trax! Lincoln Avenue empire on Chicago's North Side. Rather than the colossal skyscrapers, wailing sirens, and screaming passers-by I was fully expecting, it was a somewhat collegiate and semi-residential neighbourhood. There were a couple of small cinemas, a few restaurants—a nice, little middle class scene. Of course, this is hindsight. I was fully certain that the Latin Kings or some other random trigger-happy gang were just around the corner, waiting to mug me for my Amex traveller's cheques. The Wax Trax! office was an apartment above the Wax Trax! record store, and I was led up to be immediately introduced to the self-named "El Presidente" Jim Nash, who turned out to be an instantly loveable music fanatic. Camp and hilarious, a kind of indie rock John Waters, he had a desk in a large office in the front along with his niece, Liz, a loud woman with a southern accent who seemed to be an amalgam of a few generations of Robert Altman characters. Information was relayed to me from different corners of the room. There is this kind of talk that comes—perhaps this is peculiar only to me—when I seem to be invited into an alien situation. People always seem to assume that I know exactly what they are talking about: usually bands, people in bands, records, remixes, how great they might be, or how this guy is full of shit, etc. Well, I give a pretty good nod-and-smile routine, and as a joint and a tumbler of scotch were pushed into my paw, the routine kicked in well. I had no idea what anyone was talking about, but I was beginning to feel at home.

I was not used to smoking "grass" like they do in the US. In Scotland, we smoked hash in joints with tobacco mainly, so I was not prepared for the double bludgeoning of the grass and the scotch. I started to get that feeling that I was wearing someone else's glasses, along with the usual feelings that come with transatlantic flights. What better time for Al to whisk me off to Chicago Trax studio where he was recording, and where we would be recording now, and for the next eternity?

I must have given the impression that Al's new protégé was this chalk-white, glassy-eyed Scot who couldn't speak. This was apparently okay, as all these engineers and studio employees seemed very pleased to meet me and there were vigorous smiles and handshakes all round, like I had just won some kind of an award. Being from Scotland, a place where we are much more prone to a nod and a grunt, handshakes were really thought of as strange, maybe even sexist, depending on your proximity to the Edinburgh University student union. Anyway, by contrast, it seemed like in the US you shook hands with everyone, no matter how slight your interaction was going to be. It was as if you entered into some kind of mutual contract for the duration of the interaction, which may well lead to bear hugs and utterances of "I love you, man" on subsequent meetings. I do not mention this out of any phobia or mean-spiritedness. I am happy to shake hands, but I have met some train-wrecks in the past who really deem it essential to squeeze the life out of you after you come back from the toilet.

I mentioned to Al excitedly that I had heard that Trax was the epicentre of the exploding Chicago house scene—at that time becoming huge in the UK. I learned immediately that Al "hates that pussy shit, man". I would also learn that, unlike the UK, America never, ever, fell out of love with the electric guitar, and especially the solos and volume that come with it. Bands that would be put in stocks in any British town in the 1980s, like Aerosmith or Def Leppard, never fell out of favour in the US. I also found out that this is partly why Al won't ever talk about his tenure with Arista Records, where apparently they held a loaded gun to his head and made him dress up like a four-year-old girl, the scoundrels! Then they threw him into a studio and forced him—again at gunpoint— to record an album that sounded like a collection of Thompson Twins' out-takes. THE MONSTERS!!

I was introduced to the two owners of the studio: Reid took care of the pen-pushing, while Buster fixed broken equipment. Both amusing characters in their own right, I would witness years of abuse and teasing that Al levelled at that pair. Reid was a tubby, bearded, and mulletted (all the staff were mulletted or permed), shifty-eyed individual who punctuated every sentence with a nervous laugh. "A-HEE-HEE? A-HEE-HEE?" Buster, on the other hand, was slight and feisty with a huge, dick-tickling moustache that dwarfed his entire head. His usual stance was shrugging his shoulders with a pained expression going "Nyeeeeeeeah", as in, "Ah, whatcha gonna do?" This was usually in response to some recorded masterwork that had been chewed up irretrievably by one of the studio's tape machines.

After leaving the studio, we got a taxi to Al's apartment. On the way I learned that he was married with an infant daughter. I had assumed him to be some kind of bachelor. Who got married these days? Weird. I was fading fast and it was still light outside. I didn't want to meet anyone else, but Al had the rest of the day planned well into the late, late hours, and I was kind of at his mercy. Hang in there. I met Mrs Jourgensen: tall, rail thin, long crimped red hair. The first thing I noticed about *chez Jourgensen* is that you could not reach out two feet in any direction without being able to touch a remote control, a pack of Marlboro Lights, or a can of hairspray. Indeed, these things are the staple of any Jourgensen diet, and would remain that way until he lost much of his hair. Patti Jourgensen turned out to be rather striking looking, with a mouth and attitude that appeared to be more than able to deal with her husband. Their little girl was adorable, and I realized my safest bet here was to get down on the carpet and start playing with the child. There was LEGO and crayons and paper, and I had no need to be coherent. Also, I won points with the parents by being a "helpful" guest.

Time turned into a revolving entity and I was not sure which thoughts had begun, or ended, or simply not finished. I do know that I made matters worse by drinking and smoking more. I do know that I was taken out to the Orbit Room, a nightclub on the North Side, and that I shook more hands in the loud, pulsing disco, Al gesticulating and yelling incomprehensibly, backwards and forwards, wild-eyed, probably spinning tales about what I had done, and what I was about to do.

What I WAS about to do was collapse, (blank) taxi (blank) motion (blank) doog thgin dna uoyknaht!!!!

Handwritten note on photo: 11:59 we'll take this & put it on Wax 028 royalties.

**Top left:** Christmas in Golders Green, London, December 1987.

**Top right:** With Jim Nash of Wax Trax!

**Bottom:** Working at the Wax Trax! store with Frank Nardiello.

# 2

## IN THE NECK

The next ten days were little more than a very surreal adjustment period. Al lived with his wife and kid in an apartment just a few doors north of the Wax Trax! store, and I was staying in the attic, which served as a third bedroom. Although I was now meeting all of Al's many friends, I couldn't quite place his position in the social strata, and it was hard for me to tell who was a friend, who was an acquaintance, and who was "just a fuckin' jagoff, man". There were certainly a lot of enthusiastic sycophants who seemed to hang on to his every world when he held court. I think that Al's tenure at Arista, despite his near pathological phobia and hatred regarding that time—though, with Al, the usual ratio was at least 70% theatre in almost everything—seemed to have earned him a "been there, done that" cache. He had indeed survived the brutal pop star machine that spat people out dancing with parachute pants, a cane, and 4 AM drag queen make-up. Al had come back fighting and enraged, tearing off the Boy George smock and the 40-inch diameter bolero hat, screaming and flailing his little wrists. People regarded him with awe, and people wanted to be his friend, understandably. It's cool to know someone with a story like that. Al had, by his own definition, "sold out", but soon his atonement would be absolute. This was just the beginning now; he had traded in aerobicizer synth-pop for something very dark, violent, and, as time would prove, completely marketable.

In all fairness, the man had been teased mercilessly and needlessly by many of his peers. That's Chicago for you. Very early on it seemed Steve Albini threw down a gauntlet of piously heterosexual indie rock to Wax Trax!'s gay dance club overtones, and it had a trickle-down effect that never went away. At least, that's the way I read it. (One thing is for certain: Albini and Al, not about to go fishing together.)

Al had something to prove. I think he still does. It was like he was a little boy who had been caught red-handed applying lipstick. It was strange though, because most of Al's immediate support system was gay, or open minded enough to allow the occasional Soft Cell/Tears for Fears facsimile. Having said that, maybe it wasn't the effected camp foppishness or the completely synthetic nature of the music, maybe it was that *With Sympathy* was a crappy record; an insipid Anglophile's cry for help in an American sea of Rick Springfields and Tommy Tutones.

So when I arrived on the scene, Al was still trying to earn his bad boy image, and build this new Al that ate children and injected drugs into his eyeballs. Part of the process had been completed a couple of years earlier with the Adrian Sherwood produced *Twitch*, which kind of sounded like *Microphonies*-era Cabaret Voltaire. It was okay, but not the vicious *Mad Max*-on-methamphetamines that he was looking for. Now things were different. The music had become this hard, evil thing, and to Al's credit, and to the credit of his then supporting cast of Paul Barker and Bill Rieflin, he had managed to reinvent himself and change gears musically.

Two other people in Al's immediate social circle were Frank and Dave, a couple who I took to instantly. (They remain two of my best friends to this day.) Frank used to front a local Chicago experimental new wave band called Special Affect, for whom Al once auditioned to be their lead guitarist. This was Al's *entrée* into the underground Chicago music scene after being a long-haired rocker that moved from Denver to Chicago in the late seventies. Frank was responsible for giving Al a more chic aesthetic, turning him from a pedestrian stoner guitarist into a tight, angular member of a very hip local band.

So between Jim, Dannie, the label, Al, Frank, and Dave, I was kept pretty busy for the next ten days. I was always on guard. Not knowing Al, I didn't know when he would jump up and announce we were going to the studio. I also didn't know what I was going to be singing on, which made me nervous. All I knew was that there were two songs for me to work on. As it happened, when he wasn't out holding court in every club on Chicago's North Side, Al gave the impression of this strange domesticity. He and his wife got along well enough, and it seemed the child wanted for nothing, although growing up in a cloud of Marlboro smoke and Aqua Net spritz may not have been beneficial. Al even made soup one day. "Okay, we got pea soup, we got lentil soup, both of them fuckin' wicked man!!!", he announced as if it was pea soup at the Buddokan.

Had he brought me over here from Edinburgh just to party? What did he want? We went to Medusa's, a famous Chicago under-age club that sold no booze. However, it seemed to me that everyone in the place was smashed. Patti and I managed to smuggle in a well-stocked bar between us, without anyone at the door really caring, using the "juice bar" for tonic water and ginger ale. It also seemed to be perfectly okay to drink a lot and get behind the wheel, provided you did enough coke to take the groggy edge off before meandering down Lake Shore Drive.

Eventually Al announced that we were going into the studio and I had better start writing lyrics. He handed me a cassette of the two songs he wanted me to sing on. The first one was a palpitating, jittery four-on-the-floor workout with synthetic car horns and slowed down inhuman screams. I wrote lyrics whilst watching a *Faces of Death* video, a ghoulish series of videos compiling real footage of grisly deaths—very popular with the nihilist set in the 80s. It seemed everywhere I went in Chicago, there were *Faces of Death* videos.

The other song was stranger, slower. Still with the four-on-the-floor, but with syncopated metal and machinery sounds, string synthesizer, and an almost robotic African chanting. This I called "In the Neck", where I chanted "I'm a killing machine" over and over again to "pervert angels, singing away". I was, of course, not yet used to Al's working methods. Our first chance meeting, like so many of my chance meetings, had ended with an empty bottle and a hangover. I had no real reason to think this would be repeated. After all, I had not been flown halfway across the world to show America how to drink, had I?

A taxi to Chicago Trax studio early on a still Sunday evening, the inside of the studio clean like a boring brown office, the scent of coffee permeating everywhere. I was introduced to the two guys who would be engineering the session, one of whom would end up going on the road with us as a live sound engineer and general Jourgensen yes-man. He looked like a hastily made-up poodle, a benign grin under a black curly mullet. To everything he would say "Yeah, cool, outstanding" and later, just "Oooutstanding". He would laugh hard at anything Al had to say, even if it was just "Get me some smokes". At first I was really worried because I thought it was some kind of joke I wasn't smart enough or American enough to get, but it wasn't me, the guy was just a moron. The other guy was a very personable, highly-skilled technician with a background in classical music; a huge hulking figure of a man who reminded me of Radar O'Reilly on steroids. One day I would witness him comatose with a blue tongue from coke ingestion, but not tonight.

Have I mentioned that Al was a strong believer in maximum volume? He played everything at full volume all the time. The Trax studio monitors were by far the biggest I had ever seen, and were equipped with red flashing lights that activated when the playback was too loud. Needless to say, they blinked furiously for the entire session.

The session itself was gruelling, I was learning quickly that Al liked to work until he couldn't work anymore. I think it may have been a habit he picked up from working with Adrian Sherwood, and that night, equipped with booze and cocaine supplied as a record company "expense", I got my first real introduction to Al, at home in Chicago, in his domain. Whether he was play-acting or not, he gave a convincing imitation of a man possessed by the sound he was creating, and when asked, I went into the vocal booth and gave it what I had. Amazingly (to me), Al loved both first takes; though thinking back, he probably just wanted to start mixing.

He did get me to re-sing the tracks six months later, which was perfectly fine. When Al was mixing, I learned slowly that I was really of no more practical use to him, I was there for casual conversation, showing off to, drinking or drugging with. However I came from a band that wanted to run democratically. When we went into the studio, the decisions were made by six people (time would show the wiser methods), so every so often I would chime in with my skinny little accent, "Eh, ah think the bass should be a wee bit more…like…punchy", "Eh, it wid be good tae put an echo or reverb on the vocals". These suggestions would eventually dissipate like smoke. Speaking of which, Al would have (and maybe he still has) two cigarettes burning at once. "One's for incense, man!"

I don't think I will ever be able to listen to these tracks again without them bringing back the essence of Chicago Trax "A" room to me: coffee, cigarettes, and the taste of coke in the back of my throat. Al played each song over and over for about fifteen hours—and this, I would learn, to my dismay in years to come, was nothing. And since this appeared to be some kind of rite of passage, I was obliged to stay alert for the whole process. Eventually I realized that you didn't have to spend this kind of time making records. We didn't in the Fini Tribe, mainly because we never had any money, but Al seemed to be able to do what he wanted— and I'm not knocking his working methods, but a painter doesn't have to watch the paint dry.

Throughout the night there was a forlorn and intermittent stream of sad-eyed, incoherent women that came by to visit Al. Nightclub antiques with unlikely names that seemed more suited to discontinued lines of perfume. Each time, Al would disappear for a while, and reappear with a huge grin on his face, the poodle with make-up laughing and going, "Out-fucking-standing!!!" I nervously pretended to read a magazine.

And so ended my first trip to the States. All in all, I thought I was seduced by America, but I was actually seduced by the protective bubble of Wax Trax!, by Jim's and Frank's whiplash wit, by Al's sheer volume, and by the music I was making. I had a few options in Edinburgh at that time, so I made up my mind to return as soon as I could.

The America I was introduced to *was* America according to Wax Trax!, but I thought that the whole country was like that. In my heart-breaking innocence, I thought I had stumbled into a country of open-minded people who loved and accepted homosexuality, were liberal with their views on drugs, and where money was never even a question. What the fuck was I thinking? I suppose I had met enough people over my short stay that would convince me that this was the norm; that all Americans were out to ridicule the American way, a campaign spearheaded at the time by President David Lynch and his *Blue Velvet* manifesto, but the thing was, there was so much to ridicule! This country, over a very short space of time had managed to build up an enviable reservoir of the ridiculous, brimming with cowboys, fatties, and televangelists. All we had in Britain at the time was Thatcher and Samantha Fox.

The Wax Trax! aesthetic, or rather, Jim Nash's aesthetic, was a celebration of 50s and 60s Americana. His domain was filled with gorgeous furniture, lamps, mirrors, and knick-knacks from another era. His walls were covered with Communist propaganda posters, and his television ran 24 hours a day, fed on a diet of unusual and bizarre videotapes. I readily assumed that every household in America was the same.

On my return to Edinburgh, I couldn't wait to get back to Chicago. I was broke, out of work, homeless, and my girlfriend had upped and moved to London to live. Alternately, I crashed at the Fini Tribe rehearsal space or my mother's flat while she was on holiday for a couple of merciful weeks. I was, best of all, incredibly bored. I had had a little taste of something bigger that I wanted. The Fini Tribe was starting to atrophy for me, partly because of my introduction to something new, partly because we had spent the last five years living and breathing each other, working very hard and for little reward. Even though Wax Trax! had shown real interest in us, the rot had set in. Rehearsals were long as we tried to write. We even started to have arguments whilst pedantically scrutinizing some minor figure in the music industry for days at a time, which used to be fun. Now we could feel the push and pull. After all, we were all grown lads now and something had to give—and it would, eventually.

I moved in to the flat where John and Davey from the Fini's were living. A girlfriend had moved out and there was a room going. The flat was in the most desirable locale in Edinburgh; the west end of Princes Street, just before you reached Haymarket, a sumptuous Georgian flat that John had charmed his way into. The irony of course being that we were all flat broke and so couldn't really enjoy the decadence of it all. Superb view, though!

Even though the Fini Tribe were suffering from internal problems, we were still busy with Wax Trax!, and still excited at our prospects. The arguments and interminable process of coming up with new material did not change that we were a formidable live force, and we were unlike anything else happening at the time. (Eat your heart out, BMX fucking Bandits!!) There was to-ing and fro-ing to London via train, where it seemed various Fini's and entourage had, in varying degrees, become romantically involved with the entire female staff of Southern Studios, virtuous Vikings that we were. These visits to London were a much-needed tonic. It was nice to have a few people who actually liked us, seeming to suffer so much from people either thinking we were too strange or not strange enough. Plus, while we were in London, we had to bond as a band. The six of us together were a force to be reckoned with and we knew it. Back in Edinburgh, we were still public enemy number one; allies were few on the ground. The actual music scene had reached a really bland plateau presided over by the flailing Shop Assistants, who were being put to a slow death by a major label contract and a name producer. We were still being labelled as sexists and fascists by the same tired old *feministas,* who would have found someone to label, it just wasn't easy to label the faux paisley-wearing Pastels or Soup Dragons such. It would be kind of like calling your teddy bear Ian Brady. The thing was that our live show had taken a turn for the perverse, playing topless with balaclava ski masks, and Davey, Andy and I worked out a kind of Detroit Emeralds/Temptations dance routine—though, please, don't even think that our stiff northern limbs even came close to the supple choreography of these showmen—whilst screaming our syncopated surrealism through megaphones. It was supposed to be funny, absurdist... oops!

At one point our dole money was stopped, the trickle-down effect from the bloodthirsty She-Devil in Number 10. Davey and I took part in a huge occupation of a government building in the city centre. Eventually they caved in and gave us food stamps for a local supermarket, which magically transformed themselves into lager, tobacco, and a bag of flour.

Eventually, Al sent for me: the much-anticipated inaugural performance of the Revolting Cocks.

"Fucking stadium-size man, we're gonna play in a fucking stadium and just come out and piss on the crowd!!", was one description that had come over the transatlantic phone line from Al.

Or, another time, jumping the gun a little, "We're fucking huge man, I'm gonna get a satellite link so we can broadcast the show all fucking over, man!!"

It was hard to get swept up in his enthusiasm whilst making roll-up cigarettes from the contents of pub ashtrays, but eventually a plane ticket was sent, and I went to London for a few days to pick up the masters for the next Fini Tribe single to take with me to Chicago.

I arrived at O'Hare early on a Saturday evening. The place was really quiet. No one was there to greet me, so I stood and waited for a while, looking like an off-duty sailor until I saw Frank and Dave patrolling their way through the baggage claim area. Apparently, Al had forgotten that I was even coming, and a conversation that afternoon had prompted his memory. This seemed to be one of a number of things that Al had forgotten about, and Frank and Dave expressed polite frustration with him. Al, I learned, was living with them, having been thrown out by Patti. When we arrived at Frank and Dave's apartment Al was sitting in the kitchen on a rowing machine wearing a jauntily placed toy Viking helmet on his head. He was purple faced and screaming the usual Jourgensen volley down the phone, "You are going DOWN man! I swear to fucking GOD, you are going DOWN!!"

There was never any argument with Al if you got into a fight with him. He would just scream one long succession of expletives that punctuated a description on the nature of your eventual death. This went around in a loop until you were forced to walk away, or he found someone else to yell at. Anyway, Al paused his daily workout for just enough time to give me a hug and welcome me back, before letting me know that, "All kinda shit is hitting the fucking fan, man, no fucking doubt". This was a vague enough assessment of the situation I had walked into to make me nervous that I would be sent straight back to O'Hare immediately. Remember, I was still new to Al, and I was definitely new to this separated-from-wife-and-any-kind-of-stability Al. My accommodation for this trip was provided by Jim Nash's daughter, Julia, who lived in close proximity to Frank and Dave's apartment—but for tonight, I would just stay where I was.

I asked Al what the plan was and I learned that Paul Barker was there already, and that Bill and Luc were arriving shortly. We were to be rehearsing at a place called Joe's, and that seemed to be all he knew for the moment. He was in the studio working on a Ministry record; the same one he had been working on for ages. There was definitely a lack of any organization, and the practicalities seemed to be being handled by either Wax Trax! or Frank and Dave at this point. No matter, it was Saturday night and I was excited to be back in Chicago. We took off clubbing. Our first stop was Exit, where I met a guy called Charles, equal parts womanizer, bassist, and coke dealer. This third trait would prove especially useful that summer. That night was spent touring various bathroom stalls, doing coke and listening to Al's rhetoric, meeting various hangers-on, listening to them kiss Al's ass and do his coke.

Cabaret Metro, situated on North Clark Street in the Wrigleyville area of Chicago, is an important musical institution as vital to touring rock bands as the Paradiso in Amsterdam. It's a marvellous venue to play, and bands have always been treated with respect by the owner and staff—unlike most small- to mid-size rock venues that lack every basic human amenity, and have suffered from clogged and doorless toilets since Little Richard's day. The club also boasts a dance club called Smart Bar, in the basement, where a weary musician can retire after a show to find coke and talk to girls, and it has a secret 100-seat theatre at the top of the building, rarely used because of fire regulations. This is "Joe's" and it is where the Revolting Cocks were rehearsing that summer.

After Exit, we went to Smart Bar, where we were met by Jay, the owner and our benefactor regarding this whole project. More than just the first concert by the Cocks, it was to be recorded for a live double album, a concept that thrilled me with the irony of 70s rock excess and the fact that, technically, it would be the first release by this brand new line-up. Jay—Gandhi with drink chips, as someone once described him—took me on a guided tour of the building. He was friendly and talkative (i.e. high as a kite), and used a lot of superlatives to describe Al. We walked around the building, a painfully coiffed mullet bouncing on the back of his shoulders the whole time. His sentences were spoken so fast that they precluded any interjections from me as he regaled me with stories about bands like the Sisters of Mercy and their shenanigans, the Godfathers and their hijinks—not that I cared. After the tour, Al and I sat in Jay's office and I studied the nature of their relationship. Jay had a seemingly endless supply of coke—although, everybody had a seemingly endless supply of fucking coke—and while we did line after line, Jay laughed harder and longer at every derogatory remark levelled at him from Al's mouth. I would learn over the years that there were many people who enjoyed this kind of relationship with Al. It made me a little uncomfortable.

After we left Jay in his office, Al and I returned to Smart Bar and caught up with Frank and Dave. The DJ had the brilliant idea of playing an old Ministry single called "Work for Love". As soon as the first bar of the song played, I witnessed Al leap across the dance floor and quicker than you could say "Mascara!" he had pulled the offending vinyl off the turntable and smashed it. The DJ was screaming at Al, Al was screaming at the DJ. I honestly thought they had come in at 5 PM that evening for a dress rehearsal. The evening wound down at Frank and Dave's with Al and Charles. It was light outside and I had a vacuum in my stomach, my face bending with the amount of drink and drugs consumed. I am sure I threw up, before jet-lag threw up on me and I blacked out.

Over the next few days, the balance of the band showed up. Apart from Paul Barker, I had met no one else. Luc Van Acker was described to me as being "bigger than Michael Jackson" in Belgium. I had no reason to disbelieve it. His record covers betrayed a faux sophistication usually found on ABC or Spandau Ballet records. I was expecting a very pompous Belgian with an iron-fisted manifesto, but I couldn't have been more wrong, AGAIN! Luc was, at some points, like a cross between Elvis and Captain Beefheart, but otherwise he was down-to-earth, charming, and a team player beloved by everyone. Bill Rieflin was steadfastly eccentric and with whom I shared a love for obscure music. Our first ever conversation was about either This Heat or Henry Cow—I can't remember which.

Paul, Bill, and Luc had one very strong thing in common: none of them were even remotely like Al. You could also tell a mile off that none of them were the sycophants that Al was wont to surround himself with, which was why this version of the Cocks was such a good band to be in. You see, with a strong core group to get the work done, to keep everything grounded and with humour, it was usually okay for Al to fly off the deep end and behave the way he did. He could be reeled back in every so often.

The next month in Chicago would turn me from being a polite visitor into a bona fide working musician and general *bon vivant* around town. While we were based at Joe's we would start rehearsing at around 4 PM, so by the time the clubs opened we had a lot of work done, and I for one was delighted when girls bearing vodka and coke drinks would come up to share with us. Some nights were just non-starters, and any hard work we had done was washed away as we swept down to Smart Bar where poor behaviour, I was told, was not only permissible, it was expected. (*n.b.* The inside of the gatefold cover of the album *You Goddamned Son of a Bitch* has a lot of photographs from this period; many taken in Joe's, many in the photo booth at Smart Bar.)

When we were not rehearsing, Al and Paul were working at Chicago Trax. Of course, any of us could drop by whenever we wanted, and often we would be put to good use behind a microphone. One endless night, Frank put a sublime vocal down on a Ministry track and named it "Tonight We Murder". In between takes, we would cross Halsted Street to one of the gay bars for cocktails. Al produced a bag of black bombers, speed pills the size of U-boats. We were eating them like liquorice Allsorts. (Why not? They *looked* just like liquorice Allsorts.) Somehow, the session managed to take off and touch down in the early dawn hours at a party being thrown by a guy called Earl, from Chicago punk legends The Effigies. We were *in situ* in Earl's back garden, Charles walking around with a glass platter of coke, offering lines, me having a very serious conversation with a girl when I gave pause to vomit at her feet. I apologized profusely, but she was just tickled and asked me to go home with her. When we arrived at her house I noticed that her bedroom was plastered with Revolting Cocks and Ministry ephemera. I felt bad for her "catch" (i.e. me), as I was not on any of the records she had scattered around. Then I was indignant that she didn't have a Fini Tribe record—but I didn't say, lest I risk my shag. It didn't occur to me at all that she might have been completely mad, which she most definitely was. It didn't even occur to me to run like hell when she grabbed me and stared dead into my eyes and sang "Close to You" from start to finish. By all rights, I should've been terrified. Instead I just fell asleep. Later on she woke me and told me she was going to church, and did I want to come? I tried to encourage her to drop her knickers, but she told me that she was a Catholic and could not, but perhaps in the future, when we were settled, and we were thinking of a family… her last words eaten up in the cloud of dust I left.

Rehearsal days began usually with me accompanying Paul and Bill on numerous errands; strings, drumsticks, impossible to find software. It was on one such errand that Bill leaned out of the window and yelled, "You goddamned son of a bitch!" at a delinquent motorist, thus giving a name to our as yet unborn double live album.

Paul and Bill were in the front of Paul's van, "Icky"—the affectionate name given to Paul's wreck of a van that had clearly served the band so well for years, and miraculously, would continue to do so for years to come)—rapid-firing their surreal wordplay at each other. We would dart around Chicago, occasionally picking up Al or Luc on the way to the Metro. Luc was staying at Jim and Dannie's, who, it turned out, had moved into Al's old apartment, which meant I could not vouch for Patti Jourgensen and the child's whereabouts. Perhaps they were just disembodied voices on the phone; either way, the disembodied voice of Patti seemed to wind Al up good and proper.

The dim theatre was in very stark contrast to the impossible heat and sun outside. Chicago in the middle of August was torture for me, my chalk-white skin used to the more sullen climes of Scotland, so walking into Joe's Theatre every afternoon felt delicious. The darkness was enveloping, interrupted intermittently by the sound of samples being bent and twisted in all direction by Paul and Bill as they tried to recreate the Cocks sound. They looked like a couple of unhinged technicians poring over sophisticated weaponry.

Eventually Al would show up, accompanied by a volley of complaints or considerable boasts about last night's Caligula orgy he claimed to have attended, though I suspect he probably just went to bed with a turkey sandwich and a copy of *Jugs*.

The rehearsals themselves were a lot of fun. The bulk of the material being played was from the album *Big Sexy Land* along with the two tracks, "Cattle Grind" and "In the Neck", that I had recorded a few months earlier, and the last single, "You Often Forget". About half of the music was on tape, so there was not a lot to worry about except finishing when the tape finished. We all had very specific parts, apart from Luc who, along with his cricket bat-shaped Steinberger guitar (remember them?), patrolled the rehearsal space kind of soloing from the beginning of the set until the end, pausing to sing his big number, "Attack Ships on Fire".

The support for the show was a local band/artists collective called X Meets Y, and one evening a couple of them showed up to rehearsal with

The support for the show was a local band/artists collective called X Meets Y, and one evening a couple of them showed up to rehearsal with a camera and a ventriloquist's dummy to make the legendary short film *Looking for Mister Goodcock*, starring myself, Luc, and Al. Mercifully, my thespian endeavours have never been made available to a curious public.[1]

Jay, the club owner, was becoming a rather frequent visitor. His mullet shimmered behind him as he made toasts to just about anything that happened. Even if we fucked up a song, he would toast to our all being human, his mouth so dry from coke us that eventually his speech became a sort of intermittent clucking noise; a diabolical fusion of Tony Montana with a turkey—gobble, gobble. During these visits from Jay, Al would often become consumed by an impossible bravado, working himself into quite a lather.

"I'll shoot a bunch of people in the crowd, man, I'm fucking serious, I got a buddy who's got a Sherman fucking tank. I swear to fucking GOD!" he faithfully promised Jay.

"Oh *Al*!" flounced Jay, "You are just too much!! You're incredible!!!"

"I swear to God, you better show up with a bunch of coke and money, or we are gonna trash the place," Al would roar, pissing in a trash can, "Get us more coke, now!!"

"Oh *AL*!! A hoo hoo hoo hoo hoo!!!!" gurgled Jay.

It was on nights like these that rehearsal would collapse around us like old Pompeii. We became far too sociable with the coke, and only two floors down was the beckoning adventure of Smart Bar and its stroboscopic maelstrom, archaeological digs to the ladies bathroom to do more drugs with a gaggle of cute Goths, spilling Sea Breezes on your Psychic TV T-shirt whilst dancing to the pummelling vapidity of Nitzer Ebb.

---

1     *Of course, in this day and age, everything eventually makes its way on to the Internet... this video has made its way on to YouTube.*

# I'M A
# KILLING
# MACHINE

**Top:** With Paul Barker and others, March 1988.

**Middle:** "The Poodle" and Al relaxing, March 1988.

**Bottom:** Al and Paul playing video games at home, March 1988.

# 3

# MAKING A MEAL OUT OF STAINLESS STEEL

I was doing quite well. Exceptionally well, considering the standards I was used to while in a band in Edinburgh, which were very little. I don't know if I have complained bitterly enough through clenched teeth how the Fini Tribe always thought—or at least I always thought—that artistic validation was just around the corner. In fact, what seemed to be around the corner was, at best, an all-night bakery on the way home from a student union gig in Aberdeen. We always seemed to have two quid between the six of us after carting our gear for miles in support of CND. (Needless to say, nowadays, these reminiscences make me quite warm and fuzzy.) But right now, there were numerous people that seemed to have my hedonistic and carnal interests at heart, and without any money changing hands perceptibly.

It was about a week before the big show that the Revolting Cocks' "Stainless Steel Providers" was born. This is probably my favourite Cocks song, inspired by a glorious nocturnal motorbike ride at the speed of sound on the back of Paul Barker's hog. I had never ridden on a motorbike before; in fact, I was really scared of them after an accident involving one as a child whilst blindly crossing a busy road. But when Paul asked in such a nonchalant fashion, I just wasn't up to admitting my cowardice and said, "Sure!"

The real inspiration for the song came while we were shooting down Cortland, a street in Chicago referred to as the "industrial" corridor, not because it has rows of sidewalk cafés and bars where members of SPK, Throbbing Gristle, and Einstürzende Neubauten might play backgammon, but because it is lined on both sides with a massive foundry. During the summer, the huge doors opened for ventilation, which meant that you were squinting into what looked like hell: walls of glowing molten liquid cascading into huge vats, the street itself dotted with alien-looking vehicles that transported huge glowing molten columns from the moulding department, presumably to the cooling department across the street.

Later that night, after Paul had made a couple of victory laps around Chicago Trax "A" live room, I complained that I was bored of being in the studio. Al was focusing on a mix, and there was really nothing much else to do. Paul thought for a second and suggested that we work on a track in the smaller "B" room. The entire studio had been infiltrated, of course, by the usual familiar club fallout, nocturna-blondes with eternal cigarettes mixing endless Sea Breezes and Daiquiris in the kitchen. The familiar coke rap squawked like a parrot-mantra. "I gotta call blah blah about a modelling job." "I can't believe I broke my fucking shoe." "D'you think Al's pissed 'cos I spilled that White Russian on him? He told me to get the fuck out." Eventually the squawks would be downgraded to croaks. The bars and clubs were all closed, there was nowhere else but Trax to go.

Paul and I locked ourselves in the "B" room. After one, two, maybe three lines of coke, I was completely nauseous. My face was as numb as a glacier. I was ready to write. The music was a hypnotic two-note thump, a high-speed conveyor belt that suggested extreme danger for limbs in close proximity. Syncopated hydraulic lifts and metallic friction burns drove the point home. The opening lines, lifted directly from the Beach Boys' "I Get Around", declared a statement of intent, trading all beach buggies for motorbikes. (I have, by the way, always had a healthy appetite for the Beach Boys—what's not to love?) The song is an urban travelogue heading into the heart of the rotting metropolis, through the night streets of Chicago in the claustrophobic summer; kind of like Iggy Pop's "The Passenger", but minus doors or windows. The song is the ultimate accident waiting to happen—in the wrong place, and definitely at the wrong time.

The streets I was witness to this time around Chicago were decaying, in a state of extreme disrepair. The neighbourhood I was staying in was poor, mainly Hispanic, with a few scattered artists and musicians. There were huge nightmarish holes everywhere in the streets. On the sides of buildings, there were signs posted everywhere saying "public enemy number one" with an image of a huge rat. It looked like a war zone, but unlike my first visit, I feared very little now. Maybe it had to do with me being either frightfully hung-over during the daylight hours, or being amongst such extended and diverse company during the evening hours. "Look at the Scottish moron wandering mystified through *carnicerias* and *supermercados*, trying to find something that looks familiar, walking out with a pack of Marlboro lights and a bottle of some Day-Glo sticky liquid." Laugh as the know-it-all Scottish twit tries to look blasé, ordering food in Castilian Spanish from a confused-looking waiter in a Mexican restaurant, pronouncing every "s" like a "th". They must have thought me retarded, with a speech impediment, which in many ways, I was.

The show was days away, the event being heralded by a cumulative series of unrelated, yet seemingly coincidental, unsettling events. Someone broke into Frank and Dave's apartment and stole some sound equipment from the living room whilst Al and Paul slept like wretched babies sprawled out on the floor. Before the dress rehearsal, a video crew was in place to document the show, and a small crew for equipment and sound. As we were preparing to leave the rehearsal in the early hours of Saturday morning, a fistfight broke out between two crewmembers. As we were in the van waiting for them to board, Al yells, "Go! Just fucking DRIVE!!" Actually, a really good idea—I live in pure terror of moments like these. We simply left them on the sidewalk to get on with it.

That night, or rather morning, I could only grab a quick couple of hours sleep, as my fellow Fini Tribe bandmate, Philip, was flying in from summer school on the East Coast to witness the gig. Dannie was going to drive me out to O'Hare first thing to get him; so, to simplify things, I slept at Jim and Dannie's, sharing a mattress with Luc in the living room. What we didn't bargain for were three other visitors who had come from out of town for the weekend to attend the show. A woman named Cheryl, a guy called Richard, and his glove puppet friend were sat around a coffee table by our bed and seemed oblivious to us. On the table, of course, was a mountain of blow and as it became smaller by increments, the voices rose and mutated. I drifted in and out of a light, light sleep. I told them to shut up. Cheryl, I gathered, was from Memphis or "frum the sauwth" as she put.

"Excuse me boys, ah'm just gunna do one more line of this, and then I'll turn in fur the evenin," she continued.

The guy named Richard had a campy voice, rendered indecipherable by his bone-dry mouth. He sounded like a constipated goose as he bellowed either laughter or distress (it was hard to tell).

"Hoawah! Hoawah! Hoawaaaaaaah!"

His glove puppet boy-toy kind of sounded the same but more shrill. "Hehwheeee!"

In my fever their voices all became one until Dannie was telling me it was time to go and pick up Philip. Philip is one of my oldest friends. We started Fini Tribe together—back then we were called Rigor Mortis—a childish collision of the Stooges and Throbbing Gristle, two guitars and tape loops. Our party piece was the Barry Manilow song "Bermuda Triangle", as reinterpreted by the Futurists. Unlike me, Philip was brainy, and had won a place at some Ivy League college studying psychology for the summer. I'll wager he learned more hanging with the Revolting Cocks for 24 hours than he did in class.

Soundcheck took most of the afternoon. It was endless tweaking and thumping. Al was in a kind of frenzy. In a way he had a lot more at stake than anyone else, but I am pretty highly strung as well. Al encouraged me to "power drink" until showtime when, "a buncha coke whores'll bring by a ton of blow, man. It'll be fucking wicked!"

I had no doubt that they would, why would tonight be any different? In fact, by all rights, they should bring by a fucking pharmacopoeia, that's what they should bring the fuck by! After soundcheck, someone asked me and Philip to sign a Fini Tribe record. I was almost tearful in my gratitude. There was no time to go and change after soundcheck, so one of the girls who was "looking after" me gave me an Anthrax T-shirt to wear. I liked it because it was heavy metal, and kind of went against everything I held dear. (I didn't realise that once the live video came out, many people would assume I was an Anthrax fan. I had never heard them. Oops. Maybe they're great, I dunno.)

Things started to go really awry when X Meets Y hit the stage. Everyone in the band seemed to be tripping really hard, and things were not helped at all by the fact that they had a huge intimidating black woman with a shotgun trained at the crowd standing dead centre of the stage. Their music was a wind-up, their presence was a wind-up, but the only people who seemed to get wound up were the band and the bouncers. Eventually, we heard an altercation from our dressing room, loud angry voices and a lot of knocking and banging. It was at this point I realised that this was exactly what Al wanted. By surrounding himself with chaos, he created the atmosphere he needed to thrive. I could empathise in a kind of Malcolm McLaren-ish way, but right at that moment, I was not in the mood for it. Well, eventually the two blonde girls, Louanne and Gina, ended up in our dressing room; the younger, Gina, seemed fine, but Louanne (that's her on the back cover of *You Goddamned Son of a Bitch*) was crying all kinds of crime and allegations against the bouncers.

"They beat me UP!! These fuckin' assholes, they took me and BEAT ME!!" she hollered.

I didn't see it, so I don't know if they did or not. Wouldn't someone have called the cops? Or, being America, wasn't there a team of lawyers on the way? What I did know was that we were playing in fifteen minutes and this band had managed to ruin my pre-gig ritual (the Zen of vodka tonic).

"Yeah, maybe it wasn't such a great idea to take a fucking SHOTGUN onstage with you, huh?" Actually, I was too chicken to say anything of the sort to her. What I did do in a quiet bedside, nursey-nursey fashion was ask her if I could make her a drink. This got me a look as if I had asked John the Baptist if he would like an aspirin. Okay! Point taken! Al began yelling for Jay, who dutifully appeared in the dressing room.

"You better have someone throw a bunch of money into the crowd, you fucking thief rip-off, or there's no show!!!"

"A hoo hoo hoo hoo! Oh *AL!!!!*" and as requested Jay had someone go on stage with a huge fan and blow out probably around twenty dollars in ones to illustrate Al's solidarity with "the kids".

It was in this atmosphere that the backing tape started and the dry ice began to flood the stage. In hindsight, it was a good thing. It meant that I didn't hit the stage in a state of complacency. I have to hand it to Al, he is a genius at provoking, and therefore ensuring a great performance. It's like being paid to be a drama queen, training other people to be drama queens! I walked out onstage all cocaine nerves and Dutch courage. Through the dry ice I saw one quizzical looking figure crushed to the front of the stage.

"Who the FUCK are you?" I heard him shout at me over the din.

"Well, I'm NOT Richard 23, mate," I thought. "He would be the short guy with a *Mad Max*-meets-the-Avon-lady hairdo, and he's in Belgium sulking right now." Louanne, who seemed to have made an excellent recovery, and Gina were to be tonight's "Revolting Pussies". They would "dance" throughout our set. Actually, Gina would dance through our set, Louanne would lurch around the stage like a drunk anteater in drag spoiling for a fight with anything in her path. She spent a lot of time on the floor in a pile with whomever she could topple successfully. My show was marred because I was terrified she'd make me look like a moron in front of all these people who didn't know who the fuck I was.

Al's face was a mask of classic Al rage, top lip tucked in to reveal teeth, bottom lip pushed out. When he was like this I was always reminded of Tom from *Tom and Jerry* right after Jerry has smashed his skull with a golf club/anvil/A.N.Other appliance, so he kind of scared me too. (I would learn that it was nothing to be scared of, just part of the show.) Paul, good-humoured as ever, played with a grin, having a ball watching the slapstick chaos around him. Bill was the picture of serenity (I think he had a book on his floor tom), while Luc, done up head to toe in leather, looked like someone fired from the set of *Cruisin'* for eating all the catering. At any given moment there was a pile of band/dancers on the floor, flailing limbs seemingly unconnected with any particular torso. Al and I shared much of the lead vocal duties, Al doing a bang-up impersonation of Richard 23. He had spent so much time mocking him during rehearsals—hilarious imitation, I might add—that, when it came time for him to sing "We Shall Cleanse the World", he sounded just like the record ("We had no toime to seenk about it!!!").

With Luc's leather cap, and my and Al's shaved heads, when the three of us were singing "TV Mind", we couldn't have looked any more gay; a nightmare clash between the Village People and the Pet Shop Boys in a vodka distillery. Speaking of gay, our buddy Charles was our onstage crew that night, looking like he had just escaped from Shalamar. He was ubiquitous, probably because of his sheer size (he's a tall fellow), and striking appearance. It really looked like we had hired an 80s R&B chart sensation to do all of our heavy lifting.

For me, the funniest part of the show was when Luc came out front to do his party piece "Attack Ships on Fire". Earlier that day, he and I had gone to the record shop, Pravda, that was right next door to Metro. An uncomfortable few minutes ensued as Luc tried to persuade the obnoxious employee behind the counter to let him hear his own record so he could copy down the lyrics—which he did, pasting them into the inside of his leather cap. If you watch the video of this performance, you can see Luc desperately trying to turn his failure to learn a song into a Shakespearean "alas poor Yorick" moment, holding his hat out in front of his face at arm's length every time he sang a verse.

After the show, we continued frivolities late into the night, upstairs at the rehearsal place and downstairs at Smart Bar. That night I learned of the horrors of aftershow hangers-on, especially if they were either drunk, on coke, or (usually) both. I had my ear chewed off that night, and witnessed Luc having his ear chewed off by the poodle-faced engineer.

"Man! You should play METAL man, these guys around here, man, they KNOW you, they would LOVE to have you, man you HAVE to play METAL man, ILOVEYOUMAN I LOVEYOUMAN ILOVEYOUMAN!!!!!" …ad nauseum.

Philip and I basically reeled from one idiotic interaction to the next, until it was time to take a cab home.

The following day Philip left. We would meet up again in Edinburgh in a few days. The whole of Chicago, nay, the whole WORLD seemed to be reeling after the earth shattering first gig by the REVOLTING COCKS. I had this great feeling in my stomach, the same feeling of fulfilment I had had after a school play, or one of the more elaborately planned Fini Tribe "happenings". That night, we were scheduled in the studio to work on either Ministry or Cocks material. I was there, Luc was there, Frank and Dave were there, and Charles was there. I can't remember if Paul and Bill were there. It would make sense in one respect—what the hell else were they doing?—but the track we cut that night was just Luc, Dave, and I. Charles was in a state of advanced agitation and extreme coke paranoia. He was openly chopping together huge amounts of cocaine with huge amounts of powdered vitamins. He kept muttering to himself and leaving the studio for minutes before coming back in and chopping again. We left him to it, but I made a mental note to never become dependent on coke. Yikes.

While we were waiting for Al to turn up, Luc and I started jamming; me on piano, Luc on bass. We had discovered a mutual love of Can over the last few weeks, and talked at length about it, so what came out was what we called "Alpine reggae"—me playing off beats on the piano, Luc holding down a strong reggae low end on the bass. While we were doing this, Dave Collins came up with a rhythm using the Fairlight that was equal parts loping and busy. It was perfect. It did not take long before we had built perhaps the most curious song in the Cocks' canon. "At the

Top" was a hymn to a huge morning after. The lyric was spontaneous. I just went out there and sang it off the top of my head, words being pushed out of me by the coke I was doing. It kind of summed up the last four weeks ("accept my inexperience and learn to love my decadence") and was a harbinger of complications yet to come. Luc finished it off with a melancholy and very Can-esque guitar throughout. It was the perfect end to the whole experience of that summer in Chicago.

We said our goodbyes with the knowledge that we would be seeing everyone again very soon.

Al was excited about the prospect of mixing a live double album. "We're gonna be HUGE man, bigger than Ministry!! Wait and see man, you're all gonna be fucking STARS!" he exclaimed, amongst other declarations of stadium-size tours, etc.

Luc and I nodded and grinned. Bill had left very quickly and quietly, Paul was staying, and Luc and I were flying back to Europe together. Tirelessly, we bothered the flight attendants for extra food, drinks, and marriage.

On returning to Edinburgh, I am quite sure I could not have been more intolerable, having idealized myself into some kind of "conquering hero of rock 'n' roll".

"I did blah blah drugs"…

…"blah blah PILES of women"…

…"oh, but blah blah in CHICAGO of course!"

My long, long suffering support group (the Fini Tribe and sundry appendages) "oooh'd" and "aaah'd" appropriately while I held court as I spun tales of the mean streets of Chicago and complained that I couldn't find good coke in Edinburgh. (I wasn't looking, I had no money.) I was trying to turn myself into Scotland's own pathetic off-brand Jourgensen.

There was a more tangible push and pull within the Finis, not least to do with my high fallutin' ideas about what I thought the band should be. We were all starting to kind of grow apart, come of age, blah blah, musical differences, etc. However, still we plodded on, a few more gigs in London, some more recording, I switched girlfriends, and TA-DA!!

Suddenly, Al was back on the phone.

"Hey man, the Cocks are gonna play Medusa's on New Year's Eve, it's gonna be fuckin' WICKED!! I got TV crews comin' out, I got radio, there's gonna be TONS of blow and chicks… There's goin…"

"It's okay Al, I'm sold. I'll see you in Chicago."

Christmas was just another uncomfortable void between dole cheques, so all I could do was hone my shoplifting skills to provide gifts for family and loved ones. It was fantastic to have a reasonable out. I was also informed that Ministry would be playing on the same bill—not hard, seeing the bands shared the same three core members of Paul, Al, and Bill—and there was a week of shows planned around Texas immediately following the New Year's Eve Chicago extravaganza. This was not going to happen for me, as I had to return to partake and witness the agonising death of the Fini Tribe.

And so the Cocks assembled once again in Chicago. We were all being housed together in the rather palatial digs that Al and Paul were renting on Altgeld Street, immediately behind the Wax Trax! store and office. (Al typically used the store's cash registers as his personal ATM.) My temporary replacement for the shows immediately following the New Year's show was a lad from Vancouver called Nivek Ogre, whose name conjured up visions of a renegade from some dreadful "sword in the stone" fantasy. However, he was the singer in a band called Skinny Puppy. The only reason I had ever heard about them was that during my first visit to Chicago, Al had spent a lot of time grousing about them when he wasn't bitching about Front 242. Anyway, it would appear that whatever transgression Skinny Puppy had committed in the past ("fuckin' posers man, what kind of a fuckin' name is that?") had been forgiven, and Nivek was allowed into Al's inner sanctum. He was a shy one: polite, likeable, with a ravenous appetite for speed. He was nothing like the renaissance-faire-jousting troll I had imagined.

Talking of bitching and grousing, who should appear for Christmas in Chicago but the very soul of yuletide bonhomie, Richard 23! My predecessor in the Cocks was every bit the pompous Belgian I had imagined, with his exploited-at-Vidal Sassoon haircut, and his seemingly bottomless pit of sardonic asides and complaints. He was in Chicago because he was dating Jim Nash's daughter, but Al was convinced he was here to sabotage our show, something (as you will soon learn) we were perfectly capable of achieving ourselves. Besides, Richard's band, Front 242, were far bigger than any of ours put together, they had cornered part of the dance floor occupied by a lot of people who were too frightened to admit they were in love with Depeche Mode and liked to play at soldiers. I had heard of Front 242 before I met Al, but that's because I thought they were Level 42 with somewhat exotic male pattern baldness.

Rehearsals took place at Medusa's on an almost nightly basis. It was frigid cold in the dank club, and there was a group of strange kids who hung out nightly watching us, nipping out to the nearby 1000 Liquors liquor store every so often to get booze as we ham-fisted our way through the same set we had played at the Metro a few months before. The cold and my chain-smoking rendered my voice a strangled gasp, and I taught Ogre the songs as well as I could.

After rehearsal I generally pirouetted through the usual nightclubs, snorting, tickling, using the accent to try and charm the ladies. My days were spent wandering around, dropping by Chicago Trax to visit Frank, who along with his friend, Marston, was making his own record under the moniker My Life With The Thrill Kill Kult—a unique sound, as seductive as it was frivolous, and Frank seemed really thrilled to have something of his own to do.

New Year's Eve is usually spent, for many, in the lofty heights of revelling. However, the Revolting Cocks managed to act like the lumbering drunk at your party who might throw up in the punchbowl and on the stereo. We did not aim to destroy everyone's evening. If we had, why would we have rehearsed? Had we known that's what would happen, chances are we would have been delighted, but we did destroy everyone's evening, and it was not entirely our fault. True, we probably should not have taken such strong acid before attempting to play, but we could not have predicted the gear breaking down. About fifteen minutes into our set, things came to a stony, silent, grinding halt. We were caught tripping with our pants down. I just stood there looking out into what appeared to be a huge pit of neon snakes and thinking that the snakes didn't really care either way if we played or not, they were just snakes. Strobes and dry ice continued on stage, making me feel like I was in an indecisive house fire. I sidled from the stage to the dressing room without alerting the neon snakes.

Backstage, Al was laughing hysterically and he persuaded Luc and I to get out there and jam on guitar and vocals until the problem was fixed. (Flashback to 1980 when I saw the same thing happen to the Damned at the Edinburgh Odeon, where the band left the stage to leave Captain Sensible on his own to tell crap joke after crap joke until the problem was resolved.) So out we went, and Luc admirably blistered his way through Led Zeppelin's *Four Sticks* while I "baby baby bay baby"'d away, not knowing the song or the lyrics. Eventually, this petered out into a languid solo, and I sidled off again, detecting the first small wave of hostility coming from the pit of fiery-eyed triffids-that-were-once-neon-snakes.

Clearly, the gear was broken. We could not finish our set.

"Someone's gotta go out and tell them man, ha ha ha ha ha! I am far too fucking high!" Al was rolling on the floor laughing heartily.

I was tittering, absolutely delighted. It was soooo Pistols at Winterland!! What a great story. Eventually, straws were drawn and poor Paul got the short one.

"Okay, yeah."

He was out by himself onstage, the crowd silent… expectant.

"Well, look man, we are really far too high to play…"

That having been relayed, you could feel the bile-filled ire of the crowd rise in waves. It might have been a better idea to tell them our gear was completely crippled, but… well, it was too fucking late now. We were advised to stay in our dressing room with the door LOCKED until the coast was clear. There were a few random kicks at the door, Al hanging out of the dressing room window, throwing vodka cranberries on the disappointed crowd forlornly leaving. "Ha ha! Happy new year, assholes!!"

I don't remember any adverse consequences resulting from our actions that night. I flew back to the UK the next day, beginning to wish I could have just stayed in Chicago.

**Top:** Me in Austin, May 1988.
**Middle:** Al in Tampa, April 1988. (Connelly)
**Bottom:** Sean Joyce. (Connelly)

# 4

# ZOO DISCO

"Raow, raow, raow ya bowt, gently dahn the straaaym…" Your sad mess of an author was impersonating Bowie singing "Row, row, row your boat" on a college radio station. I was the third wheel in a Thrill Kill Kult interview, possibly their first. The show was on Northwestern's college campus radio station, WNUR. It was their Saturday night show, hosted by some trust fund buffoon who, frankly, did not know what had hit him. Frank, Marston, and I had been in the lounge waiting to be interviewed, drinking greyhounds and smoking. By the time he interrupted his little Nitzer Ebb fest for us, we were in a very belligerent mood. His poorly-aimed, tentative questions were thrown back at him with non sequiturs and surrealist wordplay, as he begged us to stop smoking, drinking and swearing. We made fun of everything he played, and we firmly established a dislike for each other. Eventually, inevitably, we were asked firmly to leave. (When I went back there, unchallenged, to play a set with my band in 1997, the people were still complete goons.)

I had been living in Chicago for about a week. The Fini Tribe had split. I had been on the verge of taking a job managing the newly opened FOPP store in Edinburgh when a phone call with Al made me decide to pursue a career in noise and solvent abuse. Just think of the stories I'd have when I grew old! Two weeks of goodbyes and a promise to send for my lady-friend in a month or so, and I could not wait to leave. I had a couple of changes of clothes, a Walkman I'd stolen (borrowed without asking) from my girlfriend, a Mark Stewart cassette, a best of the Beach Boys cassette (never leave home without one), and a packet of Embassy Filter. Any regrets? I wish I had had enough money for two packets.

Upon arriving, the current situation in Chicago was this: Al and Patti were back together occupying the huge house on Altgeld. Al and Paul were at Chicago Trax juggling several projects, the central project being the same Ministry album they had been working on previously. The other projects were Pailhead (as mentioned before), which was now six songs strong—Ian MacKaye having been to Chicago to sing just after I had left the first time. The other was a curious and nebulous concept called "Zoo Disco", which seemed to be little different than any of Al and Paul's other projects, except it was being funded by some invisible and independently wealthy character, who, I was told, owned the rights to thousands of hours of Gregorian chant recordings. Hmmm… maybe it was Jesus.

During my first week, I was given two slabs of "Zoo Disco" to sink my teeth into, that would ultimately end up being fed into the Ministry/ Cocks production line. Eventually—well, rather quickly, actually—the shadowy rich guy disappeared from conversation, or ascended back from whence he came, who knows? Al and Paul were, at this time, the fully-fledged production team known as Luxapan Productions, that would inspire legions of noise-hungry musicians and fans alike; Al being Mr. Hypo LUXA, and Paul being Mr. Hermes PAN.

Anyway, the first of these two pieces of music would end up the B-side of a single by one of the several one-off bands we would create for our own amusement over the years—this one being PTP: short for, ahem… er… "Programming The Psychodrill" (a name Al had conjured up to get his music into the movie *Robocop* without Warner Brothers noticing). The song was "My Favorite Things", a bubbling, poppy synth track that sounded a lot like it would not have been out of place on Cabaret Voltaire's *Microphonies*. (These guys had quite an effect on Al, apparently.) In a perverse act of Scottish economics, I recycled the lyrics from the last Fini Tribe song we had been writing when I quit—the song that actually put us over the edge because it took so fucking long to write. I had the engineer, Poodle (ouuutstanding!), slow the multi-track tape down whilst I was recording my voice, so when played back normally, it sounded like a creepy baby. (I have used this technique to great effect since I started recording, especially on my solo record *Shipwreck* when I needed female backing singers and couldn't find any.)

The other track became the song "Never Believe" on *The Mind Is a Terrible Thing to Taste,* which I have never liked at all. It reminds me of those Fini Tribe live jams, when I would get stoned and make the words up as I went along. Repulsive behaviour!

One bright, cloudless Sunday morning, a few days in, I had risen in the Jourgensen household and was politely breakfasting with Patti and the child, when our hangovers were shattered as Paul and Al returned from Trax having completed mixing the mighty *Anthem* by Pailhead. Indeed it seemed that the bulk of the work had been on Paul's shoulders, as everyone seemed to be calling him "Anthem Barker"—everyone being the engineer Poodle, and Melinda, a lovable but clearly insane drug dealer who would hang out with us at Trax, supplying us with all our necessary little evils. Her story, apparently, was that she had been assaulted in a Mexican hotel whilst on a drug run, then ambushed with a baseball bat to the head whilst entering her room. She was perfectly functional, especially given the fact that she truly believed that the major telephone company, AT&T, was using her head as a conduit to process all phone calls. She heard millions of voices at once, thus making any attempt at conversation with her a treasury of Tourette's nuggets.

"You gotta do that faster, yo! Huh? Buddy! You want electric shake in the form of a snake's head, give it to me, give it back, ahhhhhh Tokyo! Wouldn't it be nice?"

So this was not Sunday morning for these guys, just Saturday night with the lights on. Melinda had a huge Ziploc bag of bright white powder, which I assumed was coke, but turned out to be one of these strange drugs with a bunch of initials for a name. This I took orally, with a swig of

Gatorade because it tasted like laundry detergent (come on, it IS laundry detergent!) and we listened to the mix.

"Man, listen to this shit, man!! It's fucking COLOSSAL!!" Al was euphoric.

Indeed, it sounded great; a brooding, loud, Killing Joke inspired slab of militaristic punk. Poodle was on the couch bouncing, barely able to contain his glee, humpty dumpty grin all over his stupid face.

"Outstanding! Awww, out-fucking-standing, man aheek heeeeek heek!" This continued for nigh on eight "outstanding" hours.

Al's child was thrilled to have so many merry-making adults around ("Honey, go get your crayons!"), and whatever the drug was, it was strong. It was like you were suddenly plucked and dropped in the middle of a stage fight between the Three Stooges and Popeye. "BOING!!!" "ZWEEEEEK" "THWACKO!!" It was like the *Looney Tunes* cartoon theme would burst in at any moment. Everything anyone said was a punch line. Al and Paul were wearing homemade cloth masks that made them look like slapstick shaman witch doctors. My Beach Boys tape was found, and we listened to "Little Deuce Coupe" over and over, crying with laughter as the 6'4" Paul danced maniacally.

Suddenly, it was Sunday evening. The morning and afternoon passed like a series of jerky, high-speed home movies. I ended up with Patti in a small bar on Halsted Street buying coke from a guy who looked like my old physics teacher.

When I wasn't recycling lyrics at Trax, or ingesting chemicals with Elmer Fudd, I was put to work at the Wax Trax! store, serving customers with Frank and a guy named Sean Joyce, who would also become an enduring friend. Sean was younger than me (by a year) and divorced already; he had a wry sense of humour and was already a veteran, having worked crew on the road for Ministry in the past. It was perfectly permissible to smoke pot and drink at the store. It was perfectly permissible to take wads of cash out of the cash register to buy beer and pot, even if you didn't work there. Al and Patti did it all the time, who knew? Who cared? There was the Wax Trax! boutique upstairs, if you wanted new sunglasses or you had to have a Bad Brains T-shirt at 9 PM, having been sick on your other one whilst working—well, be my guest! It was the time of my young life where it was by no means impossible to stay out all night, pounding my poor frightened organs with booze and drugs, and then being able to breeze into work with a cappuccino from Vie de France and get on with the day. In the clubs at night, I expect I was acting as many young expatriates do—behaviour that would no doubt earn me a stiff kicking back home, yet here it just seemed to make cute girls squeal with delight while their male friends enthusiastically sneered, "Cool, man".

Eventually (sigh) my girlfriend came, and much of the above came to a grinding halt. Now I had some responsibilities; however, she did enjoy drinking and drugging nearly as much as I did, so that was nice. A small tour was being booked for the Revolting Cocks, ostensibly to earn me some money so I could rent a place to live, maybe purchase a chair or something. Bill and Luc were sent for, duly appearing at *chez* Jourgensen, as well as another sound engineer who would be joining us as crew on the road along with the Poodle (er... outstanding!). He seemed nice enough at first, but pretty quickly showed his true colours as one of Al's yes men. Let's just call the crew the Poodle and the Princess, like a little girl's storybook.

There were some interesting shows coming through town, and I found I could walk into the Metro any time I liked, which was fantastic. I saw The Fall with Howard Devoto's new band Luxuria, I saw Psychic TV, now down to just Genesis P-Orridge and his wife Paula (confusing the packed Metro), and also Wire (for whom the Fini Tribe had recently opened in London), who recorded part of their album *IBTABA* that night.

Days were spent at the rehearsal space. Although we were kicking off the first leg of the tour at the Metro, we could not rehearse there—we probably cost so much money to support in recreational drugs alone—so we ended up borrowing a room from another band (Chicago punk legends Rights of the Accused, I believe) atop the famous Cubby Bear, across from the even more famous Wrigley Field, a Chicago landmark of absolutely zero interest to me. The fans were interesting looking, like well-scrubbed, pink balloons that shouted a lot (however, at least they didn't Stanley blade "Yer fuckin' face for ye pal," as they were wont to do back in Caledonia). Rehearsals were fine, if a little cramped. The Jourgensen house was becoming more Spahn Ranch-esque, with my girlfriend, Bill, Luc, Princess, as well as Patti and the child. It was pleasurable to sit on the steps outside worrying the more well-to-do neighbours whilst passing around a bottle of something. You know, it was almost kind of cosy.

Al had an anxiety dream about the tour as it loomed ever closer.

"Man, I had this dream last night where it was the first show of the tour and we were playing outside, and there were thousands of people there, and when I opened my mouth to sing, all that came out was 'Goin' up the Country' by Canned Heat. It was fuckin' weird, man," he exclaimed.

The first show was again at the Metro, with none of the hoopla of the previous time we played there. Al suggested that I start the show by running from backstage and diving straight into the crowd. I thought this was a fantastic idea, and did so at the expense of a treasured Neubauten T-shirt, which quickly became confetti in the hands of an adoring public. Ha! There was something really thrilling about stage diving, all these closely packed bodies seemed impervious to the dead weight falling on them, and you could be passed around for quite some time without any harm coming to anyone. I liked it. The show was fine, if a little anti-climactic. We were playing almost the same set as before, except with the addition of "Stainless Steel Providers".

The next day, we were flying to Texas, girlfriend in tow. I couldn't very well leave her in an unknown country with people she didn't know. Unfortunately, between her wide-eyed apprehension about everything (and mine, to a slightly lesser extent) and Al's constant baiting of us, aided by his braying yes-men, I was on the defensive from the jump.

I didn't enjoy that first mini-tour at all. Al was still out to prove that he wasn't a bargain-bin Boy George, and I was a perfect target for him: new, unused to the ways of boorish Americans and the boorish American way, basically scared of my shadow and out of my element. I enjoyed the shows themselves, I enjoyed fronting the band, and I enjoyed that people actually showed up to see us. This was all very novel to me. However, I digress. The basic concept behind the tour was to fly to each state we were playing and then rent a vehicle from there to go from city to city.

We flew into Houston and were met there by Jourgensen's yes man #1, a gentleman named Philip Owen—"Phildo" to his halfwit friends. At first I thought he was pretending for our amusement to be a redneck, but it soon became apparent that he was just a redneck. I wouldn't say he was completely without intelligence, but he used a lot of his intelligence to masterfully cover up any trace of intelligence, lest any of his friends (who really were dumb as a bag of hammers) realise that he may not be the complete roaring imbecile he acted.

"Hooooooooo! MAN! We wus pardyin' las' night, man! We wus fuuuucked up!! Man, Bubba stole a fuckin' COW from a fuckin' FARM! Man, it was awwwwesome! Hoooooooooooo!!"

This man, I learned quickly, did little else with his time except party, and talk about Al, and do what Al wished. Hoooooooooo!!!!

Well, he was good enough to drive us through to Austin, and after we were on the highway, all Cocks and my lady-friend crammed into a van with the gear, our host decided it would be an absolute wheeze to get on his CB radio and show Al how nice it was that you could make friends with real Texan truckers…

"Hey!" he screamed into the handset, "How many a' you trucker FAGGOTS wanna SUCK MY MOTHERFUCKIN' DIIIIICK!" garnering an immediate response from our fellow road warriors.

Then, "I'm gonna kick your pussy trucker ASS so fuckin' hard your fuckin' ASS CHEEKS'LL COME OUT YOUR FUCKING FAGGOT PIE HOLE!!!!!" and so on.

Needless to say, Phildo's cordial invitations earned us a tail of about eight enthusiastic trucks, bursting with very, very angry men who were armed. You could hear their counter-threats coming over the CB. You could also hear them talking with each other about the very nature of our dismemberment, the general sentiment being pretty uniform.

"I'm gonna fuck you up, you sorry son of a bitch."

In grey, determined tones over the air… all we needed was a fast-paced, banjo-pickin' soundtrack as Phildo "WOOOO HOO HOOOOOO'D", pulled a U-turn over a wide grass median, and headed in the opposite direction away from the truckers and onto some quieter back roads.

Throughout all of this, of course, I would have been less scared if I was being thrown out of a helicopter into a yawning volcano—that sounded kind of peaceful in comparison. I sat rigid in my seat, ashen faced, to be honest. I don't know what the other Cocks were thinking. I honestly can't imagine that Bill was thrilled, but perhaps he was grimly rolling his eyes with a firm resignation and thinking, "Ah, yes, this again." Al, of course, thought this was all just hilarious, and he loved the fact that I was scared witless. Maybe Phildo had a gun. Maybe Al knew this. I'll tell you something though, I do not fancy Al's chances in a fight. He may be able to square off admirably with a lamb, or some other meek being, but…

Okay, welcome to Texas, yes, you're all great (and armed) and you all know how to shout and bully, yes, and thanks for having me. We were booked into a shitty little motel, but as I had never stayed in a hotel in my life, it might as well have been the Austin Hilton. It had a swimming pool! Vermin infested, yes, but a pool nonetheless.

Soon, our party was gathered around said pool, perched on the white plastic furniture and drinking beer. Al was holding court as more and more of Phildo's moronic cronies arrived to listen and relay their tales of alcohol poisoning and failed romance ("Man, that bitch just fuckin' slapped me and walked out!! HOOOOOOOO!"), the Princess and the Poodle braying every time one of Al's muscles twitched. Luc, being the subject of much speculation as to what a similar scenario in his native Belgium might have been like, just grinned and nodded. The performing Eurobear.

The venue for the first Cocks' show outside of Chicago was Liberty Lunch, basically a kind of beer garden, with wooden picnic tables and a dirt floor. I was excited because I heard someone from Scratch Acid and/or the Butthole Surfers might come, two bands I liked. After the soundcheck, the band, crew and Phildo's monkeys retired to the motel, carrying Jourgensen in a Sedan chair through the streets of Austin. I elected to stay and keep my girlfriend, who was selling T-shirts, company. My Beach Boys tape blared through the PA as people filed in. It would repeat itself several times before we played, much to the chagrin of the audience. After a while, I sat by myself in the grey semi-darkness of the dressing room, forlornly nursing a case of Budweiser and wondering if I had made a horrible mistake in coming to the US at all.

In a desperate attempt to try and bolster my cache with Al and his Texan pals, I tried the stage diving trick again at the Liberty Lunch, running from the dressing room, which was behind the stage, and into the air. It worked great, except that there was a gap of fifteen feet between the stage and the somewhat reluctant crowd. I hit the ground hard on my face, lost a tooth, felt like an idiot… was an idiot.

It was pretty obvious that Al was unhappy in his choice of singers, and was trying to get me to leave of my own accord, thus saving him the bother of firing me. Although the rest of the band seemed to like me, and I certainly could sing, Al wanted some kind of hybrid between Phildo and Ogre; but, for the time being, I was not about to leave and go back to Edinburgh defeated. Also, it was unlikely that Ogre would leave his own far more successful band and Ogre's many fans probably did not want to see him snatched from the dark miasma of Skinny Puppy and dropped into the fake shit-kickin' electro hoedown of the Cocks.

The next day we drove back to play in Houston at Numbers, which was kind of the Metro crossed with a gay bar. Bruce, the owner, was a flamboyant and gracious host and looked after us for the two days we were there. The stage had been decorated by a guy called Dan Manson, a soft spoken artist who seemed to possess all of the necessary requirements of a not-very-good cult leader: goatee, tie-dye clothes, extreme body art, millions of hallucinogens, and an open door policy on free love. He was a nice guy and he had clearly taken an awful lot of drugs, and had a kind of pierced and tattooed following of waifish hippy Goth girls and lost-looking androgynous boys. They had taken a lot of care and precision to make the stage look like a fleet of painted VW hippy vans had crashed badly on it.

The show itself was insane. I learned that apparently Houston was the birthplace of the drug ecstasy, and outside a pharmaceutical headquarters downtown there was a huge statue of a guy doing a really stupid dance, with a brass plaque underneath it relaying the story of MDMA. So naturally everyone, everyone, was out of their fucking gourds! I had not taken ecstasy. Of course I couldn't find any—lock me in a brewery, I'll walk out sober, I swear—but there was an incredible amount of very strong coke. And so, a numb throat and dancing electric nerves onstage, as Al jumped around terrifying me with a can of hairspray and a cigarette lighter.

The scene after the show made anything I had borne witness to in Chicago seem like a women's guild coffee morning: Goths, transvestites, punks, and outright weirdoes seemed to be melting into the club floor. Girls who had visited us backstage were being carted out by their arms and legs. I had managed to Ray Liotta myself into a complete paranoid frenzy, not knowing that the club employed off-duty, uniformed cops to patrol the place and throw out undesirables. I thought the place was being busted. Everywhere I turned, there was a cop, and every cop in the building saw this rail thin, pallid Scot with a halo of powder around his shiny beak, frenetically twitching and running away. When I eventually found an exit, I ran into the parking lot to see if I could find a taxi to take me and my girlfriend back to the hotel, having reasonably assumed that the whole world was too high to drive, only to be confronted with hostiles, sweeping searchlights and an army of helicopters bearing down on me! Of course. Eventually, someone was found who didn't seem to have a dozen eyeballs in each socket, and we were taken back to the Holiday Inn.

All things considered, I was quite certain that Texas had little time for a far-left thinking vegetarian foreigner; although, coming from Scotland and being fond of drinking ensured that I was not lynched. (I think.) Of course, I did meet some nice Texans. (And certainly have since, courting several of its daughters, thank you kindly, sir.) The first two days I spent in Texas were too much, and I was too green, Al was too much of a dick, and Phildo's friends were just… well, just, "WOOOOOOOOOOOOO! FUCKIN" SHIT BITCH FUCK, MAN, FUUUUUCKED UP, DUDE!!!" Which is all fine and well, but they were the most annoying people I had ever met. Imagine my dismay when, at a later date, I realised they were in a band, a band who would play with us a lot, a band who were not very good at all… a band called the Skatenigs.

Florida was different—slightly better by virtue of the fact that, yes, I was surrounded by morons all the time, but at least they didn't scream and roar constantly. They kind of spoke in a low growl, with disdain and sarcasm, not aimed at me, but in a kind of "I can't believe society and its tyrannical rule book is making me…." you know, "buy this newspaper full of lies", "eat this poison", "work this job where I am made to suck such corporate cock".

I suspect that the people I was talking to were trying to impress me, or more realistically, impress Al through me, but to little avail. Al was busy with Orlando's own version of Phildo. A very different animal from Phildo, being that the guy had "friendless" written all over his spherical body. His name was Mike World and he was promoting all of our Florida shows. He made the big mistake of coming down to soundcheck to say hi. Instead of a jovial "hi!" from Al, he got a pharmaceutical grocery list screamed in his porcine face.

"You better get us a 8 BALL EACH, you little FUCK, and a fuckin' CASE of Absolut vodka, or we trash this shithole and WALK, MAN!!!"

To which came the reply that no longer surprised me, "Eah hea hea hea! Aw! This is fuckin' excellent, man. Al, you are too fuckin' much."

It was as if Al and he had some code that the rest of us—including Mike's little Gothy hirelings who were standing around looking at their boss take this—were not privy to, and they were just telling each other jokes: "WHY DID THE CHICKEN CROSS THE FUCKIN' ROAD, YOU LITTLE FUCK!!" However, Mike's frozen grin and pale, sweaty pallor betrayed his absolute terror, a walking hybrid of Danny DeVito and Robert Smith from the Cure…

"Hey, fuck you, you fuckin' circus freak, and there BETTER be some bitches at the fuckin' show or we fuckin' WALK!"

Now, Florida is famous for sunshine and orange juice; it is also famous for coke (and I think coke money has bankrolled every endeavour of ours in the Sunshine State). But did you have any idea it was also famous for its UNDEAD? There were so many rail-thin, chalk-white Goths, filed down teeth, piercings, tattoos, and general all-around sun haters, condemned to rub shoulders with retirees and Disney characters for all eternity.

Mike World had little choice but to show up with a ton of coke before we played. The venue, like so many in Florida over the years, was in a strip mall, and may have formerly been a gym or a ladies' shoe store. Either way, it was highly unsuitable for our brand of redneck Eurodisco.

The next day, we took a detour and visited Al's parents, which was a very surreal event. A tacit father and a born-again mother from Cuba, they were kind enough to feed our whole party. I was relieved that we had one more show and then we were headed back to Chicago for a week. Al and his lapdogs were really grating on my nerves, and so was Florida, and so had Texas. We played in a brightly lit club, in the front window so people walking by on the street could see us from behind. This was Tampa, and the club looked like it was generally bursting at the seams with blonde hair and tans looking for a shag. They certainly would not have been looking for us. We put on a crappy show and split.

We flew back to Chicago and were met by Jim and Dannie at the airport. I was going to be staying with them until I found an apartment, being that Al had tired of me. I was also informed that, on the next leg, I could not take the girlfriend, which was a blessed relief for me—her too, probably.

After a couple of days off, we were headed to Detroit. We piled into the van. Al was behaving like I had fucked his wife, so I (regrettably) started drinking. It was a long drive to Detroit, and I was plastered when we got there. We had to attend an "in-store" before soundcheck. The idea was to show up at a local record store where throngs of adoring fans who bought our records would get us to sign them. However, there didn't seem to be throngs of fans, and the event quickly turned into a shoplifting spree. The store was owned and run by a tall, thin reptile and his tall, thin reptile wife. They were super, super, mega-Goths, and spoke just like the people in Florida, with a tone of sarcasm and disdain all the time.

"Well, what do you think of our fair city? Heh heh heh heh!"

Half the store was taken up with records, the other with horrible shiny black plastic corsets, Misfits T-shirts, and black feather boas. I managed to shove half a dozen albums down my pants, and someone else from our party stole a black wedding dress as a forlorn flock of Goth children stood around vainly waiting for Richard 23, Ogre, or maybe even Peter Murphy to breeze in and bite us all on the neck.

The venue was St Andrews, a venue I still, to this day, return to every so often, and it has not changed much: a large room which could have been a kind of ballroom, with a disco in the basement and a huge dressing room with a piano. As soon as we got to the venue, Al hijacked the van and went off in search of crack cocaine. A good while later he reappeared with a quantity of the drug and two new pals, Charles and Renee, both hardened drug addicts. Charles was on crutches, and Renee hovered by his side.

"I drove the van into the fucking GHETTO man, people were SHOOTING at me, it was fucked up, I got CHASED, they told me they would KILL me if I ever came back! I am so fuckin' high man!" Al, beaming, spun his tale. Yeah, sure you did, Al!

"Ouuuutstanding!!" exclaimed the Poodle, his voice jumping several octaves. After the Poodle and the Princess had tried the new drug, I thought that if I did, it might re-ingratiate myself to Al. But all it did was make me vomit a full fifteen minutes before I had to bounce onstage. It was horrible, and I felt really stupid.

Because of Al's hostility—or, at best, indifference—to me at this point, I was socialising far more with Paul and Bill. I would talk to Bill endlessly about music (which laid the foundation for a musical collaboration in the future) and talk to Paul endlessly, zeroing in on factoids that seemed to fascinate him and no one else. ("Okay, check it out, man, rubber suction cups!")

Bill and Paul, having a long history, could exchange non-sequiturs for hours, kind of like *Waiting for Godot,* performed by Laurel and Hardy. They were used to Al and told me to just ignore him. It was actually thanks to them that I didn't split and catch the plane back to Scotland. As well as being the rhythm section, and maintaining their Dadaist dialogue, Paul and Bill took care of all the logistics and money. I had heard that Al had tried to tour-manage before and it had ended in tears and the money disappearing with a Latino transvestite hooker. At least, that's what I had heard.

We drove back overnight to Chicago and rested for a day before heading to Cleveland and Boston. In Cleveland, Al's sorry attempt to get girls to strip onstage ended up with his being slapped and the girls running from our own Mr Irresistible as fast as they could. Boston saw the welcome return of cocaine, and also a curious war that seemed to have been going on for a while between Al and a local two-piece no-hoper 'industrial' rock band called Manufacture. While living in Boston, and during his Arista days, Al had been managed by the same company as the Cars, Iggy Pop and Suicide. Indeed, Boston is where he met his wife. It is also when he started to sing in a quaint British accent. The beef between Al and Manufacture stretched back a year or so, and I never found out why, except that bands that are within a certain genre love to fight each other, and love to gossip about each other. Indeed, later on in the genres of hip-hop and death metal, bands would eventually solve this problem by killing each other, but right now, here in Boston, it was no more threatening than a spat between teenage girls (Al, playing the role of teenage girl, interestingly, to a T).

Al had an answering machine tape of one of the guys in Manufacture gravely threatening anyone involved in Ministry dire consequences for whatever transgression had occurred, but the angered caller had such a high pitched, lisp-y voice, it just sounded silly. Now, as I may have mentioned before, at this time in Al's career, his *nom de plume* on record jackets appeared as Alain Jourgensen, a hangover from his worshipping all things Belgian, I suppose. Anyway, the Gallic pronunciation, you may remember from your French lessons is "Allahn." This was, however, typically mispronounced in the education-hating United States, and it backfired; everyone lucky to be on first name terms with Al called him "Elaine", which meant that the phone threat (which Al miked up and played onstage during our set through a boom box) sounded as threatening as, "You jutht better watch yourthelf, Elaine…", carrying with it a kind of Elmer Fudd-in-drag quality, i.e. non-threatening, and jutht kind of thad.

Intense drug abuse continued into the early hours of the morning, at least until I had safely assumed that the motel was surrounded by the police and the military, tipped off by a community-conscious motel worker. All there really were, were stray hookers and a night doorman fast asleep with his head face down on a copy of *Anal American*. I crawled under the sheets of my bed, certain that when the amassed forces finally broke down the motel room door, they would be so gleeful about nabbing the huge selection of master criminals and terrorists, they would fail to notice me.

After a gruelling drive back to Chicago from Boston, we had a week off before the final shows in Milwaukee and California. I managed to locate a dump of an apartment, my girlfriend had secured a job at Wax Trax!, and over at the Jourgensen household, in the boutique, the tour continued mercilessly as Al set up a huge paddling pool, a TV, and a blender in his back yard. The Poodle and the Princess, having taken up residency in the pool, continued to "haw haw haw!" at everything Al did or said, until Al finally threatened to throw the portable television into the pool with them if they didn't shut the fuck up. This interesting turn of events made them shut the fuck up for five minutes, but it was funny.

We had another "in-store", this time at Atomic Records in Milwaukee, where the long-suffering owner just let us take the albums we wanted to steal. The gig at the famous Eagles Club was rather sparsely attended, if memory serves. (There would be many return visits there, too.) Before the show, Al managed to find what was possibly Milwaukee's sole coke dealer, a seedy fellow wearing sunglasses with a ponytail and male pattern baldness, who sold Al Milwaukee's sole gram of coke. Al ripped a mirror off the dressing room wall and carved out one long line that he inhaled himself, making a clean plate. Good boy. Onstage that night, to celebrate his Herculean stamina, he ran up to me while singing and threw a full vodka grapefruit in my face. It stung and I couldn't open my eyes. What a fucking dick!!!

Finally, I got to go to California; I was more excited about going to L.A. and San Francisco than I was anywhere else. We flew into L.A. and were met there by Ogre, who was in the middle of a month-long speed binge. Al immediately started crawling up his ass, grabbing my Walkman and giving it to Ogre to listen to a track he wanted him to sing on. All of this outside baggage claim as we were trying to load our gear into the van. Ogre looked horrible, as if he had been up for a month… oh, wait, he had been up for a month. He had been staying with this creepy, yet affluent, couple in the Hollywood Hills whose job seemed to be taking speed. Maybe they were market researchers for drug lords, who knows? Anyway, they were playing host to Ogre as he assisted them in their research, and Ogre was bringing Al, the Poodle and the Princess, and Luc to stay there. Paul, Bill, and I, of course, were disqualified from this privilege. We spent a while searching for a motel, which we found in a seedy corner, not far from the 'Chateau Amphetamine'. It was $30 a night, and it would have sent even Tom Waits running for domestic hygiene. However, this is where we would stay.

We had the next day off, and we dropped by the creepy speed house to check in on the peanut gallery. They were all wound up tight as drums, having been on a speed binge since the night before. Al was making Daiquiris in the back yard while the Poodle morphed into a fat, blanched parrot, screeching, "That is the sound of success!!! Ouuuutstanding!!", every time Al turned on the blender to whip up some more drinks. This almost had the appearance of a scientific experiment, correlating animal behaviour with a reward system, until the fat parrot stopped dead in his tracks and turned as green as the lush hillside we were on. He started to rotate on the spot as he projectile vomited a near perfect circle around him, clearing about four feet. I mean, this guy was really projecting. Everyone fell about laughing and the poor slob excused himself to go and lie down. Outstanding.

Bill, Paul, and I soon grew tired of this rather familiar scene and drove off to the beach for a while, prior to moving our operation to a loft space where we would be staying until after the gig. Who knew who lived there, it's a friend of a friend of a friend, and it's this incredible loft downtown, like something out of *To Live and Die in LA*. I was shocked to find that the five inhabitants of this loft neither went "Wooooooooooo!", nor did they speak in the Florida's Goth growling and sneering dialect. They were five charming students and we had a lovely time and they took me to a party where I was convinced I saw Ricardo Montalbán. It was all very normal and nice. Hmmmmm... my sense of relief was palpable.

The L.A. show was great. Savage Republic opened, a band I had been interested in for some time. The Cocks played a good show and afterwards we went to the affluent creepy couple's house to continue "market research" into various white powders. The former drummer for Killing Joke appeared, as if out of nowhere. I was impressed. Little did I know that our paths would cross professionally a couple of years down the line. His name was Paul Fergusson, known as "Big Paul". A lovely guy.

In San Francisco, I made Paul take me to Mount Davidson Park, so I could go to the cross at the top where Scorpio had smashed Inspector Harry Callahan's face in during the masterful first *Dirty Harry* film. I was so excited, I almost "put my nose right up against the concrete" and stabbed myself in the leg just like Scorpio did—but then I chose not to.

Backstage at the I-Beam, I met Jello Biafra. The Fini Tribe had recently contributed a track to a compilation to help Jello with his legal fees. I politely told him this fact, and that I was excited to have been a part of the project. Mr. Biafra could not have been more indifferent, but I was pretty drunk and I may have been abhorrent, I don't know. He was always nice during future meetings. After he left, Al paraded around the dressing room, telling all, "Me and Jello got plans, man", which, as you may know, they did, bully for them. I had hit the crystal meth hard that night, trying to counteract the whiskey I had consumed during the gig. Instead, my blood turned into hair spray, and I sat by myself at the hotel pool until it was time to leave in the morning, miserable.

And that was the end of the Cocks' tour, I think that Al wanted it to be the last interaction he had with me, but he changed his tune, and everything would eventually work out in its own twisted, awful way. We had certainly had a rocky start, even though I feel like I had proven myself a formidable front man—but perhaps that was the problem. Perhaps the problem was Al was just being a dick. Read on. Read on, and make up your own mind.

# WE'VE GOT A SURPRISE FOR YOU

**Left:** Scenes from the "Stainless Steel Providers" video. (H-Gun)

**Above:** Pre-tour relaxation, 1989.

# 5

# NO NAME, NO SLOGAN

As soon as we returned to Chicago, Al seemed to make a concerted effort to get me blacklisted from everywhere. I was kind of oblivious to this, as he flounced around from the label, to the store, to any number of clubs, telling anyone who'd listen that I was a complete failure. It mattered not, really. I decided that Al eventually treated everyone this way, whom he believed to be either a threat or who wasn't in awe of his lordship. But, really, who didn't want a pale, shaven-headed Scot in their life? So nobody paid much heed to him, and the memories of Al wearing a little smock and a stupid Zorro hat were still kind of fresh, my friends.

So, I was making my own way; I had a job, and with Jim, Dannie, Frank, Dave, Sean, and many others, I had a very reliable support system. Jim and Dannie showed up at my house one early evening with a house-warming gift of a record player. Frank was always giving me clothes and books. I was very well looked after.

Al and Paul seemed to be on the home stretch with *The Land of Rape and Honey*, and apart from a couple of sessions at Trax to redo the vocals on "Cattle Grind" and "In the Neck", I felt like *persona non grata* around there. "Stainless Steel Providers" and "At the Top" were shaped into a 12-inch single, Al adding accents and drum fills to "At the Top", to my piano and Dave Collins' programmed rhythms. A guitar solo and some smartass edits were thrown onto "Stainless", shaping it into a formidable modern day "Born to be Wild"—it was a class act, even for the utterly classless Cocks.

When the master tapes for *Rape and Honey* were delivered, Al started putting together a touring band. He flew Luc back over; a few of the Skinny Puppy organisation were siphoned down from Vancouver; Bill was brought in as guitarist and keyboard player, the drum stool being occupied by Jeff Ward—or Abner, as he came to be called—a warm-hearted suburban metalhead from a band called Hammeron. He had met Al at Trax, and supplied the drum fills to "At the Top". I, however, was not invited to go on the road, and was I bitter? I was fucking furious! He flew in Luc from Belgium, pilfered as much of the Skinny Puppy extended family as he could, and, purely as a bloody-minded show of power, froze me out.

While everyone was in town, we made a video for "Stainless Steel Providers". The guys who shot it, H-Gun, had already completed two excellent videos for *Rape and Honey* and we assembled at a loft space in Chicago's then deserted Wicker Park area to shoot. Some of the scenes were shot at the Double Door, which is now a *bona fide* rock venue. Back then, it was a creepy liquor store complete with bulletproof glass, and a country and western line-dancing venue in the back. I got to attack a motorbike, douse it in petrol and push it off a roof. It was a lot less spectacular than I thought, but it was really good fun. Ogre was in the video—Al's way of name-dropping. He wasn't on the record, but he seemed to be determined to tell the world that he and Ogre were tight. He should've just thrown a press conference, or just bitten Ogre in the neck and sucked his blood, no difference.

Someone must have spoken to Al about his dress sense because, a couple of weeks before the tour he showed up at the label declaring, "I am Thor, the rock God", with what appeared to be a huge black woollen cat toy attached to the back of his head, which I realised, with some shock, were actually hair extensions. Probably the cheapest available. Along with this, he had gone on a spending spree to the "Alley", a local punky Gothy clothing store, and purchased a whole wardrobe that could have belonged to a teenage boy who couldn't make up his mind if he loved Peter Murphy or Rob Halford. Essentially, Al had just invented a look for his audience, though at the time, it just looked really silly.

Mercifully for Al, someone, probably his long-suffering Missus, broke it to him about the cat toy on the back of his bonce, because it was gone within 24 hours. I attended a warm-up show at Medusa's, but left in a childish huff. Then I attended the proper show at the Riviera a week later and left seething, although I did not stay angry for long. Left to my own devices in Chicago, I met a lot of people when I went out, many of whom had a similarly low opinion of Elaine, and who enjoyed dishing the dirt about him. Needless to say, I felt a little more vindicated and a little more childish.

The tour finished and 1989 began. For some inexplicable reason, Al decided that I was okay again. Coming by work late one afternoon, he asked me out for a beer and I accepted, happy to pretend that there had been no nastiness between us ever—such is my pathological fear of confrontation. We drank up and went to Trax, thus beginning what I considered to be my work in earnest. 1989 was the afterburn of *The Land of Rape and Honey*. Al and Paul were still on a creative high, as was I, and we seemed to have unlimited studio time, especially since the record had performed beyond anyone's expectations.

The first missile we launched was the "Stainless Steel Providers" 12-inch, which I considered my first work proper with the band, and something of a declaration of intent. With its black leather jacket cover, it was an immediate underground dance hit. A lot more streamlined than the live double *You Goddamned Son of a Bitch* that preceded it, which I thought was a great album, but it carried more of a comic value than quality music.

It was at this time that Al, wife, and child had moved into a spectacular dwelling on Ravenswood and Lincoln, a few miles from the Wax Trax! empire. It was a sprawling loft that fitted Al's needs perfectly. As well as sheer floor space, there was a hot tub, many mirrored walls, and a plethora of faux roman columns. It was hard to pinpoint who may have dwelled there before (a low-level failed Russian mobster, I offer).

Many nights were spent at Trax with a new engineer at the helm, Keith "Fluffy" Auerbach. God knows what happened to the Poodle. I am sure it was "outstanding", whatever it was. Fluffy was fantastic. Another suburban metalhead… weeelll maybe not so much a metalhead as a classic rock dork with a very Van Halen hairdo. But he was energetic and good-natured, and weathered the "Jourgenstorm" very well for years, until the drugs and the long hours wore at him. Between the four of us, there appeared a great camaraderie, and all of a sudden, I realised that I really liked Al. Although he had the potential to be an absolute bloody-minded asshole, his good side was great, and I soon began to relax and enjoy working with him.

There were a few guests at Trax in those months. The first was Cabaret Voltaire. Now, when I was in my early to late teens, the Cabs played a close second to my favourites, Throbbing Gristle. Trivia fans— if indeed this can even be counted as trivia—one of my earliest public performances was at summer camp in 1980, where me and my mate, Simon Richardson, performed "Nag Nag Nag" at the nightly sing-song in front of about 100 schoolboys more used to hearing "An Austrian Went Yodelling" or "A Froggy Would a-Wooing Go". Needless to say, I was very excited about meeting these guys. They were in town to work on the album *Groovy, Laidback and Nasty* with house producer Marshall Jefferson. (Groovy, Laidback and Boring was more like it. Sorry lads, but *Mix Up*, it was not.) Anyway, top Chicago house legend Marshall Jefferson got top Chicago house food poisoning, which meant that former ground-breaking Sheffield noise manipulators, Stephen "Mal" Mallinder and Richard H. Kirk, were kind of at a loose end. Wax Trax! were very proactive in introducing them to Al, and away we went!

Al and I immediately dubbed them "Grumpy" and "Party", Richard H. Kirk being "Grumpy". He looked like he could have walked out of a Lowry painting wearing a flat cap and stating, "Where there's muck, there's brass, lad", whereas Mal was tall, handsome and utterly charming.

They were both delighted that I was Scottish and I strung them along with the polite, soft-spoken, ex-public schoolboy bit for quite a while—about three hours—until I vomited at their feet while we were crammed into a ladies toilet stall at Smart Bar doing coke at the same time. Utterly charming.

So, in between a gruelling nightclub schedule, we managed to squeeze out a song, but it was not easy. It was far more fun just going out with these guys, and my first attempts at writing a lyric about a cross dresser were received with hostility. ("We're not bloody doin' a song about a bloody push-oop bra!!!"—Richard) The music, as well, did not know where it wanted to go, until eventually the song hit its stride as a kind of cowboy-in-a-gay bar galloping dance track called "No Name, No Slogan". One afternoon, before we were due to mix and add overdubs, Richard called me at work and asked if I could get my hands on any blank C60 and C90 cassettes.

"Oh, they have all that stuff at Trax, Richard, no problem."

"Aye right, but we're lookin' for a certain kind of cassette, d'yer know what I mean?"

I did not. Eventually Jim took the phone from me and said, "Hey, you should do another album like *Microphonies*, the only album you ever did that sold worth a shit."

Always the king of subtle A&R advice, Jim eventually realised that C60s were code for pot, and C90s for coke. Apparently, the phone lines in all the top London studios were crackling with this code that foxed even Scotland Yard! The last time I saw Richard and Mal was on the other side of Wrightwood Avenue, with Al and I pelting them with snowballs, and them giving as good as they got before fleeing for a taxi. We had been asked to leave Club 950, for any number of reasons, who knows? We had finished most of "No Name, No Slogan" and Cabaret Voltaire had scurried back to the bland confines of *Groovy, Laidback and Nasty* with Marshall Jefferson, which is why they had come in the first place. Eventually they completed their own mix of "No Name", sending it to us from Sheffield.

Amid all of our diligence in the studio, we still found hours and hours to waste; pot and psychedelics were for a brief time the order of the day. One evening Al had Reid, the studio owner, take us out for extensive Margarita research. Upon returning to Trax to work, we remembered we had taken acid, and our tiny minds could not bend around the idea of working. Instead, it was decided to fairly and squarely blame Reid for making us drink when we had work to do. So the evening passed with us calling Reid at home and leaving increasingly surreal messages on his machine, eventually realising that the answering machine tape would make a fantastic B-side. "Reid, you gotta save this answering machine tape, man, do NOT erase it, or we WILL torch the studio". The tape never saw the light of day. I am sure it was not very funny, but it was fun making it, and certainly it was fun to waste hours and hours of time doing something we could have done at home for free, and not for a hundred bucks an hour, ha ha.

A few days later, we put "Acid Horse" to bed with a marathon midweek mixing session fuelled by a huge bag of magic mushrooms. The hilarity and childlike pleasure of which was brought to a screeching halt when I went to the Trax toilet to piss, only to realise that the actual toilet bowl had turned into a huge shiny white snapping horse's head with angry black eyes. I decided it was best to back off using the toilet and quietly sneak off home.

Heroin was here. I knew it would be; it was inevitable. Al was calling the shots in all of this, and he seemed to have been "cramming" for his degree in rock myths from the Johnny Thunders university since before I met him—working harder than anyone else to scream and shout from the rooftops, "I take lots of drugs too!" Except, and I am not trying to be mean (believe it or not), he just didn't have what someone like Iggy has, which is a far deeper and wilder spirit that drugs only served to unlock. Drugs never made people like Iggy Pop, they were a side effect. Al wanted to be a rock myth as quickly as it took to buy his skull and crossbones black spandex pants. Ho-hum.

I, however, was happy to ride along, as usual. Heroin seemed to creep in during the *Rape and Honey* tour—I had heard tell from people out on the road that Al was dabbling, not very much, but dabbling. I had been there before. In my final year of high school over a weekend with the bad boys, I had lived out a tiny rock 'n' roll fantasy in a squalid flat, somewhere near Haymarket. Then later, under doctor's orders following extensive surgery, I was fed opiates in pill form. I loved the feeling, the nothing, and here it was again. Sure, why not?

As far as these next few months went, they were a crossroads for many things; mainly, the moving away musically from *The Land of Rape and Honey*, involving the deliberations for the direction and feeling for the next Ministry album. There was also the appearance of the bastard child of both of these albums, *Beers, Steers and Queers*, the next studio project by the Cocks. It was confusing times, exacerbated by the radically different drugs that seemed to pop up from session to session, and by the direction of the sessions themselves. The game plan was pretty loose: we knew we had some things to finish, we knew we had to start work on brand new material, but, we had afforded ourselves the luxury of not restricting ourselves to a name. We were darlings at Wax Trax!, so we could go to Jim and Dannie with anything we liked and they would release it under any name we wanted, knowing it would sell. Things got really blurry when the *Beers, Steers and Queers* sessions crossed with Ministry sessions, especially because we were unaware that they were. Al and Paul were spinning their wheels while they decided on the form of the new Ministry record, how to make it, or if it was just going to appear one day—which was not altogether an unreasonable supposition, given that we were, at this time, simply throwing mud against the wall (albeit loud sounding danceable mud with a retail value). Fortunately, at the end of (or during) the session, Al would say, "This could be an awesome Cocks track", or "We gotta make this a Ministry song", or "Let's make a side project with this one!!", saving any agonising decisions.

"Rubber Glove Seduction", the A-side to the one-and-only PTP single, may have started off as a Revolting Cocks—or maybe even an ill-fated Zoo Disco—song when we began work on it, back in the summer. But when Fluffy threaded the two-inch reel onto the tape machine and we listened to it again, it had a life of its own. That's why we decided to use the PTP moniker, which, as I mentioned before, Al had used before to circumvent contractual obligations and get some music into the first *Robocop* movie without his label noticing. But there was absolutely no reason why we couldn't use it now. The soundtrack to a maximum security prison's aerobics class, the track bounced along with the pep and vigour of a beach ball, inspiring my lyric about a quiet suburban home intrusion, the perpetrator asking, "Can I try on these rubber gloves", "Can I borrow a pair of scissors?" and, perhaps more tellingly, "Can I have a bath?"

My vocals were all recorded at a slow speed, so when played back, it sounded like a nine-year old. Al and Paul threw subtle, sonic splinters over the rest of the track; clicks, clocks, alarms, and cops, all sped up and razor sharp—it was like trying to eat a push pin soufflé, if you will allow the preposterous analogy. We were all in stitches as we did the backing vocals, trying to copy the dance moves of Gladys Knight and the Pips doing "Midnight Train to Georgia".

The end product was a godless collision between the first Mothers of Invention album and Dead or Alive. Again, preposterous seems to be the buzzword... I swear it had "hit" stamped all over it. Eventually, we paired it with "My Favorite Things", the Zoo Disco track from my first few days in the studio the previous spring. Actually, it was the perfect complement to the A-side. Perhaps we should have called it quits and dissolved the Cocks and Ministry at this point, concentrating on the saccharine sounds of PTP—oh well. I believe that "My Favorite Things" started its life in the hands of Keith LeBlanc and Adrian Sherwood, being groomed for a Tackhead song; you can tell by the way the drums sound, just like a Tackhead track. I remember Al mumbling about trading a gram of speed for the drum track—ultimately, who cares. Al threw on a lovely wah-wah guitar solo in the middle that gave the track its joyous effervescence. (I sound like I am writing for a cooking magazine.)

So with two "side project" singles under our belt, Wax Trax! were delighted. Jim liked to horrify us by taking the cassette we would give him, running to Smart Bar, and making the DJ play it at midnight on a weekend night to "gauge an immediate dance floor reaction"—but going from large-grooved twelve-inch vinyl to tiny little cassette causes a massive drop in volume and sound fidelity, so almost always he'd come back from these excursions drunk and furious that the dance floor had cleared off immediately. And then word would leak that our new material "fuckin' suuucked". Thanks, Jim.

We wanted to finish a Cocks album, and we wanted to put a cover version on it, a novelty song starting a kind of tradition for the Cocks. I was actually kind of inspired by the Young Gods' cover of Gary Glitter's "Hello! Hello! I'm Back Again", which was priceless. We did kind of the same thing with Olivia Newton John's "Let's Get Physical", stripping it of any playful feminine perfumed innuendo, and turning it into a lumbering 300 pound drooling stalker serenade—all in good fun, of course. Ultimately, the writer of the song—when approached by us for permission—blew a gasket. More about that later... BUT what a perfect Cocks track! Although, naturally we had changed every note of the music to suit our purposes, the lyrics remained the same, and Al even sampled and slowed down Olivia crooning "Physical", turning her from a spunky, peppy tease, into a halfwit. I chose to sing the lyrics like a vengeful Scottish drill-sergeant, barking out the "come to bed" lyrics like a psychopath in a brothel. Among the nuances of the recording, Al disappeared into the vocal booth with a half empty glass of Dr Pepper, claiming its crystalline percussive tones. He was stoned and kept drinking from the glass, thus changing the tone completely, necessitating a top up... Physsssicaaal. The final addition was thanks to me leaving a Lydia Lunch album I had just bought lying around the studio, which Al found and sampled. This would also prove to be the beginning of another bone of contention... more about that later too.

Winter stretched into spring, and with spring came hypodermic needles and the intravenous use of illegal substances. It was the beginning of the decay—not absolute yet, but Al was forcing the hand of chance, and the bad stuff was around the corner.

Al disappeared for a few weeks to Vancouver to work on a Skinny Puppy record. When he returned, it was time to start work on a new Ministry album—the one that became *The Mind is a Terrible Thing to Taste*, or, "the title is an embarrassing thing to say", perhaps. Anyway, he and Paul imported the Princess from Vancouver to work on it. Bill was going to come, too. Fluffy was on board to engineer, and we were all going to have a jolly old time. The night Paul and I picked up the Princess from O'Hare, we took him to Al's, where he was to be stationed, and who should be there when we walked into the living room? Only post-punk apocalyptic has-beens KILLING FUCKING JOKE!! I was pleased as punch, even though they were, at that point, past their sell-by date and vaguely trying to reclaim the American audience they never really had in the first place. It was nice to meet them, and they would figure heavily in my life a little later in this story.

Jaz Coleman, the singer, looking like a drunk Greek waiter, swaying about, clinging onto a Big Gulp full of Bloody Mary, roaring his proclamations—which generally, subject-wise, stayed pretty close to JAZ and what JAZ thought. Who was I to doubt? I played the grooves off *Requiem* when I was still wearing a school uniform, and who wouldn't be tickled at listening to Jaz Coleman declaring:

"OI WAS AN EEEGYPTIAN GOD IN A PREVIOUS LOIFE!!!" gulp gulp gulp

"OI BELIEVE IN THE TOTAL FREEDOM TO DO WHAT OI WANT!!!" gulp… gulp

Then… "OO ORDERED THE MOUSSAKA???"

Just kidding about the last one.

The *Mind* sessions started slowly. I had actually gone to a rehearsal space with Paul to see if anything happened, but it didn't really. Ministry belonged in the studio, at whatever expense. That's where it seemed to happen: composition and execution. So, when Bill came, his kit was set up in the live room with a view to the band playing live, but much of the time Bill just went out there on his own and laid down drum tracks, raw or with loops. It was some of the most incredible drumming I have ever witnessed. The loops came from the hundreds of movies rented from video stores, as did the many samples on the album: *Cry Freedom*, *Full Metal Jacket*, *Dead Ringers*, and *Scarface* were all plundered for sounds and vocal samples. The first loop I remember was from *Cry Freedom* and formed the basis of "Breathe", for which Bill's drum pattern walked between military invasion and the *Brides of Dr. Funkenstein*.

The music was immediately more organic than *Rape and Honey*, much due to the fact that the drums were live and real. (There are no real drums on *Rape*, it's all programmed. Maybe Keith LeBlanc is on it, but if he was, Al ain't sayin'.) As the song progressed, it turned from being an interesting almost Eno-esque rhythm workout into a tidal wave of sound, spearheaded by a wall of guitars (inevitably). Al flew Ogre in to work on the sessions; and in one brainstorming session, myself, Ogre, and Al came up with the lyrics to "Breathe".

This, by the way, was the beginning of where my job started to get tough, because Al wanted lyrics about certain topics, mostly political or ecologically motivated, and it was up to me to encapsulate his thoughts. He was picky—now I understand why—but at the time it was frustrating. I have a tendency to perhaps get somewhat florid in my poetry. Al liked that, but had to make it easy for the average Love and Rockets T-shirted teen to digest. I considered it good training for something, I don't know what.

Al and I multied many, many vocal takes along with whoever was capable at the time until we had a "gang" vocal. The effect of the song was absolute. The point was made. The icing on the cake: a single, high synth note played quietly throughout the whole song to sustain the tension.

"Never Believe" was another leftover from the short-lived Zoo Disco period, one of the first things I wrote in Chicago, and certainly the most ridiculous, overblown Jim Morrison-esque tripe I could have spewed up on tape. When I first "improvised" it, there was only percussion on the track. Then Al built up a wall of guitars and truncated the percussion into short militaristic bursts. It did not save the track from what it was—the sound of a vocalist disappearing up his own arsehole.

Similarly, but not as nauseating, was "Cannibal Song", where Al wanted us to sound like PiL's *Metal Box*, specifically "Albatross". He told me to get out there (into the vocal booth) and do my best John Lydon impersonation. (He loved my Lydon, I do him rather well.) Unfortunately, Al loved it enough to have me commit it to tape. The session was augmented with saxophone, which came with a free bag of china white heroin. I could have gone out there with instructions to sing like Judy Garland, I couldn't have cared less.

The sessions began to lose any sense of time. I would be at the studio for days on end, awake; perhaps grabbing a nap here or there, perhaps going home to change. There was the obligatory rogue's gallery of characters visiting at all hours of the day, including Al's new "extra special friend", a junky and an incredible shoplifter who would clean off the candy racks of the local 7-Eleven at least twice in every 24 hour period. Thus our dietary needs were attended to.

I thought that the track "Burning Inside" would have been great with just drums and vocals. Bill sweated for hours over that one. I spent 48 hours writing the lyrics over a weekend with a huge amount of coke, eventually recording a version by myself with Bill producing at five on a Sunday morning. Al took what I had written and essentially doubled it in length and speed, turning it into the paranoid coke frenzy that it is and probably best illustrates the working method we employed.

Sometimes we sat down together and wrote, sometimes I would record a few versions for him, and sometimes I would just hand him reams of paper and let him have a go at it. On some tracks, like "Faith Collapsing", nothing would come, so a chain of disparate vocal samples was spliced together in lieu of a vocal. This could be highly comedic or incredibly tedious, depending on the mood.

The most awful transgression against good taste was the song "Test", where Bill and Paul had built a powerhouse of a song that steamrollered relentlessly, barrelling out of the speakers with sheer assault. All very well—until Al found a rapper, immediately ruining a great song, and helping give birth to the concept of rap metal.

Perhaps the centrepiece of the album was "So What", based loosely on an old song by the Blackouts, Paul and Bill's old band. This was actually one of the few tracks where the "band"—such as it was—set up and played in the live room, creating a smoky, dub-fuelled groove, which kind of went nowhere for a while, but the same can be said of many of the tracks. Jello Biafra had given Al a videotape of a 1950s cautionary tale film about juvenile delinquency, and Al took long sections from a monologue near the end of the film, when a judge is passing sentence on the "juvenile delinquents". This was intercut with vocal samples of Michelle Pfeiffer in *Scarface*, giving the song its identity. I dashed off a lyric about teenage rebellion and anal sex—the rest is history.

It seemed that we were, over time, amassing what promised to be a decent, if patchy, album. Half the material was strong—the rest was, well, problematic, or just filler. The song "Faith Collapsing" was one of the songs made up of several samples spliced together where a vocal might have been. The groove was fantastic; Paul and Bill built an almost slow Burundi beat, over which Al laid a loop of indigenous chanting—perhaps South American, perhaps African. Shamefully, I do not know. But he wanted to augment it with our voices, and somehow take the chant and phonetically come up with an "English" version that might somehow be relevant to Ministry in some way. So everyone sat around the studio for hours, listening to the loop, uninterrupted, as it changed and morphed in our tired drug-addled heads. We each had a clipboard and a pad of paper as we wrote down everything we could think of with the correct amount of syllables and vowel sounds: "chase and trap me", "take a last stay", "create everlasting", "Aaaaargh!"

"No!!", "um", "state of cast weight!!", "late or fast shave", "FAITH COLLAPSING!!!!"—Bingo!! I can't remember who came up with this, it was either the Princess or Fluffy. However, you are reading the short version. Like I said, it went on for hours.

As per usual, Trax was the place to go when every club and bar had shut and you had been thrown out of your friend's house because they had to eventually get up for work. With these parameters in mind, you can well imagine the dregs that appeared ashen, skull-faced, and desperate at around 5 AM, just itching to let you into their life story—especially if you were in the middle of a lyric assignment. Perhaps part of their incredible saga would catapult you into some incredibly inspired wordplay:

"I was forced into stripping by an abusive boyfriend... I..."

"Yes, but you're not a stripper..."

"Yeah, but I have come pretty close to stripping, I can tell you..."

"I thought you worked as a coat check at the blah-blah bar..."

"I gotta find some coke..." This coupled with the usual, "I have always loved you, you are such a good person..."

"But we have met twice..."

"I just know these things, my great-grandma was a Scottish gypsy an..."

"You know what, fuck off home, why don't you..."

Yes, the 5 AM coke rap—nothing says wrist-slitting hijinks quite like it.

I stayed home one day with severe backache, and when I called Al the next day to find out what, if anything, was going on, he was in a near ecstatic frenzy.

"Man, I've just recorded the best song I've ever written, man! You gotta get over here!"

Indeed, "Thieves" was pretty incredible: a mini-epic, a bit like Brian Wilson's "Heroes and Villains", if it had been written and performed by Daleks. Actually, I do maintain that this is Ministry's crowning glory. It was kind of all rubbish after that. It was hard to conceive of a lyric at that point, given that the song had three speeds; stealthy, menacing, and homicidal. We managed to put together a decent lyric between Al, Ogre, and myself, but actually singing the thing was nigh-on impossible. We called Joe Kelly, the mildly annoying, slightly skinhead-y singer for stupid local punk band, Lost Cause, who sang the song with us for a case of Budweiser. He brought his breakneck bravado to the lyric, belting it out without even slightly scratching his throat—impressive.

A couple of new British folks were starting to buzz around the sessions, one of whom was former Public Image drummer Martin Atkins. The other was former UK Subs and Broken Bones' guitarist Terry Bones. They both carried with them the slightly annoying aura of British expat awash in the USA, which I am sure I was guilty of carrying, too. But you kind of need to be another British person, or a woefully duped American girlfriend (pick-up line "Cor, blimey!! Oi used to live with Sid Vicious/ Paul Weller/the Sisters of Mercy/Lady Di"… whatever worked for that particular American girl, it was case-sensitive), to be aware of it.

Martin and his wife, Leila, were nice. They were considering relocating from New Jersey—either they were being run out of town by the mob, or there was a whiff of musical opportunity in Chicago.

Terry Bones was perhaps one rung up the genetic ladder from a garden fence. From somewhere in the north of England, all he could do was play the "eeeh by gum, fookin hell!" regional accent card that might help him get away with being thick as two short planks in the USA— it's no wonder he relocated here. Back home, he would be either laying bricks, or throwing them through post office windows—quite probably the latter. Anyway, both of these characters would start to play a bigger part in this story later on.

During the making of the album, I eventually had to call it quits with working at Wax Trax!. Not even I, in all my robust youth, could continue to work 24 hours, no matter how sympathetic Jim Nash was. After all, I was working for one of his cash cows and enough was enough. I had been getting occasional royalty checks and my girlfriend had a steady income—but this state would not last, given my usual M.O. to finance. The money slipped away pretty quickly, and I would be back to pleading for another job before too long. Ho-hum.

As the work on the *Mind* album began to slow down, there was a last flurry of activity on the new Cocks album, too. Most of the material was odds and ends from the last few years that was dragged out to be tarted-up with lyrics and guitars.

"Something Wonderful" was an empty, cascading, paranoid vortex of punk propulsion; the lyric, a nihilistic frenzy, informed by Chrome (in my very oblique way, I had been listening to the album *Third From the Sun* in my time off).

But the crown, unfortunately, went to Phildo, who sent up a tape of his rap "Beers, Steers and Queers", giving Al the backbone of what became the title track. I have to hand it to him—in terms of puerile poetry, fit to be written by a 14 year-old bored in class, Phildo really was the poet laureate of his own sorry-ass cowshed. He managed to encapsulate the essence of the Cocks that I never really cared about—the kind of Beastie Boys, *Licensed to Ill,* stupid-young-people-with-tons-of-money mentality. (Wow, that's twice already I have alluded to how much I loathe the fucking Beastie Boys!)

So we were well on the way to having two albums, and a few singles as well. Really, in terms of the way Al and Paul worked, this was lightning speed, and it would never be like this again.

*The Mind is a Terrible Thing to Taste* turned out to be an uneven record. Apart from a few gems represented, it suffered from a lack of focus—a focus that was definitely the forte of its predecessor, *The Land of Rape and Honey.* This lack was due largely to an ensemble cast, rather than just a star and co-star. Al wanted a wall of guests to hide behind. I think he wanted to be the kind of Brian Wilson or Phil Spector mad genius hiding behind a puppet army and pulling strings. However, he also wanted to be a public figure, and be a frontman with his silly stick-on hairstyle and Bauhaus-joined-the-army uniform. Poor old Al.

The record was done, and the beginnings of a tour were being planned, which I was going to participate in this time, playing keyboards and singing. I was definitely back in Al's good graces, spending more time at his house with his family and my girlfriend, watching movies, playing cards, or snorting piles of white powder. All was apparently well.

ATTENTION
CYCLE
NEVER
BROKEN

**Above:** *Mind* tour pre-production with Jello Biafra.

**Left:** Paul Barker during pre-production, December 1989.

**Below:** First show soundcheck with tour manager, Jolly Roger, May 1990.

# 6

# BREATHE, YOU FUCKER. BREATHE!!

The *Mind* tour was a pivotal period for everyone involved; a real coming-of-age movie, from its conception and inception until its incredible cliff-hanger conclusion. It separated the men from the boys, the boys from the girls. It was rolling thunder bullied by power tools. It was definitely the beginning of an end. It polarised a madness and gave birth to many terrifying and doomed side projects. It was when I dyed my dreadlocks black.

Before the band assembled, I paid a visit back to Edinburgh to check in with friends and family. I found late-80s Britain not to my liking; it seemed miserable. I liked my miserable life in Chicago so much better, I high-tailed it back there in time for my 25th birthday and for the album's official release.

I can't remember if there was a release party or anything. I have to admit, I have never noticed any particular brouhaha upon the release of anything I have done, perhaps I am oblivious. But anyway, out it came and nobody in my immediate circle seemed too concerned.

But soon, oh, such a gathering! Like the forest on its way to Dunsinane, here was an army out of nowhere. The band, for a start, was huge. Apart from me, there was Ogre, Al, Bill, Paul, Joe Kelly (the annoying little punk rock singer from "Thieves"), Terry Bones (the moronic ex-UK Subs guitarist and probable sub-post office vandaliser), Martin (the drummer with the Rupert the Bear outfit who used to be in Public Image), and last but not least, Mikey.

Mikey was on loan from the band Rigor Mortis (which was, trivia fans, the name of my first band, before we became the Fini Tribe) and he hailed from Dallas. A long-haired and tacit gent, he played the guitar. He played it fast; it was incredible to watch his fingers chop the strings, as if he was making a smoothie out of his axe. They call it "shredding", but I hate these stupid skateboardy/hard rocky phrases, dude. Mikey was going to be staying with me in my humble apartment. Mikey? He was alright; he liked to drink, he liked to drug, he liked his slasher films, his steaks, and his rock 'n' roll. We were very different, but not really so different.

Preambles to the tour took place in bits and pieces around Chicago. Bill and I, or Paul and I, in the van, moving gear around, picking up people, waiting for Al, who was being kind of annoying. He had decided to get liposuction before the tour and ended up just reeling around in agony for 48 hours. "It felt okay, man, and then I took a fucking shower and now I can't fucking bend over or up and down or anything man!!" What the fuck? Poor baby. I will never forget the image I have of him on an exercise bike in his apartment, cursing under his breath whilst smoking, with a bottle of Jack Daniels at arm's length.

We had amassed quite a crew as well. A few of the guys from H-Gun, who had done such an incredible job of the last few videos, were going to come out and build a set every night, which would consist of a huge chain-link fence across the stage—a stroke of genius, as it meant the band could keep the stage for themselves without any intruders. And it looked amazing: the right kind of post-apocalyptic, netherland of rock 'n' roll that many bands would line up to ape in years to come. Oh, the H-Gun guys also made a huge fire breathing metal dinosaur. Hmmmm... well, you can't win 'em all, can you? Sean Joyce was taking care of the two drummers—a thankless task, and I am sure there is a joke about it somewhere. A gentleman called Lee Popa was doing sound—no easy feat, however, he was pretty amazing. A stocky Italian with a grin wider than our chain link fence and an unruly mop of curly red hair, he looked like a slimmed-down Leslie West. The guy, beloved by all, had an incredible respect for the working rock 'n' roller, treated everyone the same, had a bottomless pit of rock stories, and would not hear of anyone poking fun at the elders. ("Hey!! Don't be dissin' Townshend, man. Do you know he goes home and has dinner with his mom, every day??" Enough said.)

All of this hubbub and furore was taking place during a rigorous and punishing schedule of bar hopping and drug taking, *naturellement*. We also took time to shoot a video for the first single from the album, "Burning Inside", at a disused Ludwig drum factory on Damen Avenue in Chicago, which is now a yuppie condo apartment complex. (What isn't a yuppie condo apartment complex?) We shot all day on a Saturday, doing some cutaways the next day. The band set up on a soundstage, the chain link fence, wheels of fire (not the Cream album, silly) spinning on the factory floor, and a rent-a-crowd who were supposed to go all loony when we mimed to the song. The highlight was someone catching fire and scaling the fence. This was all conducted under the safest of conditions—the guy who was on fire a lot was covered in some super fireproof suit, but I was still terrified for him. Not for long though, as Al, Mikey, and I crammed into the filthy bathroom to take a bunch of drugs. The rest of the day was spent groggily wondering why the English drummer's hair looked like David St. Hubbins' out of *Spinal Tap*. Fuck knows how, but after shooting the video for twelve straight hours, I managed to go drinking at Smart Bar, high and groggy. However, never fear, I quickly found some coke, and became quite buoyant again. Y'know… run across the bar for your new pals, dance ironically to "Personal Jesus", throw up on a girl in the girl's bathroom.

Stress!! Things were getting stressful, as they are wont to do during the lead up to a big tour. I say this with hindsight, but thus far, the *Mind* tour was the biggest production I had been involved with. It also involved me learning how to use the samplers and the Fairlight—not necessarily complicated, but a lot of the responsibility for the loops (which kept time for the entire band) and the length of time between songs (the samples took time to load) was on my shoulders. (I would quickly learn to load sample disks whilst playing. By the end of the tour, I was reading *Viz* whilst onstage, ha!) That, coupled with the all-out assault of the music, meant I was a bag of nerves, but who wasn't? Al was a bag of nerves, and because of this, he was putting on his asshole armour and he was also doing far too much heroin. Ogre was living with him, so the pair were drug buddies, and that did not help. They always carried around an air of what-I'm-going-through-eclipses-what-you-are-going-through— fraught meetings and journeys, part drama, part show-off, part stupidity.

Dabbling seemed to be off the menu; it was full-on drug abuse or nothing. I stayed away. There was plenty of camaraderie between the rest of us. I could even tolerate the bovver boy Terry Bones in short doses socially, mainly because he had a really pretty wife. What in God's name was she doing with him? I was going to say it would be like Britt Eckland dating Rod Stewart, but I suppose I won't say that.

Evanston, Illinois is a suburb of Chicago. It is called a suburb, but it is really a very polite roommate of the more loutish, blue collar Chicago, and a small extension of the northern part of the city founded on dismal craft fairs, a piously stuck-up university, and prohibition. It made little sense why the rehearsals for the 1989/1990 *Mind is a Terrible Thing to Taste* tour would take place in Evanston, miles away from our comfort zones, and in a dank, disused theatre, in the middle of December.

The daily timetable, enforced by some God of Cruel Jokes, ran thus: the band arrived at 12 PM; heating sneaked in very quietly at 3 PM; Paul and Bill would sit in the dim light preparing samples, truncating and speeding them up, or slowing them down, tuning them to our instruments (this involved long periods of silence shattered rudely by searing sounds of larger-than-life dentist's drills, gunfire, and people being eaten by crocodiles); his royal highness would bustle in with the *drama du jour* and his posse of foul tempers at around 6 PM, trailing his factory-fabricated black dreadlocks that looked for all the world as if a squid, suffering a cardiac arrest at high speed, had managed to attach itself to the back of his head. Commands and unanswerable questions were barked into the half-dark silence, the band dotted around the theatre as if someone had flash-frozen the contents of a porno cinema.

The rehearsals themselves were torture. There is definitely a science to creating a sound that's like an army of lawnmowers colliding with *Sabbath Bloody Sabbath* at high speed and at maximum volume. However, it is by no means an exact science, and if one of these lawnmowers made a mistake it was back to the very beginning again. Even if there wasn't a mistake—if Al was just in a bad mood (he usually was)—then it was back to the beginning again, like writing "I must not talk in class" a hundred times with an Uzi. One day we played a song twenty-one times. I know we did, because I counted them.

The great thing about rehearsals was that we had a curfew. The caretaker turfed us out at 11 or 12, which meant that a hard-working, weary musician had time to reflect on the day's accomplishments and follies before lying down exhausted for a few hours and then doing it again. Or you could go out to somewhere like Smart Bar and do a heap of blow and a brace of shots before ending up "reflecting" on how the fuck you were going to be able to play the songs in a straight line in a few hours now that the wan light of morning was stabbing you in the face. All that after you just tried snorting instant coffee and doing a shot of melon schnapps in your kitchen.

In all fairness, playing that music, with that many people in the band, was a challenge. Al wouldn't settle for anything less than the album sound, and I can scarcely blame him. But in these early rehearsals, it was chaotic. Terry Brains—sorry, Bones—was way out of his league, coming from an extensive training in lowest level "Oi!" bands. Al had made a mistake in choosing him; it wasn't as if anyone liked him particularly either. If one tiny part of the Ministry "machine" was out of sync, even slightly, it all went pear-shaped quickly. I had horrible problems with the song "The Missing", which is a perfect example of a Ministry song in that it is short, runs at breakneck speed, with everyone playing in a different time signature. I had to relearn a lot, which I managed to do without anyone noticing. Paul and Bill were excellent bandleaders, not only having been responsible for the music's creation, but they were patient, and could explain eloquently and scientifically to you exactly why you were fucking up.

Almost a week until blast off, KMFDM were here—the band imported by Wax Trax! from Germany to open for the whole tour. Al had already made up his mind not to like them, and he kept muttering things about them when they were brought to our rehearsal space to say hello and dump their gear. There were four of them, and four more disparate souls you could not meet. The singer, Sascha, was a compact man with boyish, almost pin-up good looks. The other sort of singer was Nick, or En Esch, incredibly tall, gaunt, and gawky, with sandy hair and a worried expression on his pale sandy face. The drummer, Rudi, looked like a cross between Elton John and an aubergine. The guitarist, Gunther, looked like he had escaped from a prog rock band, such as Marillion. They were joined by one of the most strikingly beautiful women any of us had ever seen; we would all take turns acting like idiots in front of her throughout the tour. Her name was Julia, Sascha's girlfriend and lighting engineer. After rehearsal that day, we all went out with KMFDM to welcome them to America. They were nice people, if a little bewildered, with varying degrees of English language skills.

A hearty Christmas was spent doing ecstasy in Al's hot tub, and we were in the home stretch. We had gotten to the point when everyone else connected with the tour made themselves present. Enter William Tucker, who would have been playing the guitar that Terry Brains was playing, if his audition had not collapsed in on itself. Martin had recommended William for the gig, having known him for some time from when they both lived in New Jersey. Al had told William to come out for an audition, which he did, meeting up at Al's house at the agreed time one afternoon. Al had immediately forgotten about the audition and taken William on an intensive tour of local heroin and coke dealers, followed by an extensive tour of Al's hottest nightspots—he usuals. Anyway, to cut a very long night short, the audition, which was scheduled for 4 PM on one day, actually happened at 8 AM the next day. William was incoherent. Al told him he failed, but he could come out as my keyboard tech. Thus began a very close and productive/destructive friendship that lasted up to William's very untimely and sad death in 1999. His opening gambit was to tell me that he had heard I was a fan of the band Can, to which I grinned and started talking about the same, probably boring the pants off him. He lived in Manhattan, I learned, and was every bit the embodiment of that city: short attention span, loud, passionate, hilarious, and very, very irreverent about every topic. It was love at first sight; we were inseparable for the whole tour.

We got a tour manager, a giant of a man called Jolly. There were many legends concerning Jolly—there could be a book about him alone. He cut a formidable figure, dressed in a ubiquitous dirty-old-man raincoat, and always carrying a three-foot long monkey wrench, brandishing it for the benefit of financially reluctant club owners and promoters. But I was convinced he was hired because his voice was the only thing in this world that was louder than Ministry. It was incredible.

We had shifted operations to the Riviera Theatre. We were playing there in a few days on New Year's Eve, and on the day before New Year's Eve also. We were allowed in for a dress rehearsal—the theatre in Evanston clearly not being dank, freezing or cavernous enough—and had to rehearse in the empty 3000-seater for two days. We were, in fact, playing a warm up show in Milwaukee on the 29th, but for now, the huge Riviera was playing host to the entire touring party. Of course, playing the songs in such a huge and empty cavern of a theatre confirmed one thing for sure: that we sounded empty and cavernous. The sound billowed out into the dark canyon and bounced straight off the back wall, sending Al into little pirouettes of rage. What more perfect a time to introduce a "VJ" from an MTV show, here to "hang" with Al for a couple of days and see "what's up" with Ministry. Who knows what that poor slob said to Al, but they were screaming at each other and fighting within a minute, girly fists flailing in the dark, dank air. I guessed he wouldn't be "hanging" after all.

The warm-up show in Milwaukee could not have been worse. The venue was the Eagles Club, the same place where Al threw a vodka drink in my face when the Cocks played there. Being a huge ballroom, it was not built for the acoustics of a rock band, let alone an eight-piece, very, very loud rock band. I was in the most trouble. My samplers had remained on all day, without much ventilation. They were stacked one on top of the other, and all the samples had either doubled in speed, or halved in speed. I was so alarmed I honestly thought it was some kind of practical joke. This was exacerbated by the fact that I had left my cue cards—little cheat-sheet postcards I had drawn up to guide me through the songs—at home in Chicago. Fortunately, everyone seemed to suffer a similar fate, and we all sounded terrible, the venue ensuring that even the most discerning and critical ear would only hear a hollow roar. We were joined by Jello Biafra—perhaps his frantic squawk was able to transcend the sonic canyon in which we were trapped.

Battle-scarred and wary of disaster, we returned to Chicago for the two completely sold out New Year's Eve shows. I certainly had a "what could possibly be worse than Milwaukee?" attitude as I took the train from my house to the venue. Backstage was the kind of Fellini-meets-Tales-From-the-Crypt scene of absolute strangers that I would soon get used to. People who wanted beer, drugs, or worse, to talk to you about themselves. People for whom, in years to come, I would cultivate an impatience and rudeness I had previously lacked.

Well, look who's come all the way from TEXAS!! "Woooooooooooooooooooo!!!" It's the Skatenigs! Phildo and his band of failed motor functions were to play before KMFDM. Well that's all we fucking needed. I watched the beer supply dwindle forlornly, hours before we played.

The gig was a lot better. We came on to the soundtrack of *Psycho*, before we counted in "Breathe". The front line of the stage went: guitarist, guitarist, guitarist. Al wearing a Stetson—as was Terry, because he tried to copy everything Al did. With Mikey's long hair, the three of them looking exactly like the cover of ZZ Top's *Fandango*, heads bobbing in time to the music. Ogre and I were at the back with our keyboards in line with Bill and Martin, Bill sombre in a dark suit, Martin wearing his trademark black and white striped top (ahaaaar! me maties!). In another universe, they could have been ventriloquist and dummy. Paul moved around the stage grinning, using his eyebrows for cues so us dimwits didn't screw anything up. During the show, both Ogre and I got our chance to bathe in the limelight, me with "So What", Ogre with a Skinny Puppy song called "Smothered Hope". Li'l annoying punky boy Joe Kelly got to run out and play at being Ian MacKaye too, delivering a couple of Pailhead songs. (Later on in the tour, he would prove how brazen he was by seducing girls with the "I used to be in Minor Threat" line—now come on!!!! The shame, Joe!)

The next night followed suit—except, it being New Year's Eve, Al counted down to midnight and we kicked off 1990 playing "Breathe". It was the 90s—a brand new decade—and I was in a starkly lit dressing room, slurping cheap champagne and snorting cheaper coke. Wait, was I slurping the coke and snorting the champers? Did it matter? I had survived the 80s and I was where I thought I wanted to be, in a mildly successful rock band, in the States, doing blow and fighting off pretty girls with a stick, right?

There were a few days to kill before we left Chicago for the tour proper. Al and Paul were in the studio putting the finishing touches to *Beers, Steers and Queers*, and there was a problem. When approached for permission to use the lyrics to his magnum opus "Let's Get Physical", the writer of the song heard our version and blew a gasket, point blank refusing to let us use his… er… poetry. So this really fucked us as we were, for the most part, done with the album, and we had to deliver the master for a 1990 release. I had a few hours to come up with an alternative vocal to throw on the top, remove the "official" lyrics and be done with it. I tried several different approaches with very little success: the first being outright rejected by Wax Trax! ("I fucked her in a Burger King restroom," I bellowed), the last version being executed at the eleventh hour so Paul could fly to L.A. to master the record and be back in time to join us in Cleveland for the first date. I did a crappy job—no one was really expecting anything better. After all, we were being forced into changing it, and none of us were happy about it. I left the studio for a last night of sleep in my own bed before leaving, but at 6 AM the phone rang. Al, sounding incredibly contrite for rousing me, "Chris, man, you gotta come down and sing this again." I bellowed like a snared moose for a minute and then wandered down the freezing Chicago streets to the studio. The final version of "Physical", the version that is on *Beers, Steers and Queers*, is frankly embarrassing—to me anyway. Yuck! Horrible! The lyrics sound like the runt of David Coverdale's litter. I hate it. Oh well, a few white label bootlegs snuck out of the original, it was not all for nothing.

TOUR BUS!!! TOUUUUR BUS!! FUCKING HELL!!! I was trying to be as blasé and nonchalant about this as I could, but, outside of Al's loft, were two of 'em!! Yes, you may have gathered, I had never set foot on a tour bus. I had no idea. Of course, everyone else was completely breezy, taking it all in stride, "Oh, we grew up in these things"—flash American gits. Except Martin, he was a flash English git who shared one of these with oh, you know, JOHNNY ROTTEN!!!! (Or so he maintained.) Oh, and Terry, but his lentil-sized brain had a ten second memory (as evidenced in rehearsal). But okay, I was excited. I had no idea they had bunks, televisions, video players and cassette decks (no CD players for a few years), a kitchen, microwave, toilet (but you can't shit in it, pee only, no vomiting). So, apart from the necessary annoyance of having to get off for about two hours a day to play, you were—as long as the booze and drugs were siphoned in regularly—in heaven. There were very few responsibilities. If someone did not like what you were doing and they were a member of your touring party—say you were smoking pot, or injecting something in your EYE VEIN—then you merely crushed them like an insect by organising a little gang of your like-minded fellows and childishly ostracising them until they either left the tour or poked needles in their piggy little eyes too! Squeal!!

Of course, I was an ingénue. I was resolute in being a peaceable, good-natured bandmate and a sport, a "ha ha" chuckle after the show over a couple of beers and the occasional joint. I was there to work, I told myself in a pious internal voice. Let's worry about the shows first, and maybe the fun later, I said, fluffing my pyjamas on my comforter, then sitting down in the front lounge for some light chit-chat with the lads.

We arrived in Cleveland the night before we played. At the end of the journey, a very few of us smoked an awful lot of weed and bustled into the Holiday Inn like the Keystone Cops. Thus began a long, long legacy of trying to appear completely normal when high in conservative areas of the USA. Oh fuuuuck!! Will you pleeease stop pretending that I am not high??? Upon being handed a hotel room key, I immediately put it in my mouth! We all piled into my room and I tried to order pizza from a local delivery joint, but I was laughing too hard, wondering if Gene Simmons and the gang, or, oh I don't know, the guys from Tygers of Pan Tang, had ever done this—maybe in this very room!

We played Cleveland the next day, just like in the *Spinal Tap* film. We played in a theatre underneath the former seafood restaurant where we'd been with the Cocks. The show was, as far as I could tell, fine. Tons of us got laid after the show and I had a party in my room. I think I was rooming with Al, of all people! I must have been, because Ogre had taken Cyan, his girlfriend, out on the road with him and they had their own room. I can't think for one second why Al decided this was the best idea. Sigh. There was always a part of Al that at least tried, I suppose. Anyway, this arrangement would not last for the whole tour.

Apart from the many goings on of keeping the tour on the road, there was definitely a "first day at camp" vibe. Everyone was showing off their little personality traits, pissing on their territory, telling stupid, boring road stories much like this one: "… and I yelled at the guy, 'HEY! DOUCHEBAG! Either PICK UP the guitar and WALK it to the stage, or GO THE FUCK HOME!' Jesus, local crews, right? So he turns round and says, 'Oh, I'm sorry, man,' and IT'S FUCKING ALICE COOPER! I ALMOST FUCKING SHIT, MAN!!!"

After Detroit, we gingerly tiptoed into Canada. I was worried, as I had to pick up a work visa whilst there for the next few months. Otherwise, I would not have been allowed to re-enter the States, which would have been disastrous. So, on a snowy day in Toronto, I dragged my scrawny ass down to the American Embassy and agreed with the officer that yes, my band bore more than a passing resemblance to the Moody Blues. He stamped my passport and I left, pausing in a mall to enjoy decent coffee and marvel at the availability of Jacques Brel albums in Canada. That night Al and I held court in our room with Ogre, a redhead, and a ton of heroin. It was truly disgusting, and I did not wake up until soundcheck in Ottawa the next day. I fell in love with Montreal, and was sad to leave Canada.

Prior to leaving, I found a grocery bag about half full of syringes underneath a sofa in the back lounge of the bus. I decided to make an executive decision and discard these prior to braving the US Customs on our way back. I walked down the streets of Montreal at three in the morning looking for an inconspicuous drop, hoping that no one would think that a gangly, dreadlocked guy with a look of absolute panic on his face looked in the least bit suspicious. I found a dumpster and sighed relief.

Of course, Al was really annoyed at me, "What the fuck, man, do you know what I had to do to get these???"

I reminded him of the impending customs stop.

"Yeah, whatever, man," he sulked.

The next port of call was New York, which has always, for me, provoked two separate emotions: annoyance and excitement. It is kind of like looking at porn with dust in your eye. There is never any parking for the bus (or later in my career, van), hotels are a problem, and the dressing rooms are jam-packed with people wanting to guzzle your booze. And they are never people like Kate Moss, Christie Brinkley, or Robert DeNiro—at least not in my time.

We were there for two days and we were joined by several wives and girlfriends, all arriving from their destinations with that grim resolution on their faces that characterises a loaded rolling pin, i.e. "I assume that I know what you have been doing on the road, and I am going to get to the bottom of it." However, as we had been out for just over a week, it was easy to assume the expression of the wrongly accused. "Oh, my God, how can you say that? I'm really, really hurt, I am out here WORKING, there is no time for anything else, and I couldn't, I JUST COULDN'T!" This resonated from several rooms, forever haunting the hotel!

Whether Al was the full-on absolute junky he claimed to be, or he was still renting space in the rock myth he wanted to be, he announced that he was "going coooold turkey, man". In one of the heroin capitols of the U.S. this announcement yielded very little other than a lot of cooing, "ahs", and sympathetic "aaaaws" from the visiting Mrs Jourgensen, and a magnificent performance by Al, during which, apparently, he claimed, with no little pride, that he had managed to void his bowels on stage! Ha ha ha ha!

After the first NY show, there was a party being thrown in our honour at the Pyramid, organised by Tucker. I went there with him, my girlfriend, and his girlfriend, and drank strange red drinks seemingly designed with an especially horrible hangover in mind. The next day it was as if someone had sewn a generous handful of sharp surgical instruments into my head, which they may well have done. I don't remember anything after a certain point, except that I secretly fancied Tucker's bird.

Someone had convinced Al that the obnoxious English MTV presenter had his best interests at heart, and that he should allow himself to be filmed and interviewed for a piece on the band. They filmed the soundcheck while we were playing "So What". Terry Brains begged me to come over to his side of the stage and put my arm around him in a show of band solidarity. "You know, like what Angus Young and Brian Johnson do." Sure, Terry, wow, that's a great idea!! When it came time for shooting, I made sure I stayed as far away from his sorry English ass as I could. Wanker. This was followed by an interview which Al chose to do with Ogre and Martin—which was annoying, as it should have been Paul or Bill, but Al was still showing off his new toys to the world. I remember Al being Al, Ogre being silent, and Martin being pompous. His interviews always make him sound like a Time Lord elder from *Dr. Who*—or worse, Davros, creator of the Daleks.

We had an extra band on the bill for these two New York shows: either Controlled Bleeding or Joined at the Head, both of which were pretty much the same thing, actually—the same "mastermind" in Paul Lemos, who may well have poisoned himself with his own pretentiousness and utter pomposity. They had recently signed to Wax Trax!, and were busy shedding their skin(s) of the Throbbing Gristle/Whitehouse bandwagon, and more recently the Einstürzende/SPK skin(s), only to sashay languidly into an industrial-dance-anything-goes skin. This meant that they appeared with a fey opera singer and some nitwit lamely brandishing a disc saw about four years too late to shock anyone in the crowd, especially a Manhattan crowd. Didn't they remember the infamous Einstürzende at the Danceteria debacle? They drilled through the stage into the dressing room? I didn't want to sit through this and KMFDM. I was bored.

The Boston show was hilarious. Some person, or persons, from the audience figured out a way to disengage our scary authoritarian fence from the stage, and we watched it being carried away like ants carrying crumbs into the Boston evening. Al got hit with a nut and bolt, but he remained unfazed. After the show, I had occasion to go onto the "crew" bus to pick up my wages. I was baked, having enjoyed about eight bongs in a row with fans after the show. While I was waiting for my pay packet, I tried to make (stoned) idle chit chat with one of our "set designers". His name, I cannot recall, but he was very clean shaven, extremely bald, and he looked like a tall, angry baby.

"Well, well! That was pretty funny, right? The fence coming down like that? It was like an uprising of the people, wasn't it?" I chortled to him.

Angry Baby scowled at me, "It wasn't funny at all, actually, it could have been disastrous. If one of these fences had fallen straight down, do you know what probably would have happened? Do you have any idea?"

I was grinning so hard my face hurt. I thought he was going to crack up too after a minute and slap me heartily on the back and say, "Oh, who cares?" But no, he didn't, he had made up his mind to be Mr Stick-in-the-fucking-butt.

"PEOPLE MIGHT HAVE DIED!!! THEY WOULD HAVE BEEN CRUSHED WITH THEIR HEADS SMASHED FUCKING OPEN, AND YOU WOULD HAVE JUST STOOD THERE ON STAGE GAPING!!!"

I burst out laughing so hard that a gob of snot came out of my nose at jettison speed, landing on Angry Baby's shirt. I turned around and ran off the bus, howling with laughter. I never spoke to him again, ever in my life, thank fuck.

In Washington, DC, we played at the famous 9:30 Club. It was a fantastic place, but tiny. We had to split the day in two: an afternoon show and an evening show. This suited us just fine because we got to, justifiably, start drinkin' at 3 PM! Al went out to be interviewed by long-suffering but diamond fellow Jason Pettigrew for *Alternative Press*, a nascent music magazine that really has been more than kind to us over the years. Big, big mistake on Jason's part, as Al, in a mischievous mood, got the poor chap so drunk on Margaritas that he was comatose in the alley of the 9:30 before the show began. Not that we were much better! Of course, after the first show, out of my tiny mind, I was making out with these adorable twin girls in the dressing room, and in walked Ian MacKaye (he of Pailhead, Fugazi, and Minor Threat). "Hi, Chris," he said with a good-natured and conspiratorial grin. I knew he was trying to make me feel better after walking in on me behaving like a typical wannabe rock star. He is a sweetheart. I grinned my watery grin back and immediately felt guilty. I know, whatever, but I'm a Catholic. My cats make me feel guilty.

Like gears on a sports car, the *Mind* tour kept going up a notch. The drugs changed. The people and the climate changed. The only certainties were that we kept getting better as a band, and it all kept getting more and more insane, like a bucking bronco getting faster and faster. Tucker and I grew closer, we were too similar not to. We had each other to refer to if the going got too crazy. DC was done with, its blurry alleys were disappearing fast. The entire party had "had a bit too much to drink". Oh *quelle surprise*, darlings… but now, it was time to head SOUTH.

**Top:** KMFDM and Connelly backstage, 1990. (Sean Joyce)

**Bottom:** With Tucker at the Holiday Star in Indiana, February 1990.

# 7

# GUITARS, CADILLACS, HILLBILLY MUSIC

Oh look, we're in Florida! And it seemed that the Red Cross has parachuted a parcel of crystal methedrine onto our tour! Yummy. We wasted little time—oh, ok I wasted little time—embracing what it was like living in a suspended reality. Basically, I did not need to go to bed any more. I could drink through the sunny day, into the balmy night. And my playing? Apparently not affected. I had become a superhero, being followed around the beach by a gang of toothless Goth ladies, cackling in the sun, bird skulls around their necks on blackened sinew. I could barely wait to get onstage and push myself. It was all second nature, now. I paused between lines to go jet skiing. I loved my bandmates. I loved KMFDM. I was a moron. I could not help myself.

You know, Tucker kept a diary. Who knows where it went. He died in 1999, and there were a few items left to remember the great man by. He insisted on keeping a diary, because he "…knew we would all forget."

We did Florida. There is none more GOTH than Florida. It was so fucking GOTH in Florida that, on my way to the beach in Miami with KMFDM, we bumped into NINE INCH FREAKIN' NAILS!!! But we couldn't really say it like that because they weren't that famous yet. They would be in about two months, but now we were just, "Oh, that's nice, Nine Inch Nails". I invited them to join us jet skiing, but they muttered something about sharks and split.

The bus had become permeated with country music. The best fun you can have on tour is not the sea of drugs, nor the river of women, it's not the storm of rock you play every night; it's the truck stops, it's the cassettes you can buy at the truck stops, it's being in the truck stop high, and looking at the rednecks who want to kick your ass, it's the celestial bliss of a strawberry milkshake whilst tripping. …but, back to the tapes. Al had bought a Hank Williams one, a Patsy Cline one, and a Dwight Yoakum one. After shows, the sounds of "Walkin' after Midnight", "Crazy", "Honky Tonkin'", and "Guitars, Cadillacs, Hillbilly Music" permeated the bus as we sat around with fans, yelling in fake hillbilly accents. My God, I was turning into PHILDO!! Yes, fine, when in Rome and all that—but the wonderful thing I was learning about touring was that you became part of a tiny little macrocosmic universe, that meant you forgot where you were from. You forgot being at home; it was all suspended. Your family was around you; they were your band and crew mates, the ones you get fucked up with after the show. I never considered country music for a second before, but now? Fuck yeah! It sounded so great on that tour, especially Patsy Cline, especially whilst watching slasher films, which Mikey had in abundance.

What could be more fun than Florida on speed? Well, New Orleans, of course. And the best part is that we had no gig there. We had an entire day off. Tucker and myself set off on our own. We had never been to New Orleans. Tucker decided to enhance our experience by taking half a Rohypnol—as did I, why not? It was 11 AM, it was a day off, and it was New Orleans. I found a fantastic record shop and we spent a busy half-hour looking for Sensational Alex Harvey Band albums. I did find a sealed copy of *Aloner*, the first Scott Walker album, and I gleefully turned around to show Tucker… only to find him curled up asleep, using a stack of Juice Newton albums as a pillow. Hmmm, perhaps we better leave. Once I had slapped the kid awake, we decided to find some food, quickly situating ourselves in the outdoor patio of some Mexican joint. The waitress didn't mind that we lit up a joint, as we were the only people there. She took our order and then sat down and smoked with us. We left her an enormous tip (by Scottish standards).

Bouncing around the French Quarter in an existential fog, we bumped into KMFDM and joined them to explore. Eventually we wound up with Paul in a bar. We glugged down Hurricanes, because we were supposed to—though, I have to admit, they were disgusting, and I was rewarded with the same open-surgical-instrument-in-the-brain hangover I had earned in New York.

We were now on our way to Texas; priests and holy men up and down the freeway were crossing themselves as we passed ferociously in the "rolling womb". Blazing our asses off, we set our minds on fire with coke, methedrine, and acid for a crash landing in Houson. Houston was going to be fun, because we were there for two days, and we were going to do an "in-store". We were like the Beatles in Houston, nay Texas—at least that is what I was told. The line of fans stretched around the record store and down the next couple of blocks. There were obviously a lot of kids here who wanted to get their stupid Ministry records signed. We were all behind the counter, passing around a bottle of Bushmills Whiskey (this was Al's fave, and not a bad tipple), so by the time we reached soundcheck—we were playing for two nights at Numbers, the place where, with the Cocks, I had the paranoid freak out—I just curled up on the floor and went to sleep. In certain circles this could have been considered unprofessional, but I was being unprofessional every day so far. So what? I was just fine for the show. A verve and peppiness returned to my tired bloodstream with the ingestion of some ecstasy.

It was at this point in the tour that I came up with the term "human washing machine" to best describe the way the audience was when the music was at its most pummellingly fast. For example, during "Thieves", in the really fast bit, it really was kind of transcendent in a way—but thank fuck we were behind the fence. The crowd became one huge ball of body parts, all moving in different directions at an incredible speed.

Texas seemed to explode for us. Texas loved us. I am sorry about all the meany-mean things I said about Texas in the earlier chapters, I was beginning to really love it back… was I turning into PHILDO?? I met a lovely and shy girl after the show—who I would continue to meet, with diminishing returns, for the rest of my touring life—who was clearly insane, but we enjoyed our 8 hour relationship. We watched an anime with Tucker and stayed up all night, leaving the hotel in the very early hours to take pictures of each other and goof around in the bland downtown area. The next night was considerably more subdued for me. There was no drunken "in-store", thankfully, and my after-show heroics were restricted to a very Spartan pharmacopoeia. I had to think about my constitution and my wellbeing, don't you know.

Al was joined by a mysterious and exotic travelling companion; beautiful and adored by all, she would remain with us for a couple of weeks. This necessitated a room change; finally Tucker and I were together, Al got his own room, and everyone was pleased. Not so with KMFDM: it would seem there had been unrest within their ranks. They were not content with the van they had been allocated, nor the driver, nor the offer of the front sofa of our bus (which we have made available nightly to one of their number, always hoping against all hopes that it will be Julia), nor—and this would be the straw breaking the dachshund's back—their supply of beer. After every show, prior to their leaving, they would send the obnoxious Timo, a roadie hailing from Lapland or some such, to fill his shovel-sized paws with as much of our beer as he could possibly carry.

"What do I know? I'm just a craaaazy Laplander in the USA," he would say, trying desperately to pass it off unnoticed. Or a lame type of joke like, "Ha Ha! Maybe ve see J.R. EWING SOON, YA??"

Until one night, when Tucker ran out of US/Scandanavian diplomacy and shouted, "YO, TIMO, MAN, YOU WANNA LEAVE US SOME OF OUR FUCKING BEER??" Amongst murmurs of aggrieved concurring, the sheepish sleigh-builder slinked off the bus empty-shovelled.

A few minutes later a furious Sascha appeared. "VOT EES THEES I AM HEARIIIIING??!!!!" he roared down the length of the bus, sending

Al into a complete fucking benny[2]. It was heartening to see Al go to bat for the band, for the beer, for freedom. I don't think poor Sascha got it completely. First US tour, there was a lot more to the "code of the road" than just keeping extramarital affairs a big secret. This shit ran deep... team spirit, and all that. Anyway, a gauntlet was thrown down, and nothing between Al and Sascha would ever be the same—not that it ever could, they both had Herculean egos. This town ain't big enough for the both of them (da na na na) and it ain't Al who's gonna leave. (Sorry, had to.)

Of the many epicentres of madness on this tour, Dallas was awe-inspiring. There were still multiple Red Cross parcels of speed falling from the sky from invisible helicopters and, after the Dallas show, we lived about four different nights in waves—starting at a party after the show at a warehouse loft somewhere downtown, where Paul elected himself as guest DJ: playing the turntables and eschewing the records, filling the space with an oppressive white noise while his 6'4" frame flailed around behind the decks. I eventually wound up back at the hotel with a friendly couple and their huge Doberman Pinscher, running around the corridors trying to outwit security. Eventually they tired of running and left me to my own devices, where I focused my energy on helping my bandmates with the logistics of fitting a grand piano into an elevator—no easy feat, I tell ya! We would have been fine, save for the arrival of the long-suffering security guard who said nothing, but his face betrayed a kind of stoic pleading. Shamefacedly, we locked ourselves in one of the hotel's many conference rooms. Sitting around a huge oval table, we snorted speed, drank beer, and smoked joints, whilst carving a beautiful—if abstract—tableau into the table. We wound out the evening (by now it was 9 or 10 in the morning) sitting around a table in the hotel restaurant sheepishly hiding our Heinekens under the table and pretending to munch on dry toast, which was like eating cotton wool. The phone in the kitchen of the restaurant would not stop ringing. It started to jar our glassy nerves to

---

2      *Benny: Scottish 1970s colloquialism, to go completely berserk.*

the point where we couldn't stand it anymore. I marched into the kitchen and, seeing it was deserted, picked up the phone.

"Kitchen!" I chirped.

"Yeah, could you send a pot of coffee up to room 2056, please?" It was Al, and he was clearly pipped at waiting on the telephone for so long.

"Could you send a pot of coffee up to room 2056, please??" I replied, mimicking his voice back to him as childishly as I could before slamming down the phone and chortling my way back to the table. What a wag!!

The tour's mood rudder was pushed in a slightly new direction with the arrival of another of Al's truck stop purchases, *Psychedelic Classics of the Sixties*. You can imagine a mix of Top 40 draft-dodgin' greats such as "White Rabbit", "Magic Carpet Ride", and the bus favourite, "Green Tambourine". He also bought *Grateful Dead's Greatest Hits*, which he conceded was nowhere near as good as Hawkwind, as far as psychedelic music went.

By now, Tucker had joined the band for a few numbers on stage—Al relenting when he realized that Terry Brains couldn't count in the songs. (Probably because the guy couldn't count, period.) Always one to make the most of his stage time, Tucker's debut with Ministry was duly noted.

"Yeah man, so I told Tucker to come up and play on 'Thieves' during the show, and he wanders off, you know; baseball hat, crew gear, dirty pants. Then I look around when it's about his time to play, and it's Gary Glitter!!" Al was clearly enthused about Tucker's 30-second glam rock makeover—silver lipstick, a roadie's best friend.

Cain's Ballroom, Tulsa, Oklahoma, had paintings of old C&W icons on the wall, all of who'd played in this historic venue. Someone told me the Pistols played here on their famous 1978 US tour, which was far more exciting to me. During soundcheck, a less belligerent Sascha approached the stage with a peace offering for Al—a Patsy Cline T-shirt—which Al accepted with good grace, hatchet buried (but not forgotten). After a rowdy, rootin'-tootin' show, the bus was invaded by fans. I saw William receive the first of many slaps in the face by female fans when he acted out of order.

"Darling, it's perfectly fucking simple, it's called UP PERISCOPE. I stick my head in your shirt and yell 'UP PERISCOPE!!!' What is so hard about that, woman?" he asked plaintively, a millisecond before her hand cracked his jaw and the female stormed off the bus.

Two other fans brought us a gift of mescaline mixed with Nesquik chocolate milk, to make it more palatable. We all took a spoonful that induced a giggling fit for six hours. It was as if everything started to display its true, inner Hanna-Barbara quality. That night Al gave me the nickname "Pinky", because of the hue my face took on from laughing too hard for too long. We watched *Eraserhead* three times in a row, each time Al giving a hilarious *Mystery Science Theater 3000* type of running commentary. At some point we stopped at a Jack-in-the-Box, a burger chain famous for its tainted meat. The staff were so stunned at thirty dishevelled *Mad Max*-types swarming in that they did not notice Al's lady friend steal a drive-thru microphone and begin to serenade the staff and customers with an *a cappella* version of the Morris Albert 70s smasheroo, "Feelings", over the tannoy. This was typical of her spontaneous and charming behaviour, but she had to leave us in Phoenix, which was the following date… sad. We were playing in a hall adjoining our hotel in Phoenix, with Tucker and myself riding the crest of an acid frenzy. It seemed like we were plugged into it all the time, never giving the psychedelics enough time to exit the body, making way for new psychedelics. Why bother?

(Side note: Recently—in fact, late 2005—I was at a social function at Columbia College in Chicago, when a guy came up and told me solemnly that we had taken acid together when Ministry played Phoenix in early 1990. I was tickled, needless to say, making sure that I had been nice to him and not been offhand. He assured me I was pleasant.)

ACID! ACID! ACIIIIID! Yes, I was tripping onstage again, and hold on… were my eyes deceiving me, or was annoying punker-boy, Joe Kelly, burning an American flag on stage?! Oh, bless him! He's really not so bad! Of course, it did not burn like it would in a movie—instead the blackened, flaming flag was becoming disengaged from the body of the pole, and was floating perilously close to, well, everything, really.

There was a scene: everyone was yelling, the staff were rather displeased. "How can you do this???", blah blah blah, "America!!!", blah blah blah, "SACRED!!!" … yeah, blow me.

After the gig I had the usual unhinged feeling that LSD diluted with a good few belts of Bushmills will do to ya. We were pulling out of the place soon, and Al was nowhere to be found. I had to move his luggage onto the bus from his room, mainly because no one else was around either. Tucker was found at the front desk, harassing the concierge into giving him the key to Dante's "Inferno" and one of the seven circles of hell. When all was said and done and we were all safely on the bus, we stopped at a truck stop so Al could make one of his now-famous mashed potato sculptures. It was actually pretty good, bordering on Giacometti-meets-Casper-the-Friendly Ghost. So we rounded out another warm and fuzzy evening smoking weed, drinking, and watching numerous women get their heads slashed open. Nighty-night, pals… we all better get a good night's sleep. Well, an hour maybe, because we were on our way to HOLLYWOOOOD!!!

Two days in Hollywood, two shows at the Palladium. We were staying in one of the more minor-league rock motels, but that's not to say it was not a good place. The rooms were suites: kitchen, private bedroom, etc. No sooner were Tucker and I situated, than Jolly was hammering on our door, roaring through the corridors that "MICHAEL SCHENKER IS DRINKIN' IN THE BAR NEXT DOOR, C'MON YOU FAGGOTS!!!" Thanks, Jolly, maybe we'll meet you over there. Both the gigs were blistering, and on the second night, I had a very interesting rendezvous.

Let me backtrack a little… For a while back in Chicago, I had been getting a lot of hang-up calls, to the point where I needed to change my phone number. Up until then, my name was in the book. Some of the calls would not hang up immediately, but, after a pause, the silent receiver would erupt into girlish giggles—so I knew the caller(s) to be female, or maybe, seven-year-old boys. (Which is not unreasonable. One of my preferred pastimes as a child, with the famous Andy, on a rainy day was prank phone calls. Still would be if it weren't for double-crossing technology.) This of course, drove my girlfriend insane. I, of course, was absolutely delighted. Tonight, in Hollywood, California, I was going to meet the source of these calls.

After the show, a girl approached me. "Hey, Chris? My friend really wants to meet you. She's really hot, she's a model." This was delivered in a deadpan, just like, "Hey Chris, there's a phone call for you."

We shall call her Vogue, being that she had been featured numerous times within the pages of that periodical, as well as Harpers, Sassy (cover!!), and Vogue Italia, no less. We went back to my suite—along with Tucker, Brains, Mikey (who would be affectionate with the friend of Vogue), Al's wife (who was visiting)… perhaps Al too, I can't remember… and pretty much anyone else from the audience who was still remotely interested piled in. I led Vogue to the bedroom and let the party rage on. After a pleasant liaison, Vogue, who it must be said, was piss drunk, leaned over and threw up into an arbitrary shoe. I liked her style. Romance was in the air. Afterwards, we joined the party, a subdued one, everyone sitting cross-legged on the floor passing around a mirror with a pile of coke on it, rapping, the usual preposterous stories flying around.

"I'm gonna go fuckin' hot-air ballooning tomorrow!" I spat through gritted teeth. Until HARK! I heard a knock at the door! And of course! It's Vogue's boyfriend, a red-faced, angry Luke Perry clone (actually, it could have been Luke Perry, I dunno), screaming at me that he was going to "… kick your motherfuckin' ass you faggot fuck!!!"

I smile a smile of benign, patronizing tolerance while I asked him, "How can I be a faggot fuck, if I just screwed your girl?"

To which Mikey burst out laughing, "Yeah, man, you better just chill the fuck out or we'll kick your fuckin' ass, and fuck you for fucking interrupting us, get the fuck outta here!"

Well, he could scarcely argue—it was about twenty-against-one, unfair odds. But I didn't know she had a boyfriend, now, did I? Vogue left a few minutes later to placate him. I resumed my rant about a hot-air ballooning expedition. All was well. I did not expect to see her again— but I would, and next time, without the hostile Luke Perry guy.

The person suffering the most on this tour, the man who would be a martyr and soak up all of Al's frustrations was Bill, our monitor man: a soft-spoken, easy-going lad who should have been born with a crash helmet instead of a mane of long hair. You see—and please excuse me if you tut and exclaim, "I know what a monitor guy does!"—the job of the monitor engineer is to provide the band with a balanced onstage sound, and it is far more frustrating than engineering the out-front sound. What you have to do, in a perfect situation, is give every single prissy-pants in the band what they want: "more guitar, less bass, a shade more snare drum, no kick, and less vocals," or, "no vocals, lots more guitar, keyboards, tons of drums, no bass," or best of all, "just lots of me." And of course, this may change a lot during a show. The monitor engineer also has to learn to read fleeting hand gestures and tense facial expressions. This, I have found, is especially true with new bands who maybe want to make the guy feel wanted, or who just don't know what to listen for onstage.

The trouble with Ministry was that, well, there were so many of us for a start, and in all fairness, the rhythmic loops that I was playing via my keyboard had to be heard clearly by everyone, or else the song would collapse, because inevitably someone would start playing in the wrong time signature. The other thing was that Al, whose voice was processed into a satanic growl every night, wanted to hear his satanic growl onstage, and not just be safe in the knowledge that the kids out beyond the fence were enjoying his nightmarish reflections. This, along with the loooong echoes he liked, meant that the stage sound could get pretty "swampy" quite quickly. And when Al got frustrated, he would take it out on Bill the unfortunate monitor guy. Whatever came conveniently to hand— whiskey bottles, for example—would be thrown at Bill's head. This would go on until either the problem was solved, or there was a long enough song that Bill could not be in fear for his life for at least six or seven minutes. Of course, after the show, when Bill was summoned to Al's office (the dressing room: Stay Out!), you could here the tortured screams and incredible thumping noises for miles around. It was louder—and, if we weren't so nervous, more entertaining—than the concert itself. This, of course, would be forgiven and forgotten by the next day. We needed the monitor engineer more than he needed us, and he was a fantastic engineer. It's just that we were such a pain in the ass to work with.

I mean, at the very least, we had two drummers. This was a lot of work for Sean, who described it as, "good cop, bad cop". Sean had enjoyed a friendship and working relationship with Rieflin for years. Martin was the new kid on the block and was determined to flaunt his "This Is Not a Love Song" credentials. Acting equal parts Bonham and Streisand, he kind of made Sean's already tough job into a living hell, making Sean sit like a little servant monkey so he could pour water onto the snare so that, when struck, the water would explode like a fountain, all a little bit Liberace-in-Doc-Martens.

We arrived in San Francisco the day before the show at the Warfield Theatre. A party was being thrown in our honour at some club, and another miraculous Red Cross parcel of crystal meth just happened to parachute down on the Bay Area—corner of Eddy and Larkin to be precise—at the infamous Phoenix Hotel, another "rock" hotel. The party was fun. I met up with a friend who worked for Alternative Tentacles, an English girl I had known for a while. The DJ played something from the first Throbbing Gristle album. I was impressed. When we all made it back to the Phoenix, too wired to sleep, I invited a few people onto the roof to play "Dirty Harry". The next morning, Al, Tucker and I went out for breakfast with a few people who'd crashed the night. Breakfast was neat Bushmills in the first bar we could find. Thus went the rest of the day.

We were joined onstage by the repulsive "El Duce", front man for the repulsive Mentors, a God-awful band whose instrumental prowess and band politics made the Skatenigs look like contenders. I mention them only because they will figure later on in this story, I'm afraid. So yes, the famous "El Duce" joined us onstage—not that the guy could do anything except drink, which he did in spades. He came out onstage and, I think he was sort of dancing? He had on a two-piece-suit with the trousers inside out, and he had his arms outstretched, inviting the crowd who probably thought—and rightly so—that he was a bum who had wandered in off the street who security were too scared to approach.

San Francisco marked the beginning of the end. Not in any negative way: it was the last third of the tour, and rather than things winding down, they were taken up a notch. You see, the mass "consciousness" of the tour did not want to go home. I know I certainly didn't, and I know Tucker certainly didn't. I guess I can't really speak for anyone else, but it kind of felt that way, in our own fucked-up little universe. So the activity became more frenzied, more psychedelic, more country, more western. A cancelled gig in Reno meant another day spent tripping with Tucker, wandering around the endless fruit machines, looking for a way out.

There was no way out—instead, there was Salt Lake City, Utah. It was Paul's birthday, and since we were the only ones awake we went out for a walk, eventually finding a café with a pool table. Happy birthday, Paul—now watch me kick your lanky ass at pool. Actually, he hammered me, which is easy to do in any competitive sport, I'm afraid. A relatively innocent start to the most sordid date of the tour.

The Speedway Café was kind of a safe house for little punk rockers trying to escape the oppression of Mormonism, multiple moms, and a booze-free existence. A dank cavern decorated from dumpsters and assorted garbage, it boasted a few threadbare rugs, a crooked pool table, a forlorn darts board, and a stage at one end. Apart from being a bit on the "home-made" side, and without a bar, there was nothing particularly unusual about the situation. Before the gig, I watched *Throw Mama from the Train* with Al in our motel, and then we were shipped back to the Speedway Café. The crowd was fucking mental, because that's what happens in a repressed minority religion community when Satan comes to town, I guess. After the show, we purchased a lot of acid from a cute hippy couple. I put about thirty hits behind the tray of a CD for safe keeping, as the back lounge of the bus was occupied, but that was not unusual for after-show shenanigans. It wasn't until the door burst open, and a tearful girl ran screaming from the bus, that I realized something was wrong.

Out swaggers my buddy Terry Brains. "She were bleedin' askin' for that!" he said with an assured grin—what a dick.

Very shortly after this, we are informed, "Hurry up, the gear is being packed and we have to leave town now!!" No waiting, no hanging out with fans, go go go go go, go!!

The tearful girl had called the cops and we needed to disappear before they appeared. Oh, tooooo late!!! Here they come, five or six squad cars, all dying to arrest a rock band. Brains is told to go and lie in his bunk until it's all over. Meanwhile, the rest of us are ordered by the cops to line up against the bus. It is at this point that I witness something so incredible, that, although alluded to before, to see it in full flight was truly a thing of awe: Al Jourgensen's stand-up routine. We are all up against it, literally, and Al's survival instinct kicked in. His comedy routine might not reduce the cops to helpless guffawing wrecks, but it certainly turned them from blood thirsty rock 'n' roll loathing Mormons. They just got really sick of listening to us, their inner voices saying, "Okay, okay, OKAY!! Leave already!" while Al strutted up and down the tarmac on an avenue between the cops and us. The stunned girl was unable to make an ID. It did not occur to anyone that he might be on the bus hiding, and that, in good faith, we had all vacated the premises for a line-up at the police's command. Perhaps getting the necessary warrant was too much hassle, and no one was going to suggest, "We are far too busy for any kind of nonsense sir. Why, we have approximately 200 hits of acid we bought from a teenager tonight!!" So we were told in no uncertain terms to get the fuck out of Utah, and never, ever come back. We were escorted from the town while Mr Brains is yuk-yuk-yukking with Al and his pit bulls. I hope he shits a hedgehog, the motherfucker.

This proved to be the overload point for the tour. Things had to start to give, and they did, of course. Nothing really had a sobering effect on us to the point where we would pass each other and grin grimly, suggesting, "That was a close one, let's just keep our heads down. We had a fright, let's play the shows, get home, no trouble". Oh, please!! We went bananas after that, and to help reaffirm our status, our bus driver had a breakdown—a mental one, not an automotive one.

Ray drove the band bus, and his wife, Kate, drove the crew bus. Ray was an even-tempered, good-natured cowboy with whom I would sit up front a lot, learning about the geography of the States, listening to band stories—but nothing prepared me for the scene that confronted me in the hotel only an hour or so after arriving in Denver. I was on my way to the elevator and witnessed Ray being frog-marched by two cops off the premises. Following them out cautiously, I saw a few of our party staring at the bus, which stood in the middle of the parking lot, surrounded by our luggage, and an ever growing swamp of fuel. "There must be a sensible explanation for this!!" I thought, and there was. Ray had taken a mixture of crystal meth, Halcyon sleeping pills, and a bottle of scotch, and retired to his room with his wife, whereupon he proceeded to threaten her with a gun, at which point she abandoned her spouse to call the police, and he left in a rage to cut the fuel lines to the bus. See? There's an explanation for everything.

Luckily(?), we were in Denver for a couple of days for two shows at the Gothic Theatre, so, ha ha! Ray, we didn't really need the stupid bus anyway! And who cares that we can only smoke cigarettes naked because every item of clothing we collectively own is soaked with fucking diesel fucking fuel, you fucking redneck drunken asshole!! After the shock of all that had happened, it was relief to note that there was a happy hour in the hotel bar. This was a huge hotel. There were about a zillion different stupid conventions all going on at once, and the bar poured free Margaritas between 5 and 6. Since we no longer needed to soundcheck, this suited our needs perfectly.

The Denver shows climbed to legendary status. On the first night, we invited teenage Colorado back to the hotel. Tucker and I had about fifteen kids in the room. Nothing sordid—we were drinking beer, smoking pot, and watching cartoons whilst holding court. Of course, the police arrived, Johnny Law getting a taste for all of this back in Utah, and telepathically transmitting it to their mountain dwelling fascist pals in

Denver. We just didn't open the door, studiously following a strict ignore-it-and-it-will-go-away policy, and they did. One kid decided to climb up the hotel wall outside the room to try and reach Al's room, two floors above us. Meanwhile, I'm trying to come up with the perfect headline—they probably have a stock "Drug-Crazed Teen Rocker Falls to Death in Satanic Band Hotel Nightmare", or, "Children Force-Fed Pot and Made to Jump from Building by Jeering Cult Rockers", or "Chris Connelly Sent to Prison, Forever"... something like that.

The next evening showed more of the same. Al had spent some of his teenage years in Denver, so some old high school pals showed up to reminisce and crack open an envelope of good old home-made, pharmaceutical MDMA powder, which they were delighted to share around backstage. The end result of this being that our entire party of thirty people, plus guests, ended up in the hotel pool—some with clothes, some without. The fire alarm was sounding, yet for some reason, no one on the staff or security detail seemed to care. The night seemed to give birth to other nights, and before long, I had dried off and was in En Esch's (from KMFDM) room with Tucker, recording on Tucker's 4-track tape machine.

One more show had been added at the Gothic Theatre, due to popular demand. We were ecstatic, because it meant another night at the hotel. After the show, Tucker and I took our regulation dose of LSD and went to the hotel bar to wait for the acid to kick in. Martin-the-English-drummer was there, drunk, and getting into a bloodthirsty argument with an airbag salesman, about airbags—apparently, a subject in which the percussive hero of "This Is Not a Love Song" is quite the expert.

By the time the acid started to have its effect, we could no longer listen to the clucking of conventioneers or the drummer from south of Scotland, as they batted back and forth stories about golf swings, net profits, and Johnny Rotten's sweater collection. We went upstairs to watch TV. We were sucked in and hours went by until we decided to move onto the next thing. A little restless, Tucker produced a couple of screwdrivers from his toolbox, and we silently and diligently went about disassembling the entire room: the beds, the television, the closets, the desk, everything. All the blankets and towels were folded neatly and placed in the bath, which we then topped off with water, at around about 7 a.m.

Tucker and I looked at our handiwork. "Dude, what the fuck have we done?" he asked.

"If we flush the room key down the toilet, they'll never know it was us." That steadfast Connelly logic coming to the fore and dealing with the situation. Then I suggested that, "We could just hide on the bus until it's time to go." Brilliant.

So we flushed both of our room keys down the toilet, grabbed our luggage, and made off to the bus—acid logic making me anticipate the smug staff member who might step out at any minute and say, "You forgot to dismantle the in-room surveillance camera, boys. A HA HA HA HA HA HA!" But we made it to the bus and went to our bunks to hide. Eventually, the wheels started turning and we were on our way, with apparently no security staff or police inciting any kind of cross-state chase. Oh well, I supposed we were invincible. Ha!

(Of course, Ray was no longer driving the bus, and the fuel lines had been repaired. Just so you know.)

Omaha is—bar none—the most boring place on Earth. Subsequent visits over the years have not changed my opinion. There are three things to do in Omaha: purchase gasoline at the Circle K gas station, purchase a beverage or a snack food item at the Circle K convenience store, or go to the car dealership across the street. (There is rumoured to be a Circle K museum, boasting a replica of the world's biggest Twizzler, which was sacrificed in the Depression.)

The show itself was not without its charms. Clearly, if you were a teenage boy in Nebraska who liked to wear dark clothes and makeup and you simply didn't have the time or energy to take firearms to school to ice your classmates... well, here was Ministry! We will happily scream at you for two hours about your oppressors. Funnily enough, this show has been bootlegged many, many times. The most frequently seen release, titled *Power Department*, has a glass skull on the cover. It's a good representation of the band, super tight, and half on drugs. I wonder who taped and sold it? I have my suspicions… it had to have been an inside job.

Quite by sheer chance, Al collided hard with a Mai Tai. Between the end of the show and bus call, Al had sucked back an unholy amount of the rum, citrus, and fruit syrup cocktail (with shaved ice). I can't think where. It certainly was not from the Circle K, so it had to have been the car dealership, right? Tucker and I were exiting the venue via the *Spinal Tap*-ian labyrinth of corridors that had frustrated us prior to the show. We stopped dead in our tracks when we thought we saw the mythical Minotaur, however it was just a flailing Al: clearly lost, horribly drunk, collapsed on all fours, and making a sound like a seagull with a lobotomy. He didn't look up or notice his aghast bandmates, so we doubled back and left by a fire exit, hoping against all hopes that he would just get left behind.

On the bus, things were looking good.

"I didn't see him," I said with a look of concern and pensive thought. "Right after the show, he was there, and then I thought he had come on the bus. Did you check his bunk? Maybe he's asleep." (Hee hee hee!!! This is gonna be great!)

"I think I saw him get into a car with a bunch of kids," said Tucker, straight-faced, "maybe he mentioned something about meeting us in St. Louis."

It was almost time to leave and still no Al. The bus had a bustling good-natured peace about it: a card game, a joint, *Blazing Saddles* on the TV, but this was short-lived. The lobotomized seagull had turned into Hitler with a Cher wig, hammering with all fours on the bus door, screaming at the top of his lungs. I knew from past experience that this was the beginning, not the finale—this was going to go on all night. Weighing my options, I went to bed with my headphones on, but Al was definitely not going to allow anyone to miss his performance. He crawled up the bus corridor on all fours screaming—just in case anyone fell asleep—"Come on you dirty-ass motherfuckers, BURN with me. Get up you FUCKS." Oh, who could resist the invitation for an audience with the Dean Martin of cybertechnology? I was in!! I got up and sat patiently, and listened as Al roared his way through a two-hour monologue detailing exactly how "fucking WAAAAASTED" he was. And yet somehow, it became endearing. As long as he had an audience agreeing with him, he wouldn't lash out. He was just being himself—I had witnessed it before, and certainly would again. So I sat, smiled, and nodded until his battery went flat, and I made sure his cigarette was out before I went to bed.

The dubious pleasure of a day off in St. Louis. The company you kept during free time depended on who was up when you woke up and left your room, or got off the bus. I liked this randomness and got to forge a lot of friendships by just going to do laundry with whoever was awake at the time. In St Louis, I spent the day with Ogre and his girlfriend, Cyan. Al had relegated them to scapegoat status on the tour, probably because Ogre had brought Cyan—he was being treated much the same way I had on the first Cocks tour, and I felt badly for them. They kept to themselves and it was nice to spend time with them. Although shy, Ogre was a sweetheart, and his girlfriend was charming. We went to a horrible mall and then we went up the stupid St. Louis Arch, apparently the gateway to something… boredom, I imagine. We had the day off so we were in no hurry. There was a party for us that night, no commitments. I went to the party later that evening. It was dull, but as I was about to leave either Brains or Joe the Annoying Punk Kid got into a fight. This reaffirmed my determination to leave.

I found out the next day that Joe the Annoying Punk Kid was in jail! Hilarious!! Although I did rather wish it had been Terry Brains, or better still, both of them—but still, I was tickled pink. Good going, Joe the Annoying Punk Kid! Unfortunately, they let him out, which was a shame, because we could have managed just fine without him and divvied up his stuff and shared his rations.

Afterwards, another party—this time in the basement of the club we were playing, a basement I still to this day find myself in. This time though, I was down there with Tucker and his girlfriend, who had flown out from NYC to join us. She had brought a heap of ecstasy, and we were high as kites. Highlight of the party: I threw up on the floor.

The clock was ticking, and we were playing our way back to Chicago. I was not happy about this, neither was Tucker. Tick tick tick… Kansas City…. tick tick tick… WE WERE OUTSIDE AL'S APARTMENT IN CHICAGO. WE WERE HOME!! There were still a few dates left; regional, gigs and locations that we could drive to and from, so we waved goodbye to the bus and we were getting a Winnebago to cut costs. I didn't know what a Winnebago was—I thought it was a kind of covered wagon like they have in cowboy films—and, as it was mid-winter, I was concerned. It turned out to be a large mobile caravan, like a mini tour bus. There was even a shower, which Brains broke when he tried to have sex in it.

The next day we were headed to Joliet, Illinois—a kind of a suburb. After a day being cross-examined and de-briefed by my girlfriend: "Yes, I slept with someone on the road, she was a Vogue model! Ha ha ha ha!! Jesus, cut me some slack, please!!" (Oh! Vogue-vogue-vogue-vogue-VOGUE!!!!!) It would be a few days before she discovered my phone book ("Oh, they're just friends I met on the road who happened to be girls…") and blacked out the female parts.

Horrible news as we assembled at Al's to leave for the Joliet gig. The night before, En Esch had been staying at a girl's apartment. The apartment caught fire, and he was left with the choice of burning to death or jumping from a third storey window. He chose to jump and nearly broke every bone in his body. He spoke hardly any English. Tucker took over guitar chores for KMFDM for the last shows.

After Joliet—the venue was an oversized game room with pinball machines, etc.—we drove to Grand Rapids, which was a longer haul. I was in the front quietly drinking wine and listening to music on my headphones when there was a lot of shouting from the back. It seemed that Terry Brains had picked a fight with the English drummer—over punk credentials, or something, who knows. Fisticuffs! And a lot of:

"Ah'll bloody (pronounced Blue'dy) well 'ave you, mate."

"Coom on then ah'll tek yee now."

"You foockin coont!" and perhaps "I say, you need a jolly good whacking!"

All this did nothing to ease our driver's nerves. The vehicle was swaying around due to strong freezing winds and ice anyway, and the British seemed to be importing soccer hooliganism in the small, confined lounge area.

We were almost done. The Holiday Star Plaza is a large, horrible, modern theatre adjoining a Holiday Inn. Bands like Gladys Knight and the Pips, the Temptations, maybe Styx, or REO Speedwagon play there. It's for people who want to be entertained, have a night out swooning to Frankie Valli and the Four Seasons, and then go back to a hotel room to have disappointing sex. It is not usually the scene of 3,000 rabid teenage fans. Jello came to join us. He found a cape backstage somewhere.

"The janitor told me this belonged to Liberace!" he gurgled, sounding, as usual, like a verse from "Holiday in Cambodia".

Tucker and I were on a roll, drinking like it was nearly the end of the tour. We all went to Smart Bar afterwards.

The following show, the last, was in Ann Arbor, Michigan. Before we went on, the crew hijacked the stage and started to play their own version of the set. Someone had changed my sampling keyboard to play the word "crazy", taken from the Patsy Cline song, every time a key was struck. There was Silly String and much hooting, but we soon retaliated with the good old Ministry hammer-to-the-back-of-the-skull wall of sound.

After the show, in a celebratory mood, Al got into a fight with a college student trying to interview him for something. The guy was tiny and probably only 18 or 19. The bouncers of the club were interested in pummelling us into a pulp—we needed to exit the building efficiently, and NOW. In a more reflective mood, in the Winnebago, Al screamed himself hoarse while discussing something with/at his wife and made her cry. He was obviously trying to end the tour on an "up" note.

And that brought the tour to its conclusion. Over the next few days, people started to drift home. I shut myself in my house, ignoring the many messages left by Tucker, who was staying with almost everyone else on Al's floor.

"The mutants are starting to wake, please help me!" he pleaded. "Call me man, help!" "Hey man, can you hook me up with some pot?"

The tour was over, but really it was not, as the next couple of weeks would prove. It was just changing shape…

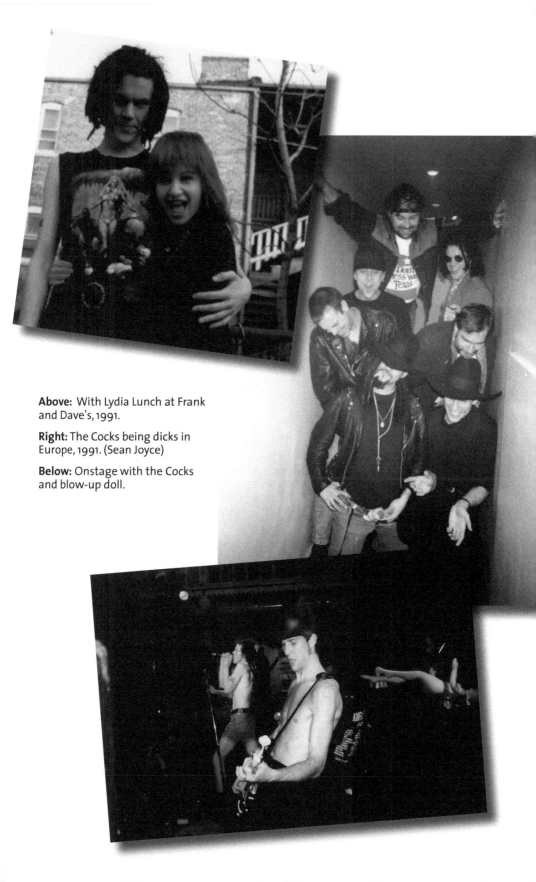

**Above:** With Lydia Lunch at Frank and Dave's, 1991.

**Right:** The Cocks being dicks in Europe, 1991. (Sean Joyce)

**Below:** Onstage with the Cocks and blow-up doll.

# 8

# POINT BLANK

Whilst we had been cavorting, snorting, drinking, and slinking on the road, the two drummers—specifically Martin—had been plotting a kind of "super jam" (yikes! run!) once we were back in Chicago. This spontaneous studio experiment was to harness our talents, or perhaps it was simply a way to usurp Al's authority and prove to anyone who'd listen that drummers could be just as bossy. Martin booked the studio and hired Steve Albini to record whatever happened. Although he was a fantastic engineer, it was interesting to witness the caustic Albini working along with the black-clad Goth icons he found completely abhorrent. He loathed Al, he loathed Wax Trax!, and he had new people to loathe in Ogre and Tucker. He seemed to like Martin and Bill though, and I don't think he had a beef with me. I certainly enjoyed his terse, caustic wit and he had a seemingly endless supply of good jokes. The biggest problem was having Fluffy the engineer, who Steve especially disliked—their personalities an incredible clash of dour, sarcastic realism against coke-fuelled optimistic gloss. KABOOM!!

However, the sessions ran "smoothly" enough, with people coming and going over the next couple of weeks, but the idea of bringing twenty-odd people into a studio environment to be spontaneous, simply because they were all connected by one mid-level rock tour, was a flawed one. Anyone on a mid-level rock tour is predisposed to have mid-level delusions of grandeur, and, just because you are a decent musician from another band, it does not necessarily follow that you will shine in any musical situation. Thus, the main problem with the first Pigface album, *Gub*, is that its creators wanted a finished product with a minor celebrity line-up, without paying any heed to the content. Talk about putting the cart before the horse! All objectivity was lost in the assumption that this particular collective would achieve lofty heights of musical greatness purely on the strength of its component parts, and also the assumption was that everyone would blend together in a marvellous "Kids from 'Fame'" kind of symbiosis, *i.e.* as soon as the participants came together, a higher instinct would take over, and the most incredible musical epiphany would be captured, right there, on tape.

What actually happened was a series of forced experiments speckled with barely written songs. The recording was so horribly dry, it was dying of thirst. If ever there was a case for taking the defibrillator of studio effects to a dying recording, this was it.

The best song—perhaps the only song—"Little Sisters" owed its debt to a fantastic Dick Dale-meets-The Seeds guitar riff that Tucker provided; the only problem being that it was sucked out of the song during the final mixdown and left out until the fadeout—either as a calculated mix-move by Albini or because he just hated Tucker.

In other areas, the two drum kits battled each other like Godzilla and King Kong on Rohypnol. Although I sang in a couple of places, the vocals were not much more than parched squawks provided by myself and Ogre, with a fleeting cameo by Trent Reznor, one from Paul Barker, one from David Yow (the singer from The Jesus Lizard), and a Blixa Bargeld-esque monologue from a now-under-repair En Esch. Hollow, throbbing basses battled against scratchy guitars, all in the stark relief of the studio lights, peppered with pointless tape loop experiments and boring "found" sounds. Other people drifted in and out, other experiments were undertaken. My own vocal contributions were self-conscious and floundering at best.

When one thinks of great improvisational albums, one might think of *Agharta* or any of the great electric Miles Davis albums, or any of Can's late 60s/early 70s output, or Amon Düül I, or even Throbbing Gristle. This was not one of these records, no siree.

This was all a far cry from the tour that had ended just a few days ago; it was kind of like a rock 'n' roll "monkey's paw". The tour that had been horribly disfigured and killed had subsequently been "wished" back to life again by desperately grieving parents. But the tour had come back all wrong: a lumbering, agonised, broken wreck.

During the months that followed, I went through a leisurely breakup with my girlfriend, started work on my first solo album, continued a correspondence with Vogue, and became—albeit inadvertently—friends with Lydia Lunch. The day I had recorded my vocal for "Physical", I had gone to the studio via the Wax Trax! store, having just purchased the new Lydia Lunch album, *Oral Fixation*. I had left it at the studio; Al had put it on and realised there were several great samples there. He sampled Lydia and stuck it at the beginning of "Physical". Lydia heard the record when it came out and was none-too-pleased—mostly because Al had sampled from a spoken word album, something that was so unmistakably Lydia's words that she had every right to be pissed. Lydia was a very old friend of Frank's, so we learned from him that all was not well, that she was coming to Chicago to work, and that she would like to discuss this. She actually called me at work. I, of course, was terrified, and we arranged to meet at Frank's apartment later that day. In the event, Jim Nash "compensated" her for her work and when I went over to Frank's that evening, it turned out that we got along great, and have remained friends ever since. She did not like Jourgensen though, noooo!! This would rear its head a few months later.

*Beers, Steers and Queers* was released and, all of a sudden, because of this, and because of Thrill Kill Kult and other sundry musical endeavours on the label, British journalists were sniffing around and wanted to write about the "Chicago scene" that seemed to attract so many "edgy" continental European dance floor guerrillas (read: pompous disco boys).

I am sure they had just squeezed the Touch and Go/Big Black situation for all it was worth by this point, and there was no real scene happening anywhere else—too early for Madchester or Seattle. Funnily enough, this would all happen again on an enormous scale when the Smashing Pumpkins broke four or five years later, finally putting the last nail in the pompous Euro-disco coffin, sniff! The owner of Wax Trax!'s European affiliate label, Play it Again Sam, paid a visit, and spent a few minutes telling me how great *Beers, Steers and Queers* was. As the man had always been at best condescending to me, I paid little heed as he tried to crawl a little. Almost everyone I would eventually encounter from that label viewed me with mild contempt.

So, a few features appeared in the British music press. "Physical" came out as a 12-inch with a cover that I put together with Wax Trax! graphic designer Brian Shanley—there I am on the back cover talking dirty into a payphone. I also worked with Brian on the *Beers, Steers and Queers* cover, which we based on the album cover of the soundtrack to *Caligula*.

As we started making plans to hit the road again as the Cocks, my oldest friend, Andy, came over to stay. As I was enjoying bachelor status and living alone, there was plenty of fun to be had. We bought a couple of bikes and rode around the city. The new bar to go to was Crash Palace on Lincoln and Diversey; it had taken over from clubs like Exit and Smart Bar. It was just a few blocks from my house, and it became a bit of a drug haven, amongst other things. I would end up spending almost every night there for a while, Jesus…

Andy was ostensibly in town to make a video for the first single off my solo album, which was nearing completion at Trax. I had been going into the studio once or twice a week, and, with the help of some musicians and a lot of amazing contributions from Bill Rieflin, I had a record—one that was as far away from the sound of Ministry or the Cocks as you'd care to imagine. (Why would I wish to make a record that sounded like Ministry or the Cocks—but not as good—if I was currently involved in the real deal? This is all part of the quandary that has dogged me ever since. I had no interest in doing what many people from bands do when making solo albums—*i.e.* sound exactly like the bands they are from.) We shot the video in various locations around Chicago: Martin's headquarters, the roof of Martin's headquarters, various street locations, and a slot machine rental business. We were trying to make a kind of surreal *Dirty Harry*-themed video, if you can believe that.

Rehearsals for the *Beers, Steers and Queers* summer tour took place in—of all places—a novelty soap factory, which was the property of the father of one of our crew. Although the place was crammed to the gills with pink champagne bottles brimming with bubble bath, it looked like it had long since been abandoned, a veritable Marie Celeste of personal hygiene. The overpowering sickly scent of chemically generated flowers—"Moonspring", "Morning Tide", "Summer Cascades", "Evening Forest", "Dog Vomit"—permeated everything to the core. Even the guitar strings took on the aroma of Eastern Bloc luxury. It was like rehearsing in one of these soap-on-a-rope/aftershave-and-talc sets I always got from my aunt at Christmas.

Jeff Ward on drums, ladies and gentlemen—on loan from Midwest metal merchants, Hammeron. Bill would not be joining us this tour, he was just sensible; nor would Luc, who was about to become a daddy. We were, however, being joined by the famous Phildo, and his band were going to be the openers. And you know what? I was warming to them. Perhaps because—stacked up against the other openers, the God-awful Mentors—the Skatenigs sounded like *The Lamb Lies Down on Broadway*. Now that Phildo was integrating into the Cocks, I was starting to realize he had more strings to his bow than going, "WOOOOOOOO!!" "AN' TAWKIN LAHK THIS". I think we both had to bend in the middle—I mean, he couldn't possibly be like that all the time.

We were also being joined by Michael Balch, a Skinny Puppy alumnus and former member of Front Line Assembly, a general all-around tall boy—he was up there. Mike was quiet, charming, with a sinister undercurrent; I loved him. He would be playing keyboards.

Once Al had breezed into rehearsal after a busy morning's hustle-bustle scoring heroin in Chicago's seedy underbelly, he—and whoever else wanted to be a junky that day—would go and ingest the drug between two towering pallets of Big Bird soap-on-a-rope, then we'd get down to it. We sounded okay. At one point Al told me, "Man, you're starting to sound like that chick from Yazoo," (that'd be Alison Moyet, Al) which I took as a compliment.

Someone conspicuous in his absence was Ogre. He and Al had been working on their much-touted collaboration project called "W.E.L.T." ("*I am the mornin' d.j.....*" sorry, sorry) at Trax, and then... well, he wasn't there. He just slid out the door, perhaps to get cigarettes or something, and he never came back. I, of course, was quite pleased: one less person to be upstaged by, although I did like the guy a lot. I don't know what happened, but one can speculate it may have been drug-related, or the rift Al had opened up on the *Mind* tour had not yet closed.

We were playing two shows at the Riviera Theatre in Chicago to kick off the tour, and because of my Roman-themed album cover, we decided to dress in Centurion drag, Caesar chic, whatever—"Let's keep it ROMAN you guys!!" Andy and I sat in my downstairs neighbour's apartment, smoking pot and putting the finishing touches to my costume: a huge red curtain fashioned into a toga, with flip flops spray painted gold, and some plastic Christmas holly painted gold for a wreath to put on my head. The phone rang: it was my (almost ex) girlfriend. She was upstairs and wished to see me IMMEDIATELY. I went upstairs and she swooped down, talons outstretched, brandishing aloft a photograph of Vogue!! (Actually, one cut from the pages of *Vogue Italia*, which she had sent me after scrawling "Aren't they enormous????" on her considerable cleavage.) She must have been doing one of her periodic wallet 'n' phone book raids and come across it. I was busted. I was also really stoned. And I was also dressed up like Caligula. I started to laugh uncontrollably at the comedy of the situation, which sent the (almost ex) girlfriend into a high-pitched frenzy, evaporating the photo of Vogue and her tits into dust. I think I managed to slip quietly out the door while she was looking for matches to burn my phone book, and any other evidence of Vogue she could find. Oh well, we were breaking up, and I would see Vogue in her Manhattan dwelling in a couple of weeks. Ha ha!!

The next night at the Riviera, the Mentors lived up to my expectations of being inexcusably dreadful. They also played for far too long; three miserable guys wearing KKK-style hoods, caught somewhere between racism, misogyny, and pig-ignorance, but it made the Skatenigs look a little better. Now it was our turn.

"On behalf of the Senate and the people of Rome… Let's rooooock!!" I am such a ham, but how can you not be when you are wearing a toga and in the Cocks? Al, of course, had rented his costume, and was, in a wry indication of his state, connected to a fake IV onstage. He looked a bit like a failed actor "between roles", waiting tables at some suburban Italian joint. Paul was dressed like a kind of soldier who had lost his helmet. I think we had the desired aesthetic effect of the Cocks, kind of getting it all just a bit wrong—which was great—however, the music was a very different story. It was collapsing around us as tidal waves of white noise swept the stage. The sound guys were panicking, stopping only long enough to sign their own death warrants as a purple-faced Jourgensen, IV flailing, quit playing guitar to signal across the stage, confirming to the sound guys that they were, indeed, going to die—probably via a Gladius sword to the throat. He then, in the interest of equality, stared at each of us around the stage, promising the same fate.

At some point in the show's death throes, an army of strippers descended upon the stage, each one dancing as poorly as the next and to a completely different tune. By no stretch of the imagination was this at all sexy, as our equipment was stepped on and tripped over by thirty pairs of pink fleshy legs, united perhaps by one brain cell. I managed to get quite annoyed, and eventually slinked off the stage to find something to make out with.

I am not being lazy when I tell you that the second night was exactly the same as the first—the only difference being that Al threw up on his rented toga or something, so he was back to "civvies". Apart from that, same three shitty bands, same crappy strippers, same foul tempers lost. A party after the show, followed by a short blackout (this serving the same purpose as a pallet-cleansing sorbet between courses), and we all had to meet the bus at Al's to go to Cleveland, a whirling tornado of shattered glass in my skull. The scene at Al's was not much better: Chernobyl in leather trousers, the floor strewn with the ugliest chapter in rock 'n' roll history. We were late. Everyone (except Al's wife who had let me in) was fast asleep. We were being joined by Jason from *Alternative Press*, who, clearly wishing to exit this world in search of something better, had thought it would be a great idea to join us for the whole tour and write about it. Fine, if your idea of a summer holiday is waking up in Conrad's *Heart of Darkness*, over and over again.

In Cleveland, we picked up Trent Reznor, whose star was on the rise with the first Nine Inch Nails album *Pretty Hate Machine*, but he was clearly not enjoying the fruits of his stardom:

"I don't have a life, can I come with you guys?"

"Sure… if your idea of a summer holiday is waking up in Conrad's *Heart of Darkness*, over and over again.

The tour was born into problems. The bus we had hired for the tour had got us from Chicago to Cleveland but then promptly broke down. Our tour manager was a backwards-thinking Texan hippy—I am not sure exactly how he'd come to be our tour manager, I think Al had won him in a card game. We had a "stage" manager who was affronted at every turn by our "sheer unprofessionalism", so he kept threatening to quit. We had also brought along a variety pack of Al's drug buddies, some of who were on the bus, some of who were in pursuit in a car. Fortunately Sean was with us, happy to roll with the punches, no matter how ludicrous those punches were. And we had a new front-of-house soundman in Critter, who had started engineering our studio sessions. He too, was very much a team player and would complain not once.

The Cleveland show was much what you would expect. One of Sean's jobs on this tour was to round up as many trashy looking females as he could find (and this was pretty easy at a Cocks show) and ask them to join us onstage. I actually didn't know this, and for the first couple of shows marvelled at my apparent charms when these women flooded the stage—and then I became perplexed that I was such a freak magnet. Eventually, I twigged that Sean was siphoning women from the club onto the stage.

The next day we couldn't go anywhere, so we waited in the hotel bar as the hillbilly tour manager ran around trying to get the bus fixed or trying to find enough horses to make the trip to New York, whichever happened first. We listlessly threw back "Jell-O shots", Trent's manager fussing around his charge. Eventually, at about 1 AM, we were presented with two vehicles, both tiny: one, an SUV for the band and as much of the crew as would fit in it; the other, a car driven by a blue-haired gentleman called Steve. He looked a bit like Tin Tin, and had disturbingly manicured eyebrows. This sullen fellow would drive Al and his posse to New York and seemed to fit the parameters of what Al required in a driver: namely access to a supply of narcotics and the capacity to agree with everything Al said. The band crammed into the SUV, six or seven of us for the next 500 miles. We had two cassettes. I seem to remember lying upside down for most of the journey, which took until late morning of the next day.

Feeling like I had been smuggled over the border, I slipped backwards out of the van and into the busy Manhattan streets, physically repulsed by myself and everyone else around me. Some genius of the aesthetic had arranged a photo shoot, during which I quietly left and hailed a cab to Vogue's apartment. I must have been excited to see her, in retrospect, I don't know why else I would even consider this an option, given the journey I had undertaken and my general state on that day. However, she welcomed me with tolerant and charitable arms, and let me shower.

The gig was great. Everyone in the crowd seemed to be on their own different designer drugs, so the band had an easy job—everyone was far too high to notice if we actually sucked or not. Eventually, the stage was invaded by the dregs of possibly every strip joint from Newark to Poughkeepsie, and back again. (They were far too ugly to be from Manhattan strip clubs, darling.) Both Tucker and Andy were there—

Tucker's girlfriend begged me to take him with us—and we all moved *en masse* from the backstage area of the Ritz to an open bar party for us in some bar across town. I took a quick break from drinking to get into a fight with a fan.

"Yeah man," he said in an accusatory tone, "so what the fuck is up with that 'Physical' single? That fuckin' sucks, man." The guy is a boorish, hectoring, square-headed type.

"Actually, I couldn't agree with you more, it's dreadful," I told him.

"Hey FUCK YOU, MAN, I'm gonna kick your ass!"

Well, you just can't please everybody all of the time, can you? So I slipped back into the bar to wait for my fabled ass-kicking, which, of course, never came. However, when we poured out of the bar later, he was still there, and still yelling at me. Note to self: remember to make records that "don't suck".

We dropped Vogue off at her exclusive Chelsea address and went on to the hotel. There was some kind of a tour bus waiting for us. Andy and I said our goodbyes, and I expired for the day, knowing I would wake up *en route* to Orlando.

Trying to act tough in full STAINLESS STEEL glory, Summer 1992. (Cyan Meeks)

**Above:** The Fini Tribe, enjoying one of their frequent band meeting/showers together, Autumn 1984. (Peter Ross)

**Below left:** Wax Trax! El Presidente Jim Nash tries to teach a disinterested Luc Van Acker how to run a record label, Spring 1988. (Connelly)

**Below right:** Al, scanning the stage for his Vodka Cranberry cocktail between verses. The Cocks live, Spring 1988. (Connelly)

**Above:** The Fini Tribe try to con the DHSS for mental Disability compensation, 1987. (Peter Ross)

**Below left:** The Fini Tribe's Simon Mcglynn trying to look deadly serious in his Ultravox outfit, Winter 1984. (Peter Ross)

**Below middle:** Jim Nash browses gay porn when he should have been writing our royalty cheques, Spring 1988. (Connelly)

**Below right:** My first week in Chicago, trying to fit in with a Charles Manson T-shirt and a Baader-Meinhoff beret, Spring 1988. (Frank Nardiello)

**Above:** Me scouring Sassy Magazine for possible love interest whilst Phil "Phildo" Owens triesto understand why the British press fears Texas so much. January 1991. (Sean Joyce)

**Below:** The quintessential Cocks' gig, Glasgow 1991. Everyone in the room on every equation of drug at all times—except, perhaps, my mother, who was also present. (Sean Joyce)

**Above:** Paul Barker tries hard to bring culture to Ministry whilst wondering how Ogre can smoke and shred at the same time, January 1990. (Sean Joyce)

**Below left:** The combined force of the Cocks trying to stop the King of Belgium, Luc Van Acker, from devouring the rider and draining the booze, January 1991. (Sean Joyce)

**Right top:** Me holding court in a Glasgow pub, pre-gig siphoning off everyone's pint whilst they mug for the camera, January 1991. (Andy McGregor)

**Right bottom:** The inimitable Sean Joyce considers leaving the Cocks posse to become a German sheep farmer, January 1991. (Paul Barker)

**Above:** The clean living Cocks feel each others muscles, Spring 1988. (Bobby Talamine)

**Below:** Intense and diligent rehearsals for the Cocks' inaugural gig, Chicago, Summer 1987. (Brian Shanley)

**Above:** Sombre pre-gig meditation in Berlin, January 1991. (Sean Joyce)

**Below left:** The hapless Mark Durante tries to dissuade Luc Van Acker from driving the tour bus back to his mum's in Tienen, Belgium.
**Below top right:** Al and Patti Jourgensen organize hors d'oevres and fancy cakes at my 25th Birthday bash, November 1990. (Connelly)
**Below bottom right:** The late, great William Tucker having just done something awful, or just about to do something awful, 1992. (Connelly)

"I can drink all day, as long as it's only halves of lager, any objections?" Summer 1990.
(Brian Shanley)

# 9

# HELL IS NOT A PLACE...

The Cocks in the South—we perhaps should have established this before—was a very different animal to the Cocks in the North. The South polarized the redneck mentality that we both seemed to abhor and celebrate.

In Florida, you could throw a crucifix in any direction and be sure to hit a Goth—they were everywhere. If you broke Florida down into its main component parts, you would have: tanning salons, tattoo parlours (Why are they parlours? That's such an old lady afternoon-tea word), fetish clothing stores, dance clubs, and trailer parks. There are contributing agents such as heavy metal, which goes in the trailer park test tube.

I awoke with the customary headache and dehydration knowing two things were certain:

1. The air conditioning was not working.

2. There was a female voice coming from the back of the bus, and it was spouting poetry.

There is no advice or protocol as to what action should be taken in the event of bad poetry: no covering of windows, no hiding under kitchen tables, no lining the walls with tin foil. You have to either wait it out or stage an intervention; and, as I was too polite for an intervention, I tried distraction. I opened the door of the back lounge to see our hippy tour manager sitting with Dr Frankenstein's facsimile of Stevie Nicks, journal open on her lap (always a red flag), gesticulating every nuance of her braying rhyme with her over-bangled and theatrically serpentine arms. The hippy tour manager, of course, was hanging on to every word, gasping at ham-fisted alliteration and war-torn onomatopoeia. The "poetry" seemingly channelled through her from the souls of millions of dead inspirational self-help books, the ones you find nestling between the *TV Guide* and True Zodiac at supermarket checkouts. This was a real piece of work. Where had she come from? Did she come with the bus? Was she the driver?? She either jumped on at a North Carolina rest stop or had come on this morning in Orlando—either way, I did not need to know. I left the bus in a hurry with a view to finding some breakfast. Instead I found a taproom and whiled away the afternoon by myself, drinking 75-cent drafts in a semi-morose mood, writing postcards to friends, family, and Vogue.

That evening's show was shaping up to be another stellar evening, with the arrival of Al's parents and little brother—and of a small Coke bottle full of liquid LSD. While Al entertained his family somewhat reluctantly, we busied ourselves by using an eyedropper to administer the drug directly onto our eyeballs. Who knows how we played that night. I do remember that, at the zenith of my first wave of hallucinations, there was a huge fight outside the venue between fans and over-testosterone-fuelled bouncers looking for trouble. Then, fractured memories of walking on the beach with everyone at dawn, eventually curling up in a paranoid ball.

The bus was overheating. There seemed to be more hangers-on than band and crew, but they all seemed to be pretty small in stature, so it was the same as carting around a bunch of eight-year-old heroin addicts—manageable, I suppose. After the previous night's LSD fiasco, I decided to shift my focus onto alcohol—drugs were seemingly being handled very well in other "departments" and there was always tons of booze.

We were playing at a dump in Melbourne called the Power Station, probably named after the Duran Duran side project, fronted at different times by Robert Palmer and Michael Des Barres—how very Florida-in-the-late-80s. The club, like so many in Florida, was in a strip mall that boasted, of course, a tanning salon, a tattoo parlour, some kind of vile eatery, a fetish store, and I think someone said there was a gun 'n' run emporium. The singer of the Mentors, El Duce, had drunk a bottle of Listerine mouthwash, after having been banned from drinking booze by his "band" mates. It didn't matter because they all wore hoods anyway; their roadie pretended to be Duce for the evening.

The carpeted stage was punctuated with mirrored columns—it was a bit like playing in a clothing store. Michael Balch and I half-heartedly chatted up random cocktail waitresses, bemused that they were so unimpressed that we were in the band—the HEADLINING band, no less—but, at the same time, certain that these 19-year-old beauties almost certainly had scores of children, and very angry and armed men close by. One of the waitresses, dressed as a sexy cowgirl, kept us at bay by feeding us test tubes of liquor that she carried around her purdy l'il waist in a holster belt: Jack Daniels and/or vodka, I think. Eventually, during a lull in the conversation, poor Michael's cheeks ballooned with vomit as he made a somewhat staggered beeline for the bathroom. No sexy cowgirl for you, tonight, tall boy! Or me, for that matter; I managed to hiccup my way through the entire set on all fours, another proud moment in the pantheon of rock 'n' roll.

Laughing gas is nitrous oxide, N2O (more properly called dinitrogen oxide). It is a colourless gas with a sweet odour and taste. Inhalation leads to disorientation, euphoria, numbness, loss of motor coordination, dizziness, and ultimately a loss of consciousness. The gas is used as an anaesthetic, as a propellant in whipped cream cans, as an oxidizing agent in racing cars... and as a recreational activity for the Cocks when in New Orleans. All day we wandered around, having stopped for a day's R 'n' R on the way to Texas, inhaling huge balloons of nitrous oxide; laughing, reeling, and calming down with a slurp of Hurricane. I was now well off my high horse and completely at one with the Skatenigs, hootin' and hollerin' with the best of 'em, until I threw up in the Mississippi in front of a plague of curious rats.

We had brought along a second guitarist: Mark Durante, who had been a guitar tech on the *Mind* tour, was now doing a bit of that and playing onstage with us every night—a fantastic guitarist. However, his first tour with the Cocks was not to be a happy one.

We were playing two shows at Numbers in Houston; again, two blurry days with sold-out shows and apparently every stripper from the Mexican border all the way to Arkansas joining us on stage. It got to be that you just couldn't see the band—in fact, people were paying top dollar to look at the girl whose cleavage they had probably stuffed with twenties the night before, ha ha ha! "Ever feel like you've been cheated?" Ha ha ha!!! There was a tall stranger wearing shades and an outlaw mask on his face the whole time, dancing away; this turned out to be Billy Gibbons from ZZ Top, a haw haw haw haw!

Apparently, after the second show, Mark, drunk and disorientated, had tried to hail a cab outside the club. This is something you cannot do in Houston. You have to call for a cab. Of course, Mark did not know this, and, frustrated that no one would stop for him, he decided the best course of action would be to throw a stone at the next cab in an effort to persuade them to give him a ride. Of course, the "cab" that the stone hit was not a cab, but a police car. Of course, he had some Valium on his person… so, so, so much trouble. He ended up in a cell and would be absent from the tour while we tried to figure out how to liberate the poor guy.

Meanwhile, in Dallas… Vogue came by the hotel and picked me up (this is where she is from), and off we went joyriding around the town. I was kind of surprised that she'd have anything to do with me after NYC. The Cocks on paper and on record are much easier to appreciate than in person, I have always thought. She came to Austin as well, also hometown of the Skatenigs. Hence we were surrounded at all times by a flock of guys just like them orbiting at high velocity and screaming

"WOOOOOOOOO!! HOOO!!" It was kind of like how seagulls pursue fishing boats, except with baseball caps on and slugging malt liquor.

Mark was back: they finally let him out pending a trial, but for the meantime, he was safely back with us... or was he? How safe, exactly, is "with us"? Not very. We left him at a gas station somewhere between Austin and Los Angeles. Okay, somewhere between... that's a long, long way, and who knows how long we had been driving before we looked up from our card game and noticed he wasn't there. A wry, unassuming man, he was low-key, and apart from his wealth of curly locks, it was conceivable that we would not notice his absence for a while. Plus we had picked up Mikey Scaccia in Dallas, who was going to come along for the ride and play, so there seemed to always be a surplus of black-haired, black-jacketed guitarists at any given moment. The poor guy finally caught up with us in L.A., where Al almost took his eye out smashing a guitar onstage. This was something Al did a lot when he was in a bad mood. Unfortunately, he was really crap at it, so rather than some incredible Moon/Townshend climax, he was still always beating it against the stage long after the song was over and the audience had drifted to the bar.

Who knows what set him off in L.A.? It may have had something to do with Paul's showing up for the show drunk—God forbid Paul should have a little fun without Al. Anyway, the tantrum continued offstage in the dressing room; I had gone in there right after we played and got a chair to the face. I decided to stay well clear and sat and watched Mark's bleeding eye socket instead.

The next night, in San Francisco, was just as annoying; another photo-shoot in the early afternoon, after which I slinked off on a bar crawl with an old friend. By showtime I was paralytic; however, there was plenty of horrible, sharp, stinging crystal meth to help me autopilot through the show. We were playing a dive called The Stone, a hideous metal bar that would not have been out of place in somewhere like Florida or Oklahoma. During the show, a delegate from a rival band—whom we did not actually know were rivals (I think it was a horrible preachy P.C. band called Consolidated, standing high on their pious tower)—thought he would set us straight from our deviant ways by letting off a smoke bomb. At first I thought it was dry ice, but then I realized it probably was not, as I projectile vomited over the first few rows of packed crowd—sorry! But, we did get to finish early, which was a relief. I was suffering from my all-day booze schedule. Not professional enough to "Bukowski" it, I left the stage citing sinus problems or something, while everyone else deserted the venue.

We left California and enjoyed a day in Reno, pissing our wages away (not me, I am far too cheap to gamble), before shuffling off to Salt Lake City, to the same venue as before, the Speedway Café. No one was sure if the Cocks were banned from Salt Lake City, if the ban applied only to Ministry, and if the local interfering busybodies would indeed connect the two Mormon-hatin', rape-charge-avoidin', police-escort-out-of-townin' rock bands as being pretty much the same animal. Mercifully, Terry Brains was not with us this time; he was probably back in provincial England throwing fireworks through letter boxes and being a roadie for Infa Riot or Vice Squad or something. Utah is a rather beautiful part of the world, inhabited for the main part by bear-frighteningly ugly people. Anyone with any brains will not hang around too long after high school, for obvious reasons.

So the bus pulled up outside the Speedway Café, same dump-of-all-dumps as it was in February. The pool table was so warped it was like playing on a field of sleeping rodents—maybe they were sleeping rodents, it was too dark to tell. There were a few random work lights barely illuminating the joint, an ambivalent crew of teenagers to help move the gear… thousands of lawsuits waiting to happen.

I got up early with Paul, much like the last time we were here; we went for a walk, stopping for a while at a pawnshop where Paul studied wristwatches with the zeal of a fanatic, expounding upon the idiosyncrasies of various date and calendar features. I studied the idiosyncrasies of the old couple who ran the business, as they studied us in barely concealed horror. On the way back to the bus, we stumbled upon a cinema where we were just in time to catch a matinee about a

Japanese family slowly burning to death from radiation in the wake of Hiroshima. Afterwards, suitably buoyed in spirits, we set off at a jaunty clip to the bus for soundcheck.

Everyone was awake. Al busied himself with a few others, crushing up pills with a view to shooting them up; they were also trying to collect as much spit as they could in a jar—purpose: unknown. We also had a houseguest, a young lady called Nutmeg, or Ginger, or vanilla extract—I cannot remember now—but she looked like a feather duster of deepest magenta, her body an anorexic black stick to her mad plume of purple spikes on top. She was sitting in the back lounge, pushing safety pins through the flesh of her arms, like you do, from her wrists up to her shoulders, her alabaster white skin covered in septic scabs and bruises and cigarette burns. Turns out, Daddy was some kind of high-falutin' senator, and when forced to attend a recent dinner party hosted by her parents, she enlivened dinner conversation by stubbing out cigarettes on her forearm whilst screaming "THANK YOU, DADDY!! THANK YOU, DADDY!!"

More than a little relieved to be gone from Utah, we were again in Denver, again at the Gothic Theatre; this time outside, with Trent smashing tables, the promoter looking on at us mystified. This would be Trent's last show with the Cocks, perhaps realising that he did have some kind of a life that was a lot better than hanging around with us; I know I would have scarpered ages ago. It must be said that, on this tour, whenever I was not with the band, I had "Hey Trent!" or "Hey Ogre!" yelled at me from across the street enough to make me start to resent my third fiddle status in the pecking order of industrial rock. (Nowadays, I am fine with it; I am probably 20th fiddle, I stopped counting in 1993.) But when we got onstage in St. Louis, I introduced myself as "TRENTNOOGRENOTRENTNOOGRE". After the show, I took acid with a girl and sat in my bathroom in the dark with the shower on, listening to the rainbow droplets. Jesus, get me out of here!!

A triumphant homecoming gig at the Cubby Bear, where we played a charity show for the hapless Mark Durante. Again, I was less than pleased to be home, with the eternal break-up making home life no more comfortable after the "girlfriend" had moved back in while I was away. So I leapfrogged to Crash Palace to carry on the tour-at-home party along with everyone else. Good Lord! The girl with whom I "listened" to rainbow drops in St. Louis is at the bar! Did she follow me? I persuaded Jeff Ward to entertain her. I was screwed; unwanted in my own home, and with not really anywhere else to go, I called Vogue and she told me to come to NYC for a week. Why not? It'd be fun. She had modelling assignments all day, so I entertained myself by writing and wandering around record stores, at night hitting clubs. It was a good week, but I knew this wasn't going to turn into anything. So did she.

Finally, the girlfriend was leaving the country and we could get on with our lives. My life was about to get a lot more impoverished and needlessly complicated—between tours was always a lean time. I picked up a few shifts at the record store, but couldn't make a commitment to anything particularly. Royalties were thin on the ground, rent had to be paid, and I had to go out, although now I was by myself. I soon discovered the joys of drinking alone and listening to my Kevin Coyne records, which no one I knew seemed to like. But before long, I took in a roommate, a girl who operated on the periphery of my social circle whom I met whilst high on coke at the Smart Bar. I stupidly told her she could move in the next day after she spun a tale of woe about having nowhere to live. I did not know she had no job, and she proceeded to seemingly make a career out of inviting everyone back to my apartment to do coke at four in the morning.

At this time both Tucker and Mike Balch moved to Chicago. I was very happy about both of these developments, and it heralded in a new era of my life in Chicago. Mike and William moved in together, Mike had become a full time member of Ministry for the time being, and Tucker was just here having also gone through a break-up in NYC. There seemed to be a lot more going on musically in Chicago for him.

My life was becoming a very dark netherworld. Even during the day, I was completely unhinged, with no job or partner to stop me. (Vogue was out of the picture.) There were plenty of girls in Chicago, and plenty of free drink and narcotics. I was young and resilient, and I certainly didn't need food... behold! The salad days of drugged-out slutdom!!

*Beers, Steers and Queers* was poised for imminent release in Europe on the beastly Play It Again Sam label, home of the humourless. Al and myself were volunteered to travel across the ocean to discuss in detail why we had been banned from touring the UK. We had been scheduled to go straight after the summer tour, but for one reason or another, we had not. It certainly wasn't anything to do with the band. However, a spin from our British publicist meant that a rent-a-quote Tory cabinet member had refused to let us tour, whew!! Face saved again!! Rumours abounded about our "fwankly disgusting onstage bahaviour", which apparently included live cattle, a bucking bronco onstage, as well as, of course, tons and tons of strippers and loose women all engaging in sexcapades with the... er... live cattle. Of course. This was an incredible spin that had been passed from our publicist onto the "penny dreadfuls", a huge lie detailing our depraved stage show, and the kind of thing some journalists will crawl and lick boots for. Of course, Al and I did not know anything about it as we boarded the plane with a chaperone to Heathrow from Chicago, charming the flight attendants out of whiskey and coffee the entire journey. Wax Trax! had indeed liaised with the publicists in London, but they either neglected to mention it to me or Al, or were too scared. Either way, the journalists got what they wanted with Al and me—as soon as we touched down, we tricked our chaperone, Scott (he worked at Wax Trax!), out of our *per-diem* money, which was supposed to last us all week. Al grabbed it, chuckling, while Scott was taking a shower and immediately called our publicist's office, demanding a bag of speed.

"Come on man, we got the money to pay for it." The publicist was furious, which in turn made Al furious, which in turn made me furious. "Who the fuck do they think we are?? We're the motherfucking Revolting Cocks, and we want DRUGS!!"

Scott came out of the shower and became furious that we'd taken all of our money. "Guys, that's for food and everything for a whole week!"

"Hey, relax, man, we'll be careful with it. I just feel better if we hang on to it, no extra stress for you," reasoned Al. Within an hour it was in the hands of a grubby little speed dealer, and Al and I were snorting lines in the Columbia Hotel bar toilet before getting ready for our interviews.

For the duration of our stay, Scott looked like a parent who had just walked in on his eight-year-old son having a party with about ten other eight-year olds—which fire to put out first? He claimed to be there on business for the label. "Guys, I have my own stuff I need to take care of, I'm not here to look after you, you're on your own." Sure, Scott. A car came and picked us up and whizzed us off to do a television interview for some "bwilliant new pwogwamme" called "Blimey!!! *Sound Xplosion*!!!", or something. I managed to fall asleep under my Stetson and behind my mirror shades, to the point where I am sure the interviewer thought I might just be a stuffed dummy, and not the singer from shock rockers, the Revolting Cocks.

"Can you tell me how you expect to be able to get a herd of loive cattle onstayge with you? I mean, aren't you worried about animal roights activists and such?" inquired the interviewer.

"Er… we weren't planning to bring any cattle with us. That'd be kind of difficult to organise, don't you think?" Fortunately Al spoke for the two of us.

"What about strippers and girls? Aren't you worried about feminist activists?"

"Hey man, we don't ask for that kind of thing. We don't stop it, but we don't ask for it. I'm just a bloke who wants to play guitar, man… and get pissed."

It was always really funny when Al tried to use British terminology on British people—what a bloke! I eventually chimed in telling the interviewer that cattle onstage would be boring. They would also shit everywhere.

Andy came down to egg us on, and my recent ex and the ex before marched round to the hotel—not together, of course—to do battle with each other and lay claim to their forlornly drunken ex-boyfriend. (Why?? I was a disgusting mess, frankly.) The bloody finale between me and the recent ex happened in my room, after she gave me a black eye, after which I poured a full pint over her in the bar.

Two photo shoots had been scheduled for the most awful of all newspapers, *The Star*, a right-wing wank-rag filled with ridiculously sized tits—ever since the advent of Samantha Fox, Britain's appetite for tits had grown to epic proportions. Al and I were obliged to stand with our arms around these women with breasts large enough to have their own school systems and public transportation. The photographers were middle-aged, dishevelled men with Coke-bottle glasses and tongues hanging out of their livery lips, unkempt toupees and years of self-abuse.

"Cooooor, that's luuuuuuvely!!! Roight moi san, grab an 'andful! Luuuvely!"

Later that night, I went to a very sleazy nightclub in Soho, directed by our publicist—more photographers, more page three dolly birds. Time for a bath.

Later in the week, I introduced Al to early morning drinking. You could order as much to drink in a restaurant as you liked, as long as you ordered some food.

"Yes, we'll have the slice of toast please, and forty pints of lager."

They were well used to us in the Columbia bar by now. The bartender called Al "Ahhhh! Meester dabble voadka!!" in his Italian accent. The bar was full all the time, everyone in a band. They all looked like an amalgam of the Happy Mondays, the Soup Dragons, and the Inspiral Carpets to me.

I suppose we did what we set out to do—we set the record straight about the cattle nonsense—but I think we still managed to piss off every journalist we encountered. Not because we were rude—in fact, Al was on really good behaviour. I just don't think we were what they wanted, which was in keeping with the Cocks' philosophy.

The week had, as we knew it would, collapsed in on itself, a wall of powdered sulphate awash on a beach of lager. I had to stay for a few more days while I sorted out some visa problems, but soon enough I was back in Chicago, in my cosy little nightmarish netherworld. My "roommate" had used up every resource in the apartment, and had clearly thrown a number of parties. The place reeked of spilled beer and ciggies, and there was an interesting random pattern of cigarette burns all over the carpet. Oh well, I was angry for about fifteen minutes... then I became distracted by something else.

Killing Joke were on tour again, promoting a new album, and hosting a private party at the famous Star Top restaurant. It was here that I first made the acquaintance of Paul Raven, the bassist—whom I was told I would love, and sure enough, we hit it off immediately. I had met Geordie and Jaz before—and, of course, Martin was there, in agony thanks to a splinter being lodged in his eye. After we had drank and eaten everything we could, we went to visit Al at Trax. Mike Balch was there, and I was thrust in front of a microphone to do a vocal. This was not possible, I was far too drunk—which was kind of the shape of autumn 1990, not a particularly good shape: blackouts and random women stuck between sporadic musical outings. Things were not going to decelerate either, there was really no reason for them to do so. I was learning fast that once one life collapses around you, there is another one right behind it to collapse as well, so why worry?

# I'VE BEEN STABBED IN THE BACK BY A MANIAC

THE CIRCUS hits town: no cattle turn up so the audience attempt to take its place

Leo Regan

# Give 'em enough grope

## REVOLTING COCKS
### Charing Cross Road Astoria

"WE ALL think the war sucks just as much as you do, but for the next one and a half hours we're gonna have a good time."

A man resembling nothing so much as masked Saturday afternoon TV wrestler Kendo Nagasaki — complete with trunks — introduces the Revolting Cocks' show. And what a show it is — more of a sex carnival than a bunch of musicians cavorting around onstage.

The Astoria is packed to the gills with what is, to all intents and purposes, an anarcho S&M crowd, those at the front heaving forward in a desperate attempt to get involved.

Which is hardly surprising. Because what begins with three blow-up dolls propped against the drum riser, while a band of five or six people play hard, a hypnotic, thrashing dance music, quickly turns into a performance featuring various forms of simulated sex. Two immodestly clad pussycats take up position at either end of the stage and proceed to writhe around in suggestive fashion, first alone, then with around in suggestive fashion, first alone, then with the audience.

Even minus the ___ come across like a ___ ten gallon-hatted ___ 'Beers, Steers ___ appropriate "Y ___ Revolting Cocks ___ whatever subst ___

By far the m ___ attack is the p ___ the drummer' ___ noise, punctu ___ produced by ___ the dry ice a ___ whether this ___ performance ___

One Cock ___ described ___ which he sh ___ the (ahem) ___ out of idea ___ reasonably ___ Physical' ___

At one ___ "I'm a kis ___ oral sex, ___ fighting ___ soft-___

—New Musical Express 2 February, 1991.

# Cocks at centre of 'strip' storm

**NEWS**

REVOLTING COCKS were again at the centre of controversy after last week's London date turned into 'a gratuitous peep show', with two models from *The Sport* newspaper joining the band onstage during their set.

Some members of the audience walked out of the Astoria theatre when the women stripped off their clothes and simulated sex with each other and members of the group, before being lowered into the crowd.

Revolting Cocks regularly perform with two go-go dancers in tow, but the representatives from *The Sport* allegedly offered their services when the paper interviewed the band last November.

One angry audience member said: "We're used to seeing extreme behaviour from the band and it's obvious that the controversy surrounding them is part of their appeal. But tonight was too much. Nobody should be immune from

prosecution for turning this int___ gratuitous peep show."

Revolting Cocks' guitarist Al Jourgenson claimed after the gi___ had no prior knowledge of the w___ actions. "We're just a bunch of o___ blokes trying to play our gear," h___ tonight, because we're Revolting___ they provide us with dancers. We ___ hire the f—ing dancers. I don't kn___ those f—ing people are."

The UK music press reports on RevCo: Sounds (top) and NME (bottom), February 1991.

**Middle right:** Caught with my pants down in 1990. (Sean Joyce)

## 10

## "IT GOT IN THE WAY, SO I SHOT IT DOWN..."

The UK had built us up into something prior to our first visit. I do not know exactly what we had been built up to, but following my visit with Al a couple of months prior to the tour in October, it seemed we had fanned quite a few flames. Simply being ourselves, we had passed muster as the complete degenerates the UK music journalists wanted us to be. It was kind of like that *Monty Python* sketch where the guy is completely determined to make the other guy's wife into a nymphomaniac ("Your wife, does she go, then, eh? Nudge nudge, say no more"). So yes, okay, fine, we are bringing a whole Nebraskan plain of cattle with us, and four generations of strippers, and all of them go, eh? Nudge, nudge!!

So we were, indeed, going to Europe. It was mid-winter, and there was a healthy wave of anti-American protest sweeping Europe due to "Desert Storm". There was also a wave of ecstasy and "rave" culture taking place, but I was quite certain the Cocks would not have been welcome at a rave. The Cocks in Europe would be me, Al, the hapless Mark Durante, Bill (back after his summer sabbatical), Paul, Mike Balch, Phildo, and Luc, who we would pick up in Tienen, near Brussels. The crew consisted of Sean Joyce, Critter, and Tucker. Managing the whole fiasco would be Patrick, the French manager of The Young Gods, and to this day the best tour manager I have ever had. Before getting to the Continent, we needed to rehearse, and we needed to play a New Year's Eve show in Chicago with Killing Joke.

Rehearsals took place at a horrible space on Lake Street, dire by even the Cocks' lowly standards. The dampness, the freezing temperature, and the constant volume battle with the Viking rock band next door meant that my voice was lost almost immediately. I was left with nothing but a rusty squeak, exacerbated by my death-defying forays into Smart Bar every night. Tucker had the unenviable job of doing onstage monitors; I'm sure he remembered only too well from the recent *Mind* tour just how terrifying that could be.

We were playing the double bill with Killing Joke at the Vic Theatre, and on the day of the gig, as we were loading in our gear to soundcheck, it became apparent that no one had seen or heard from Al for about a day, nor Phildo, for that matter. We set up the equipment and started soundchecking anyway. Eventually, from the back of the Vic Theatre, you could hear a strangled cry, "UNACCEPTABLE!! UNACCEPTABLE!!", with all the compassion and tenderness of a Dalek. Al came storming into the building in an absolute fury, a sheepish-looking, gape-mouthed Phildo by his side. Al was dressed head-to-toe in a pure white formal cowboy suit, complete with an insanely large Stetson with a brim that practically filled the theatre. He looked like the nightmare offspring of Cher and J.R. Ewing. To say he was in a horrible mood would be like saying Genghis Khan was an interfering busybody. He stood, purple-faced on the Vic stage, pointing in the direction of either band members or equipment, screaming "YOU ARE AN ENEMY OF THE DALEKS". No, he didn't, really—he just kept yelling, "Guitar: unacceptable", "Keyboards: unacceptable", "UNACCEPTABLE". I really wanted to chime in quietly, "Stupid hat: unacceptable", but it was neither the time nor the place. Besides, I did not want him to notice I couldn't sing, hoping that Tucker and Critter would swamp what little voice I had left in some robotic disguise. It was apparent that Al and Phildo had been out on a long drug binge, and that he simply was feeling completely "unacceptable".

Al was making Killing Joke play last, out of respect. They were deserving of a top billing because of their sheer longevity and influence, especially on Al. Thrill Kill Kult were playing at the Metro at midnight, which was very close by, and Al wanted to make sure that no one left before the Cocks played—in the event, the crowd haemorrhaged out of the Vic almost as soon as Killing Joke hit the stage. Oops!

If the soundcheck was the great fire of Chicago, the gig itself was Armageddon. Al being the six-headed beast, as you no doubt know by now, every inaugural gig we played sounded like a dog's breakfast. It's not like it would sound just a bit off and could be remedied with some fine-tuning, it has to inspire biblical imagery on these pages. Tidal waves of white noise towered over the stage, breaking on the equipment and sending out white-hot sprays and splinters of feedback… just like that! My voice, of course, was just not there, but that was my fault. Even Paul looked a little nervous as Al screamed from the stage to where William stood at the side at the monitor board. William, greeny-white with fear and nausea, could only shrug and make his hands flurry on top of the forest of nobs and buttons that made up the desk, lamely trying to give over the impression that it was out of his control, which made Al scream even louder, alternating "YOU'RE DEAD" and "YOU'RE FIRED!!" He looked like the mythical Minotaur, a bull's head on Dwight Yoakam's body, as he lunged across the stage and pulled William out in front of the capacity crowd, shaking him like a bad dog. Incidentally, I think the crowd was far too fucked-up to notice. I mean, come on, it was the Cocks, and it was New Year's Eve.

After the show, Al's tantrum had consumed him completely. Having reached Homeric proportions and showing little sign of subsiding, it was just a case of riding it out. He fired William, and rehired him almost immediately. This went on for a while until everyone lost interest and went up to watch Killing Joke as the audience made a beeline to the Metro.

I stayed late at the Vic, doing coke with Killing Joke and chatting up stray females. The next day I had to walk over to Al's to pick up my wages. His wife answered the door and gave me an envelope with my money in it, not inviting me in and politely making it clear that I was not coming in. I found out later that someone had overdosed after the show whilst at Al's apartment, and had died for a few minutes.

London: a drunken flight over, resulting in our being cut off from any more booze; although we certainly were not being unruly, I think the flight attendants just got sick of attending to us. Of course, at customs in Heathrow, we were convinced that the government ban on the Cocks would still be in effect and we would be sent back from whence we came, and indeed, our entire party was singled out and taken to a remote part of the airport. Fortunately, this was just for work permit processing. Let's face it, there was no ban. No one cared.

Back in the Columbia Hotel bar, the barman recognized Al and me from our press trip a few months earlier. "Ahhhh! Meeester dabble voadka!!" A number of old friends gathered in the bar to say hello to us; Coil, John Loder, and my two London-dwelling exes, who were just ecstatic to see each other, taking perches at opposite ends of the bar to stare daggers at one another. The one ex-girlfriend was trying to convince anyone who would listen that the other ex was a man. Eventually I got tired of trying to keep both of them happy and went to bed.

We had booked a space in London for a solid day's rehearsal before our bus arrived to whisk us off to the Continent, and things were sounding a lot better. My throat was just fucked, plain and simple. By singing like that every night, especially in winter, there was no chance of it healing. The set was about the same as the summer tour, with the addition of a cover of John Cale's "Chicken Shit", the song he wrote about his drummer who quit after Cale decapitated a live chicken onstage ("I didn't hurt it, I killed it"). It seemed very appropriate.

The tour was, on the whole, a fairly light-hearted affair, although the Gulf War cast a shadow over everything. We picked up Luc in time for the first show in Brussels, and so excited was he to be on the road again that, after the show, he overturned the dinner table backstage and drank a bottle of Jack Daniels. The next night in Amsterdam, we bullied and browbeat the pompous rep from our pompous record company into getting us some speed. Once he had delivered, we banned him and his asshole pompous pals from the Paradiso dressing room. This ushered in a long night of experimentation, with many varieties of drugs being consumed—Tucker being the butt of everyone's jokes for purchasing a crushed aspirin out on the street, giving him nothing but a stinging nostril. Eventually we cruised the Red Light District along with an old man we had found playing a harmonica on the street. I could not make sense of that night's drug cocktail sloshing about my blood with a case of Grolsch lager. Later on, I could not comprehend my hangover, a coal shovel wrestling with the Kraken. It was pain that forced tears to my eyes. It was a premonition of things to come.

We were stuck in the more robotic regions of Europe—no Italy or Spain, unfortunately, but tons of Germany. Tons of provincial metal bars and metal heads who, as you might imagine, are pretty uniform the world over. One other thing that the gigs had in common was the absence of women, and on the rare occasion that a female found herself in the dressing room, and perhaps asked back to the hotel, the reply was always, "Sure, I just get my partner and we come with you!" The silent, grumbling boyfriend dragged into the dressing room soon after to help finish our booze.

The content of the shows swayed slightly, depending upon the drugs of the region and the beer, but I feel we were consistently sloppy for all of the appearances. In Malmö, Mike caught heat from Al because the strong heroin rendered him almost unable to lift his hands to play his keyboard. He countered this by doing jumping jacks behind his instrument for the whole of the encore. A thwarted attempt by Sean and me to climb the Eiffel Tower in Paris on foot using the stairs, a thwarted attempt to win over a hostile audience the same night provoked us into playing our last (and longest) song "Get Down" for 40-plus minutes—stick that in your pipe and smoke it, Paris. After the show, the antagonistic audience provoked the "ugly American" in the poor, long suffering Critter. After taking all the heat that the audience could not personally inflict on the band—we were hiding in the dressing room—he finally broke and started shouting (what he thought was) "Fuck your mother!", the only phrase he had learned on his first trip to France.

We left for Cannes to play at MIDEM, being joined for most of the journey by Franz from the Young Gods; always a fun guy to have around, although he looked mildly alarmed as the whole touring party sat on the bus passing around bottles of amyl nitrate whilst singing along to "If I Had A Hammer" by Trini Lopez, over, and over, and over again.

And exactly who in their right mind invited the Cocks to Cannes? The balmy January temperatures and the slick casino culture were wildly out of step with the unwashed black-leather clad wannabe rednecks. We were playing in what looked like a plush porno theatre for rich folks (and I have no reason to doubt that it was, indeed, a plush porno theatre for rich folks) with a long banquet table covered in food in a huge dressing room, which we soon realized was the foyer—as the desensitised MIDEM crowd wandered into the theatre apathetically. They barely even noticed Phildo rubbing his dick on a peanut butter and banana demi-baguette and trying to get Bill to eat it. But that was fine, we barely noticed them as varying percentages of band and crew huddled at the side of the stage inhaling amyl nitrate (the new drug of choice, in case you hadn't noticed), and then taking frog leaps onto the stage to dance with each other. All this during the show, why not? The audience was seated and impassive-looking as we (surely) impressed the hell out of the Cock-hungry music business elite of Europe. My musical "chops" were so finely honed at this point, I tripped over my mike stand several times before leaving the stage in pursuit of an errant audience member who was scurrying away with at least six bottles of Stella Artois from the stage.

We took an overnight ferry and in the morning we were back in London. The gig at the Astoria was the following day, a Saturday. Thumbing through the weekly music press we could see that the gig had been built up into practically the second coming of Satan—well, we're here to disappoint!! Honestly though, the British music journos had grabbed it and turned it into something that could only be paralleled by the Pistols' "Screen on the Green" mixed with the Stooges' "Metallic

KO" gigs, with a dash of the early Mary Chain gigs thrown in. Months of speculation, rumour, and, let's not forget, a cancelled tour, had nudged our market value into the rock legend class of NME notoriety. I was suddenly being talked about (generally untruthfully) in gossip columns. Goodness me! I was the singer in a band that took live cattle onstage! MOOOO! Well, cattle it was, I suppose. No matter how hard Al and I had denied this ridiculous concept on our press visit in October, the British public wanted to believe we would be crowding the stage with slow-moving herbivores. Not for us—the rock 'n' roll tradition of covering ourselves with peanut butter and rolling around in broken glass, shooting up onstage, or decapitating bats, fowl or any other winged beast, (although, like I said, the song "Chicken Shit" was about chopping off a chicken's head, does that count?)—to be honest, we just were not, and will never, ever be, as cool as Iggy, Lou, or Blixa. We were just a bunch of prank-pulling teenage boys waaaay past our sell-by date, with a splash of technology thrown in.

So it's fair to say that the legendary Astoria show was fucking miserable. It was diabolical, we were awful. The opening acts were Godflesh and Bomb Everything, who used to be called Bomb Disneyland but found out that they couldn't call themselves that (duh!). They came with a lofty reputation; however, our friend Pierre, who lived in London, swore to us that the band just hospitalised anyone that even looked at them.

"Zey will break your legs eef you even just say 'hi' or anyseeng!!!" he squeaked.

"Oh come on, Pierre, we're going to be sharing a dressing room!" we countered.

"Zey will keeck your tees in!!!"

"Well, we'll have 'em thrown out"

"Yes, but all zee bouncers are scared of zem!!"...

This exchange went on for quite a while.

Of course, when actually faced with this menace to society, they were just sillier schoolboys than us, and one of the biggest regrets of my long, forlorn career in music is that I didn't panel at least one of them, on principle. As it turned out, between our soundcheck and our returning to the venue, the fuckers had not only drank every drop of booze in our dressing room, but they had destroyed it and left the building, not man enough to stay behind and face the Cocks. Well, look at where their career is now! ...Actually, probably on a par with mine.

The show was oversold. The feeling of sheer expectation was thick in the air, replaced very quickly and bullied away by the tidal wave of complete failure that we harnessed and aimed into the crowd. The stage was scattered from start to finish with strippers that made the ones from the American leg look like a zillion Christie Turlingtons. A few depressed and deflated inflatable sheep were kicked around, leftovers from our night in Amsterdam, whilst Phildo did his eternal dance of the herniated chimpanzee. The funniest part of the whole sorry debacle, apart from seeing people's faces gaunt with horror and disappointment ("bloody load of rubbish!") was when we left the stage before our encore. (They were getting one whether they liked it or not.) I saw Michael, maniacal grin behind aviator shades, twist all the tuning pegs on Paul's bass as it sat on the guitar stand onstage where Paul had left it. When we came back on to play "Get Down", the bass was not even in the same solar system (let alone key) as the rest of the band. Chortling and rib-tickling hilarity ensued as Michael and I watched Paul trying to figure out why the only two notes he had to play in the whole 20+ minute song were so very, very wrong.

After being thrown out of the Astoria—quite unceremoniously, I might add—we made our way back to the Columbia Hotel Bar ("meester dabble voadka!") where I held court with an assortment of Scottish pals. The rest of the joint was a madhouse; the matted butt-hairs of British indie rock were swarming the bar and destroying any breakable fixtures. (I think in the case of the Columbia, this meant a phone book and a business card holder.) The bar stayed open as long as there were people to keep it in business. Eventually, around five, I oozed back to my digs, only to be awoken as the band Mussolini Headkick (I am not making that up, they were protégés of Luc's) banged on my door, looking for their ample Belgian mentor. After screaming at them, I headed downstairs to find some coffee—only to find that the treacherous Jourgensen had befriended Bomb-fucking-Everything!!! Apparently, all was forgiven, and they were all sitting at a table "bombing everything" together with an unstoppable volley of dinner rolls. It was almost sweet... almost.

The final stop on the tour was Glasgow. Against my better judgment, my mother was coming. Al purchased a tape of bagpipe music at the first rest stop across the border; I begged him not to play it through the PA, but he had made up his mind. I was met off the bus outside Glasgow University by Andy and his girlfriend, and immediately ushered to the nearest pub where we started the day's festivities in earnest, continuing after soundcheck and into the night. I almost forgot we had a gig until an accumulated group of Fini's, ex-Fini's, and assorted partners whisked me back to Glasgow University. Outside the dressing room was a long line of would-be interviewers and drug dealers. Oh, and my mum. I had taken speed, ecstasy, and washed it all down with lager—the E was so strong that, me being me, I vomited onstage. It looked to me like the venue ceiling was undulating purple—for fuck's sake, I should've been in Hawkwind. It was the last show of the tour, and it was probably the most incredible gig I was ever a part of. The audience reacted well to the bagpipe cassette blaring through the PA (phew!); people were hanging from the ceiling, from the speaker cabinets, and generally melting into a pool of human/MDMA primordial soup on the floor, diluted by gallons of student union lager. It made me proud to be a Scot, and if I hadn't been so awe-inspiringly fucked out of my gourd, I may well have shed a tear and sang "Flower of Scotland"—thankfully though, I did not. After the show, I said goodbye to my fellow Cocks, as I was staying on for a week in Edinburgh.

I flew home into a complete nightmare. At Heathrow, I was arrested for being in possession of a stolen plane ticket, which, indeed it was—although clearly unbeknownst to me. (The booking agent for the tour had apparently tried to cut a few "corners".) I was eventually released from the little airport interrogation cell and allowed to board; all the while I maintained an excellently haughty and self-righteous "Well I never! This is an outrage!!" demeanour which, of course, with my stupid dreadlocks and my near-translucent visage, must have made the airport pigs bust a gut laughing.

I called my apartment from O'Hare to see if my roommate was home.

"You're back already??" she squeaked/croaked (squawked?) into the phone. "Oh, a ha ha ha, I figured you were gonna be gone for a while more a hee hee."

I could almost see the disaster of my dwellings, and I was right. She had thrown a number of parties; there were at least six garbage bags full of crap, unpaid bills, blah, blah... very indicative of my wretched life, I'd say. But I hunkered down and cleaned the place, knowing that I was climbing down another few rungs of the stability ladder. The same lost weekend as before but getting more lost, hanging out at Crash Palace, doing stupid drugs, meeting strange people, always strange people at the apartment, stranger people showing up at any hour. Al showed up one night with about twenty people and a case of Old Style beer.

One night at Trax, we had a bad falling out. Al asked me to go out for a drink with him after the session, and we went to Crash Palace where he flatly gave me a "me or her" ultimatum regarding my friendship with Lydia Lunch. I told him to fuck off and stop being such a fucking baby. Up he jumped and stormed out of the bar, clearly wishing no further discussion or argument. Kind of crushed, I morosely contemplated my future, which really was rather bleak with or without Al. So when I awoke the next day, I can't say I felt too badly.

There was an impending tour for the release of the first Pigface album, and although the album was indeed every bit the infuriatingly malformed and unattractive freak I have earlier described, a tour is a tour. It meant three square meals, a bed, and all of the other delights a band riding on Trent Reznor's coat tails could hope to enjoy.

For the past while, I had been receiving anonymous gifts at the Wax Trax! store; a watch, cinema tickets, cards with cryptic messages scrawled inside, all leading up to a random incident at Crash Palace—although, in hindsight, there was nothing random about it. I was out having a drink with a friend, when three of her girlfriends showed up and joined us, one of whom was called Tracey. I fell for her immediately and, subtle as a hammer-bomb, asked if I could come over to her apartment. She declined and said it simply was not possible, but she would meet me on Monday, if I gave her my phone number. After a couple of dates, I learned that:

A: she was responsible for the anonymous gifts, and,

B: she was married. So I told her,

C: I didn't care if she was married.

A friend of hers, who was on an extended job out of town, donated her apartment for maximum discretion, and we began our affair in earnest.

The Pigface album was called *Gub*. Although hotly and breathlessly anticipated, it was actually really amusing but poignantly sad to witness the jaws of every industrial rock fan in the world drop in perplexed horror as they put the needle on side one of the album; a refrigerator being thrown down a flight of stairs by the cast of *One Flew Over The Cuckoo's Nest* but in slow motion. The album cover, by Bill Rieflin's wife, Francesca Sundsten, was excellent, but this does not a great album make. Of course there was a sticker on the front, name-checking all the artists on the album, and the most financially rewarding bands we had ever been in, no matter how tenuous. I have to say, I cringed a little.

Being so highly anticipated meant there was a lot of press. I lied under oath in interviews about how, "Pigface is pushing the boundaries of pop music as we know it, blah blah", shameless whore that I am. Of course, this was nothing compared to Martin's Shakespearean soliloquies about the second fucking coming, a new era where there was no band line-ups, the band was different every night, the music changed every night, the album would be redundant before the tour even began because we would have moved onto something else. I retched and kind of hoped he'd move to a West Coast retreat or join a Grateful Dead tribute band right there.

I sometimes think he did this just so people would show up and sell out the shows, just in case Trent Reznor was indeed with us and then quote himself, "The line-up changes every night!! No Trent tonight!! Nya Nya!" (He was not touring with us, but did appear at a show.) However, we had Ogre who, in the eyes of the black lipstick crowd at that time, was a decent second best.

# DOWNWARD
# SPIRALS
# NEVER
# SHINE

**Top:** Me in London, 1991. (Sean Joyce)

**Above:** Tucker in Germany, 1991. (Sean Joyce)

**Left:** Me ready to climb the Eiffel Tower in Paris.

# 11

# BLOOD AND SAND

The line-up for the *Gub* tour was different than the album—but remember, "We're not going to be restricted by archaic concepts like line-ups or songs!!" We had two drummers: Bill, who had baulked when he learned the tour was going to be a whopping six weeks (not two as he had originally thought) and Martin. The rest of the line-up was Tucker, Matt Schultz and his "anti-tank guitar", Paul Raven on loan from Killing Joke, Ogre, and me. This would make up the core of the band that would play host to any loser with a tuba or a fucking bongo who wanted to get up at any point and ruin what was already a show questionable in its artistic merits. There were some famous guests…. um… one of the guys from Gwar, although, without his costume, who knew? Er… one of the members of that band the Lunachicks, and, like I said, Martin manipulated Trent into making an appearance in New York… so yes, a veritable who's who of not very exciting musicians from kind of rubbish bands.

Rehearsals took place at Martin's little compound, a loft where he lived, did business, and played music down on 22nd Street and Wabash in Chicago's South Loop area. It was a bit of a wasteland back then—I hear that it's very "developed" these days. While Martin was on the phone boasting to anyone who'd listen that Pigface considered rehearsals a thing of the past, we were sitting around quite happy that Martin considered rehearsals a "thing of the past". I think we got a couple in; long, tiresome improvisations, trying to encapsulate the fury and the passion of a refrigerator being thrown downstairs in slow motion.

My nights were getting more and more dangerous, and although Tracey and I thought we were being incredibly discreet, we probably were nothing of the sort as our affair turned into a relationship, with all the trappings of a real relationship—except the part where we could tell people. Holding hands surreptitiously under tables was all very good fun, and I had no idea that I had become a well-known face around town— what the fuck was I thinking? The pressure from other areas began to build. I knew the husband, via Tracey, but I was introduced as her new minor-league rock star friend, so I found myself in some incredibly perverse situations, going out or having dinner with the two of them. And, of course, the usual coked-up club fixtures had something new to cackle about. These were the same club fixtures that managed to drive the wedge between myself and Al. Coke makes you talk, and if you don't have anything relevant to say…

Fortunately, it was time to go on tour—which started in Houston. We were a large party. Apart from the band, Martin's wife was coming along. We also had a "tour manager"—a ridiculous fellow with a dreadful, dreadful coke habit, who it was decided should be Ogre's roommate on tour… to help him not do coke. Brilliant. Ogre had brought along a strange, purple-haired skeleton with a shrieking voice, who complained bitterly that the world was not vegan. She was quickly dubbed "Skeletor" by the ever-affable Raven. We all missed Ogre's last girlfriend, Cyan, who had been on the *Mind* tour. Speaking of the *Mind* tour, we also had Lee Popa doing our live sound, which, as far as sound goes, saved the tour. Lee can grab it, manipulate it, and deliver it on a dubbed-out silver platter to the crowd. In short, he can make a crappy burger taste like *filet mignon*. However, this would not save us at the first show in Houston.

Opening for the Butthole Surfers at the Unicorn, a huge converted supermarket on the outskirts of town, we walked onstage and chased our tails for an hour. If the Cocks in London had been a disappointment, then this was the Titanic. Of course, we were too high to really give a damn, as usual. I had managed to ingest at least seven conflicting pharmaceutical substances and was enjoying the battle as it played out in my bloodstream.

An old acquaintance from Houston, who happened to be at the show, found me afterwards. Usually, friends and acquaintances would humour me: "Yeah, you guys sounded cool tonight, I enjoyed that," or, in extreme cases, "Cool set, man, gotta split."

Tonight, this well-spoken woman told me, "You're kidding, right? That was just fucking horrible!"

All I could do was laugh and say, "Yep, it sucked."

At the end of the day, the Pigface shows were a means to an end, like I said; three squares, a bed, peyote, acid, ecstasy, coke, speed, pot, whiskey, blah, blah, blabbetty-blah. There was no sleep the first night of this tour, the endgame being played out in the garden of some club, and ultimately my motel room, until eventually, the bus engine revved up and we were off to Dallas.

We spent a portion of the Dallas show—"we" meaning the whole band and crowd—searching the floor for a tooth pendant that Ogre had been wearing around his neck. Eventually it was found and the show continued. He repaid the band by discarding Skeletor quietly at a rest stop and saving us the bother.

The venues were busy—had the Internet been in existence, word would have got around that the show devolved into a long drum circle every night and therefore frightened everyone away. Sometimes I pulled out my notebook and read out loud over the din, but after I almost got arrested for pulling something else out in Florida, I decided to leave well enough alone. Besides, the drum-jamming went on forever. It gave me a chance to either go out into the crowd and endear myself to the pretty Goth ladies, or to hoof it back to the hotel, depending on my mood.

The tour openers were Silverfish, featuring a vocalist called Leslie Rankine, a Scot, whose mum knew my mum, which was nice. The other guys in the band were mealy-mouthed "Spare 10p for a pint? Got any fags?" provincial Londoners, and were, at best, annoying.

Remember I mentioned the "anti-tank guitar?" Well this was a device invented by Martin's upstairs neighbour, Matt Schultz—a railway sleeper with piano wire was stretched over the guitar so that it could be played percussively, or bowed, giving an incredible drone. This he played for ten to fifteen minutes every night before we staggered and fumbled our way onstage. Matt himself was kind of like a railway sleeper with piano wires stretched to breaking point over him; he seemed always to be on the brink of absolute rage. A fan of amphetamines, which didn't help, he wore perfectly ironed military garb (he brought an iron on tour with him!), his handwriting was microscopic and perfectly proportioned (Ding! Ding! WARNING!). Oh, and, as we found out soon enough, he was carrying explosives in his suitcase (RUN!!). Matt was okay in my book. He was happy to conclude that everything was a conspiracy, thus it was easy to get him ranting in tangents about any subject, so he was quite entertaining.

The entire *Gub* show is documented fairly well on the clumsy live double album *Welcome to Mexico, Asshole*, which would be the first of many questionable live Pigface albums. But basically, after we had staggered on stage, Martin and Bill would play a spluttering, hesitant dual drum pattern, over which Ogre and I squawked like a couple of tortured parrots. I could feel the audience waiting expectantly for this to come to a halt, for the smoke to flood the stage, and for the formidable Ministry/Puppy/Nails serpent to breathe almighty fire in their faces. But what actually happened was the spluttering drums got a bit faster and we weaved in and out of bits of *Gub,* interspersed with interminable improvisations, a song from my solo album, a Skinny Puppy song, and a Public Image song, "Careering". The latter had a good groove and was kind of a high point for me—there I go, impersonating Lydon again—but musical integrity had been ditched from the tour well before the first show so, whatever.

The music began to improve marginally over the tour; the band were certainly having a great time. We played with KMFDM at Tucker's stomping ground of City Gardens in Trenton, NJ, which meant that En

Esch joined us to roar and whisper his way through his contribution to *Gub*. He volleyed onto the stage wearing his best "Man at C&A" golfing outfit—this was nothing less than chilling on a 6'6" bald German wearing make-up. He then grabbed Tucker and started making out with him. I saw Tucker's parents leave the auditorium looking decidedly pale.

We played Chicago in the middle of the tour, which was strange. After the show, I spoke to several friends who were in the audience—who confirmed that we were, indeed, probably the worst band in the world. I consoled myself by smuggling Tracey onto the bus bound for St. Louis, where we spent a rose-tinted post-show evening at the E.R.—where Michael Balch had been taken following a drug overdose in Tucker's room. The phone in my room had been ringing constantly whilst I was otherwise engaged; eventually I picked it up to hear a mumbling Tucker telling me he thought Michael was kind of blue, and not sad blue, like the Miles Davis record, but dead blue, like the _____ record (fill in dead pop star name here, please). Tracey and I went up to his room, where Tucker was sitting in a chair laughing hysterically at the situation. Michael was indeed a blue/gray shade and in need of medical attention, so we called an ambulance, left Tucker to giggle away, and followed in a cab, sitting for hours while uptight Bible Belt doctors and nurses looked at us with their "holier than rock" eyes. We were eventually allowed to fetch Michael, who, with a mischievous grin, scooped a handful of fresh syringes from the supply drawer before we took him back to the hotel, fucker.

The next day, in Kansas City, clearly atoning for his dreadful misadventure and near-death experience the night before, a monastic Michael spent the day at Chili's with his drug counsellor and Tucker, drinking pitcher after pitcher of blue Margaritas until they came back to the bus prior to showtime to grind up a variety of pills and shoot them up. I was, I must admit, rather mortified. However, Michael proved that four gallons of dyed booze and half a dozen mainlined date rape pills could NOT stop the rock!! And he stumbled onstage, dressed head to toe in a receipt roll, looking like a mummy, he hesitated in front of the vocal mike, thought the better of it, and lay down to take a nap. After the show, Tucker sat on a bathroom sink—breaking it and flooded the entire backstage area. We left KC with nothing but an invoice for damages.

Lee Popa was becoming one with the band. Out front every night, his intuition, as I have said already, saved us—by taking a weak idea, tweaking it, and dubbing it. He made even the worst of the interminable drum jams at least sound vaguely like they were from Lee Perry/Adrian Sherwood territory. Meanwhile, I was focusing more and more on hallucinogenic drugs, as they were easy to find. I even found a chunk of peyote the size of my fist one night, courtesy of a fan. Matt and I ate it and went on a 12-hour trip in the undulating Christmas tree that was our bus.

The ridiculous tour manager had turned from being just a fat, fuck-up, coke head into a dangerously paranoid psychopath. He could no longer manage the tour because he could barely manage to leave his bedroom, the windows forever curtained on whatever motel room he and Ogre were holed up in. Try asking him for either your wages, or at least a $10 advance from your wages. Go on, try it. "FUCK OFF, I DON'T HAVE ANY MONEY, THE TOUR'S LOST ALL THIS MONEY, THERE IS NOTHING LEFT… SEE MARTIN… SEE MARTIN… LEAVE ME ALONE… I GOT SOME SHIT I NEED TO SORT OUT BEFORE THE SHOW TONIGHT!!!"

Hmmmm, I had a mild hunch that he might be spending all of our earnings on cocaine, isn't that crazy? Cocaine!! His paranoid delusions, plus our suspicions that he was ripping us off blind inspired Tucker and me into playing cruel, cruel jokes on him. We started knocking on his door and running away, calling his room and hanging up from a payphone by the pool as he tried to sleep/cower, and best of all, telling him that there were a lot of cops in the hotel lobby. We also routinely and regularly asked him for money because this was certain to make him lose his temper and could end up in a chase around a motel or a club parking lot. "I AM GONNA KICK (WHEEZE) YOUR SCRAWNY SCOTTISH ASS YOU MOTHERFUCKER!!" The guy was far, far too porky to run, looking, as he did, like Oliver Hardy with blonde highlights, cig in the corner of his pie-hole, face red and flushed. Oh, one night when he was beat after a three-day coke bender, I sprinkled Corn Flakes on his bunk. I have never been able to work out why he didn't figure out it was either me or Tucker, but it was kind of like the Denver room disassembly project: really good fun to do, but at the end you start to get a little scared. He probably just slept in his leather pants and jacket and didn't ever notice.

We started buying trucker's speed for financial reasons. "Trucker's speed" is ephedrine in pill form, sold in bottles in truck stops to enable long distance drivers to legally maintain alertness. It's one of the worst drugs in the world. If you ground it up and snorted it, it made you feel like a million frozen needles were being pushed through your skin, and you dry-heaved so hard, it made your leg muscles cramp. It was probably the perfect drug for this tour. We were all delighted at the discovery; one bottle between a few of you cost next to nothing!! (Actually, it used to cost about $7, so yep, a good, cheap high, baby.)

Believe it or not, the songs from *Gub*, now that we were over two-thirds through the tour, were actually starting to find form, reason, cohesion, and best of all, power. Firstly, because we were playing them every night on a long tour without any breaks, and secondly, we all knew without saying anything that the album lacked a certain kick—as well as arbitrary embellishments like melody and structure—and we wanted to rock, not noodle.

The tour was certainly successful in defining an audience (*i.e.* those who actually stayed and genuinely liked it), and it was certainly successful in indulging its participants (*i.e.* us, the band) and giving us all a false sense of importance in the musical community. Something can become an important work of art just by virtue of the fact that you keep telling people it is. Pigface suffered from "Emperor's New Clothes" syndrome—anyone who patiently waits after a show to come into your dressing room to meet you is unlikely to tell you that you suck, apart from my friends who honestly told me that it sucked, and apart from myself, who knew it sucked from the very beginning, I was constantly bemused by people who told me how absolutely incredible Pigface was on any particular night. I would just laugh and ask, "Really?"

Ultimately, though, it is unimportant. As with most things I have done, I felt that the means justified the ends, not vice versa—even if in doing something you hated so much that it forced you to do something else—something more satisfying. So it is, that I look back on the *Gub* tour with genuine affection.

# YOU'LL WANT TO BE ALIVE WHEN IT HAPPENS

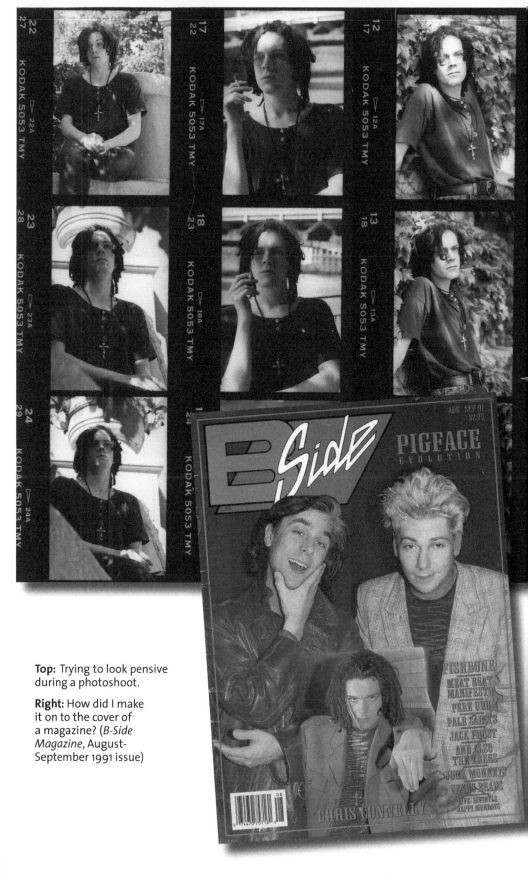

**Top:** Trying to look pensive during a photoshoot.

**Right:** How did I make it on to the cover of a magazine? (*B-Side Magazine*, August-September 1991 issue)

# 12

# IT WAS RAINING ON LOVE

Life after the *Gub* tour was no less complicated than before, and it continued to plummet downwards in terms of my physical and mental upkeep. I was still on the outs with Al, and I heard that a new Cocks album had been started with Trent taking my place. This, however, proved to be untrue. I was still continuing my affair with a married woman, both of us far too deep in it to do anything about it. It still had an undercurrent of danger that made it all a bit unreal, and it was great fun.

I got booked to do a spoken word performance in New York. Tucker's ex was the "entertainment coordinator" or something for this huge dance club, and she brought me and Tucker up there to do a Friday night performance. I thought it might be at some dusty church hall in the Village somewhere, the floorboards and walls riddled with the echoes of Ferlinghetti, Sanders, Kupferberg or Ginsberg—but no, the place was a giant, up-to-the-minute, coke-fuelled, designer drug haven, replete with the overloud necessary beats of the day. The kind of proto-rave hang written about so eloquently in James St. James' excellent *Disco Bloodbath* (he may even have been there, who knows). At this point there were plenty of "industrial" crossover 12-inch singles by bands like Front 242 and A Split Second that were being cut in with the other sounds of the day, which were not so different. You could be labelled "industrial" just by having a slightly flat sounding Belgian sing about exotic robot ladies on your record. Anyway, let's examine this, because the same basic question would haunt me for my entire career: Why, oh, why was I booked to do spoken word in a Manhattan nightclub on a Friday night? It was kind of like staging a drug intervention at your eight-year-old's birthday party.

Of course, I was in Manhattan, so I tried to call Vogue to see if she was up for a bit of slap and tickle, but I am quite sure she was off pouting her way around the Maldives with Marlon Richards or something. So I amused myself before my "reading" in the VIP lounge with Tucker, drinking away, absolutely astounded by the brick walls we were met with upon trying to hit on the army of savagely beautiful cocktail waitresses. They probably got it every other night from the likes of David Bowie and DeNiro, because my wee-laddie-lost Scottish accent and grin seemed to just repulse the spunky little debs that were fetching my Crown Royals on the rocks. I was starting to get morose when two girls from the magazine *B-Side* showed up to talk to me about my first solo album—its release was imminent—and to talk to me about *Gub*. By the time I sleepwalked through that one, it was time to go onstage.

Tucker was doing sound and running a cassette of detuned piano rumbling through the PA that sounded like slowed down thunder, which cut through the heart of whatever Deee-Lite permutation was playing at the time. Bringing the dance floor to a screeching halt, I read my doom-laden psycho-dramas to an unbelieving crowd of sweating, glittery club kids whose faces carried the expression of horror, as if the club had been a dream and they were suffering through a detention in high school. I bit it and carried on, starting to enjoy being loathed so much.

Afterwards, we took a very bizarre designer drug and met a lovely girl whose day job was running guns from Manhattan to Brooklyn every day on the subway.

Back in Chicago, the unexpected happened. I was walking down Halsted Street with Tracey when I saw Al and Paul on the other side of the street. I waved, and a few seconds later, Al and I had kissed and made up. We went out for Indian food and he graciously asked me to get down to work on the new Ministry album, which he was in the middle of with Paul.

The record was very hard work. I moved between Trax "A" room and the all-too-familiar cassette dubbing room, where I would sit for days listening to cassettes and coming up with lyrical ideas for Al, eventually getting behind the mike and singing them. At the same time, my personal life had crossed from "spicy and a little dangerous" to really quite terrifying. I was starting to be way out of my league. I was also starting a new solo album, again at Trax, when Ministry was not there. I was, as usual, penniless, and I was, as usual, doing the wrong amounts of class A drugs, both in the studio and out. Day after day at Trax, I was writing entire notebooks full of tripe to try and piece together something relevant for the new Ministry album. It seemed to me that Al had crossed a line with heroin, and he wasn't doing well. I was being very cautious with it because I had crossed a line with a woman, and I certainly wasn't doing well. Much of my social life took place at a club where Tracey worked, situated in the River North area of Chicago; I was treated like royalty when I went there, a bottle of single malt and an insane amount of coke being delivered to my table whenever I went. In another life, I may have felt quite good, but things were getting out of control.

I had been doing battle with a particular Ministry song for about a week, rewinding and playing the cassette over and over. It was a good tune, but nothing I came up with seemed to be the right thing. Then the first Lollapalooza came through town, that huge travelling circus of *bands-du-jour* headlined in its first year by Jane's Addiction, accompanied by Nine Inch Nails, the Rollins Band, the Butthole Surfers, and more. So, so, so 1991!

Trent came to visit, and Al and he took off to go to the club where Tracey worked. Although asked to come along, I elected to stay and work—which I did, until I eventually gave up and went home. The next day, the song I had been struggling with had become "Jesus Built My Hotrod", which Gibby Haines from the Butthole Surfers had come in like a fairy godmother during the night and improvised over the top of. It took him all of a few minutes, and the song became, I think, the biggest selling Ministry single, so there you go, a lesson learned indeed. I loved what he did—I mean it's so crassly catchy, what's not to love? But of course, inwardly I was saying, "but I… but he… I spent weeks on that!"

I did not enjoy working on the Ministry album which would eventually be referred to as *Psalm 69*, although the real title was a series of hieroglyphs that roughly looked like "KEBANZO". I felt like I was a prisoner in someone else's writer's block. The sense of time had disappeared and the hours were interrupted only by the clubs pouring onto the streets between 3 and 4 AM when Trax would again play host to the roaring biker clowns and the crippled strippers, all gnawing at the night.

"What are you writing about? Can I see?"

"Um… can you read?"

"You're a fucking asshole!"

"Get the fuck out…!"

So it was with some measured relief that I received a phone call one afternoon from Paul, telling me that he and Al were scrapping the whole thing and starting again—only "Jesus Built my Hotrod" and another song, "TV Song", which I co-wrote, would survive the cut. To be honest, I am not sure what prompted the change of heart, although I think there was a lack of focus in the material that was on the table at the time. Not necessarily unfocused in the way that *The Mind is a Terrible Thing to Taste* was kind of stylistically all over the map, but *Psalm 69* was headed in the same direction. Of course, there was new management in place at this point, and I am sure they chimed in with their opinion. Management liked metal, this is what they were kind of purveyors of. Metal was always lurking and sniffing around Ministry, now it seemed to be standing on the table and bearing its teeth. "Grrrrr… Metal!"

Meanwhile, I was finishing my solo album, an unremarkable venture —save for the fact that I had met a musician who would not only help change everything about the way I thought about music, but would become a best friend, too. Chris Bruce, who I had met in the record store he worked in, and through the guys in Die Warzaw, was playing guitar on my record, and he was the best guitarist I had ever heard. He overshadowed the rest of the players on the album, and is what makes the record listenable, bringing a lyrical subtlety and liquid flow that I had never encountered before. Having come from an 80s almost "no guitars allowed!!" background, into a "DAKADAKADAKDAKADAK" full-on chucky metal approach with both the Cocks and Ministry, it was amazing to play with a guitarist who was playing with empathy and intuition, and not his dick.

All this time Tucker had been on tour as guitarist with the Thrill Kill Kult, but was now back and living with his new girlfriend, Nicole. He met Nicole at Crash Palace, the same place I met Tracey; his pick up line to her being, "Wanna come see my friend throw up?" The friend was, of course, me on one of my nightly pills 'n' booze rolls. He visited me in the studio a few times and very soon was helping out with the album.

Things were starting to change for the better. Tracey and her husband were getting a divorce. I don't think he knew anything about our affair; we were already looking at apartments to move into. The husband had got a new job on the East Coast, where he was from. I was ecstatic. We quickly found a suitable apartment just a little north of Trax, and we put down a deposit, or rather she did. I was, as always, broke, but at least there was some kind of stability at the end of the tunnel.

I was beginning to pack up my few belongings one afternoon when the phone rang; it was a friend of Tracey's.

"Have you spoken to her this afternoon? Where is she?"

I had not, and didn't know where she was, which was not particularly unusual.

An hour later she called again. Tracey was at Illinois Masonic Hospital. "I don't know what the matter is," the friend frantically breathed down the phone. "Meet me there."

I did not live far, and walked quickly, my mind full of every kind of question. Most of all, did she hurt herself? Is she ill?

We lied our way to a doctor, claiming ourselves to be family. He took us into a room. "She didn't make it, I'm sorry." A deliberate overdose of Valium, apparently.

It did not take long before the husband found a substantial amount of evidence in the form of hidden letters and photographs revealing that his now deceased wife had been carrying on an affair with me. It also didn't take long for my miserable life to get worse—not only being whisked off to the local police station for interrogation in what was now being called a possible homicide, but also vague second-hand threats from the husband who, while not a mobster himself, had strong mob connections.

A fraught phone call to Andy in Scotland brought me back down to earth and put my mind at ease, "Stupid over-reactive Americans, what d'ye expect?" Friends rallied around, and I soon discovered that I had not become a leper like I thought I had—Martin, Tucker, Paul, Al, and Bill were all there for me. Al used some of his connections to verify that out on the "street" I was not a marked man, and I could go and buy cigs without fear of a knee-capping.

I tried to finish the album (working title "A Good Cheap High"), re-writing many of the songs to suit my mood in the wake of what had happened. I completed the vocals in a four-hour session, punctuating the verses with cheap beer; I am pretty crocked by the end of side two, but politely declined a chance to overdub anything. Tucker was present and trouble every day as we worked our way through various alcohol and solvent combos, doing practically everything except melting down boot polish because we were too chicken.

Andy came over for a visit and to lend moral support, adding to the general strain on America's alcohol resources, for which the 7-Eleven on the corner of Halsted and Roscoe, a few doors north of Trax, was a conduit. Facts are facts. You can buy some variation on sparkling wine that may pass for champagne at two in the morning. It may well be carbonated vinegar, but after a Caspian Sea of Maker's Mark, who cares? All cats are grey with the lights out!

The other big news in my life, apart from my girlfriend being quite dead and me fucking up my stupid solo album (it was like I was taking scissors to a Dolce and Gabbana suit), was that Killing Joke had "mislaid" their singer. Being an eccentric and somewhat pompous man, he was either acting on commands from his Gods, or he was just acting like a spoiled brat—but there was a European tour imminent, and he could not be found. He may have been sheep farming in New Zealand, he may have been sulking in Prague; no one knew, so I offered my services.

"I'll do it, when are we leaving?" I asked, rather precociously, I thought.

Although it was decided to cancel the tour, my services as singer were accepted. The band were to regroup in Chicago to write and rehearse, then go to Cannon Falls, Minnesota to record at the famous "Pachyderm" studios with Albini "recording" (he hates it when you call him a producer).

As the various members of Killing Joke made their way to Chicago, I finished my record quickly and clumsily at Trax. When I delivered it to Wax Trax!, they sat me down to ask me to please do something with it. It was, in all truth, a half-finished cadaver of a record. The band is not great (apart from Chris Bruce's performances), and this is not shown in kind relief. The songs sound like demos, and I didn't know where I wanted it to go—and that was at the beginning. When Tracey died, I lost control of the wheel completely. The record has been described as a "train wreck", and I have to agree. I should probably have abandoned the project, but there are some out there, unbelievably, who like it, which counts for a lot. I told Wax Trax! to leave it alone, I was not changing a thing.

They had, incidentally, just made me sign a contract; something they were making all of their artists do as the label's profile had grown. The lights illuminating the roster had brightened, and major labels were sniffing around, signing up many of the acts, and there wasn't a lot Jim or Dannie could do. Along with the heightened popularity of the label, there came a new crop of employees; a cloying, mealy-mouthed bunch who fancied themselves on the cutting edge of the business. They were full of casual put-downs of us old guard. Apparently the future lay with the young hotshots they were signing—laughable, as not one of the acts they signed ever went anywhere. Oh, and neither did the hotshot employees. The most they ever amounted to was that one of them managed to die from nitrous oxide inhalation—moron. I mean if you're going to die by a drug overdose, at least make it heroin or a fancy combination of pills, not laughing gas. That's like dying from taking too many indigestion pills.

One night when I was in the middle of recording, one of these slimy little hotshots was dispatched to the studio to get me to sign a contract. He told me in his legal platitudes that if I did not sign, he would pull the plug on the album. I signed, of course, like an idiot—there was no excuse except it was under duress, and I was not going to jeopardise the album, (why not? I knew it sucked). Anyhow, the slime ball got what he wanted. The only restitution I ever got was that he turned, over the years, from being a slick, go get 'em, club kid A&R hotshot, into a fat, balding failure of a man waddling around Chicago with his dejected dog called Karma (the only companion I ever saw him with). If such a thing existed, mine was certainly not the only life he fucked with.

On to the next thing, Killing Joke had regrouped and were down at Martin's little compound. They were a sight to behold. Like so many 80s heroes resurrected in the early 90s—it was too early for a reunion. Although they had released a double album recently, which hinted at their glory days, it still fell on the wrong side of Barclay James Harvest to be a serious contender. (They'd get theirs, a few years down the line in the early 2000s.) However, as I have mentioned before, they had been up and touring until the singer went AWOL, and the rest of the band were keen to continue without him. Even though for many bands, just like Killing Joke, the dark horizons were dotted only with appalling rave-culture remixes, a name change… or me, actually. I think most bands should have done at least one album with me, don't you? Iron Maiden, The Sisters of Mercy—hell, I would have even done a Blondie record!

Well, Killing Joke became nameless for a short while rehearsing at Martin's place; all tartan trousers, edgy shirts and those awful shades that aging punk rockers felt they had to wear to still be rebellious in the decades that followed punk.

I, myself, was far too busy turning my scrawny dreadlocked body into a distillery to care about rehearsing and writing with these chaps, there was time enough for that later. Andy and I were working on a video for the album, which, as far as I remember, involved a pretty girl and a pillow fight resulting in a whole city block being strewn with feathers.

Eventually Andy had to split back to Scotland, and the band had to drive up to rural Cannon Falls in Minnesota. A lovely part of the world, the studio itself boasted several bedrooms, a huge open plan living room and kitchen, a pool, endless grounds, and a studio in a separate building. We also had a chef and daily deliveries of pot and booze. Best of all, I really didn't have to work that hard. The band, augmented by a spikey-haired keyboard player, would get started in the late morning, tossing me the occasional cassette of basic tracks that I would take, along with my Walkman, for endless bicycle rides through the countryside. However, rather than gushing forth a late summer-tinged, John Denver-inspired vista of love and inspiration, my lyrics seemed to swing from black, hellish vitriol to unnerving pessimism full of scathing and antagonistic attacks on the happenings in my life over the last while. I was pleased with what I wrote; the others seemed to be too, but they were probably just humouring me. So be it.

Up late nights drinking, Geordie asking the studio in-house engineers. "D'you know where we could find some beak, then?" ('Beak' being coke.) Hardly satisfied with the answer that it might be hard to find at 2 AM in a forest thirty miles from the Twin Cities, he would respond, "Well, listen mate, oi've been at the top o' the heap, and oi've been at the bottom of the heap…." The engineers scurried off to their rooms while I sat up with Geordie listening to his tales. We found a family-sized bottle of gin in a secret cupboard at about 3 AM, which we drank while listening to *Unlimited Edition* by Can. "Oi wish they didn't use the flute so much on this wan!!"

Albini was different to work with this time—better, out of the city. He knew Pachyderm and was comfortable here, although I learned very quickly that, unlike Fluffy and other engineers, he was not about to give positive feedback necessarily. He was honest. Not brutally honest for the sake of it, but honest in telling you if something was just not working, "Hey, it's your record, you wanna fuck it up, go right ahead!" But more often than not, I would sing and he'd have his feet up on the desk reading *Viz* and I soon came to like it this way. He would set up a good vocal mike, record me, and I could pretend he wasn't there. Thus, my performances on the album were a lot better than usual. A little later in the week though, we started to have some fun when he constructed a precarious pile of planks in the vocal booth with the intention of me stamping on them as I sang. He also got me to sing whilst swinging a very expensive microphone around my head like a lasso.

To celebrate the near completion of the album, Albini took us to a strip joint in the middle of nowhere. The band got drunk and looked at tits, I got drunk and scoured the floor for dollar bills and coke. Locate! Subvert! Terminate! We eventually settled on the name "Murder Inc." for both the record and the band, another compromise that I was fairly ambivalent about. No matter...

I took a train back to Chicago and left the boys there to mix it. No one wants a singer around when you're mixing, it's as bad as having a bassist, a drummer, or even a guitarist, for that matter. It felt creepy and empty to be back, but there were only a few days before rehearsals for a Pigface tour, this time to promote the somewhat ill-advised live double album, *Welcome to Mexico, Asshole*. But, like I mentioned earlier, I was not about to not go on tour because I simply didn't like the music. Please, darling... standards in the face of hedonism? However, there was a dramatic overhaul in the line-up. All that remained from the *Gub* line-up was myself, Martin, Tucker, and Raven. We were being augmented by a female bassist (on loan from one of the God-awful signings to Martin's label), Mary Byker (former singer from Gaye Bykers on Acid), and En Esch from KMFDM. Immediately there was a better feeling about this line-up. No better or worse musically, just a good feeling. There were also a lot more people who we were going to pick up along the way, a lot more credible people who would actually be joining us for a while, and not just failed musicians jumping up to yell into a microphone—although this would happen as well. A lot.

Rehearsals? Hardly! We set up once, I think, and went over a couple of basic ideas. We would however, be playing a song from the *Murder Inc.* album, and a couple from my recently completed solo abortion too, as well as one of En Esch's songs. Oh, who cares? We were road ready as far as I was concerned. Let's go on tour.

**Above:** On stage with Pigface. (Jana)

**Right:** Backstage in Tijuana with Ogre and Bill Rieflin.

# 13

# FORCED, INHIBITED, UNRESOLUTE

I was fast asleep on the floor of Sea-Tac Airport when I was nudged. The nudger was Jonathan Formula—he was our tour manager, and he was meeting me for the first time. A spunky redheaded stranger accompanied him; she was our lighting director.

The first date was in Tacoma, and Pigface seemed to be arriving in small batches. I cannot remember who I travelled with. I can't think that it was Tucker, unless he was behaving so poorly that I requested a different seat from him on our red-eye flight. However, I'd have had to be pretty diligent to lose him in the airport, but I did wake up on the lounge floor quite alone.

Jonathan was not only our tour manager, but he was doing our sound as well. An unassuming intellectual, he bore a peculiar expression of panic and resignation. I quickly learned that he may have been in Tuxedomoon, that he definitely did live sound for the Residents and Captain Beefheart, and that he just got out of rehab, poor soul. He had no idea what he was letting himself in for.

We took a taxi to a Motel 6 somewhere in the middle of nowhere and I crashed for a few more hours. When I awoke, it was Jonathan again to get us all to soundcheck. Ogre was there and seemed to have been through a horrible patch since I saw him on the last tour. I congratulated him on his new record. Eventually the whole "band" was present, Mary Byker was like an excited puppy and scuttled around the place endearing himself to everyone. Tucker went on the hunt for pot, eschewing soundcheck for more important chores.

Of course there were problems. Pigface's biggest problem—but by no means only one—was pouring a pint into a shot glass. So many people in the band meant so much equipment on stage, and we were generally booked into clubs with stages and PA's big enough for your average 4-piece rock combo. The crew was whining, but the crew will always whine. Martin was pontificating to a high school journalist about how this incarnation of Pigface was completely different to the last, and that the world should take note: we have a drum machine as well as drums now! And, of course, the line-up will change every ten minutes and blah, blah might be joining us for the west coast dates blah, blah, blah.

Prior to the show, we were smoking some incredible Pacific Northwest marijuana in the dressing room and listening to Nirvana's *Nevermind,* which had just been released. I was enjoying it tremendously, unaware that it spearheaded a horrible movement in rock that would quickly crush my career like an ant, and allow bands to wear their dad's clothes onstage.

Our performance, as you may have been able to deduce scientifically, was not that good. We had not rehearsed very much at all, and were leaving things up to the magic of the moment—at least Martin was. The rest of us were just bone idle, so Tucker went onstage and turned on the drum machine. It broke. He tried again. Eventually, there was a loud, distorted battering onstage, followed by the trademark refrigerator-being-pushed-downstairs that slowed down and sped up at various times during what seemed like hours, until the disappointed Goths and quizzical hippies pissed off home.

It was great to be back on the road. It was early autumn, we were on the West Coast, we had a plentiful supply of soft drugs, and a never-ending line of pretty Goth girls who seemed not to mind one iota that we were dreadful. Only Ogre was conspicuous by his absence; appearing fleetingly for shows, he stayed in his bunk most of the time. Was he going through withdrawal? Trying to quit drugs? Was he sick? Did we bore the pants off him? In a display of compassion and friendly concern, Tucker and I covered his comforter with hundreds of tiny plastic spiders while he was off the bus one day, in order to lend credence to whatever paranoid delusions and hallucinations he may have been suffering. We're here for ya, pal!

It didn't take long for things to change for the better, and the band started to improve dramatically with the addition of Andrew Weiss, on loan from the Rollins Band. Andrew fit in perfectly, knew how to have a good time, and was great onstage. He immediately improved Pigface and turned it into a band with a kind of purpose.

Every day there was a new kind of acid to try. By 4 AM, after listening to *Straight Outta Compton* tripping our brains out, we would descend like berserker warriors in drag upon a truck stop. The parking lot was a sea of snarling metal horses; we would find our tables, giggling the entire time, the waitresses rolling their eyes. En Esch played up his German-ness, Andrew baited tables of cops. The shows suddenly became packed and it seemed like people were enthusiastic. We worked the entire West Coast and ended up in Boulder where our bus driver could be spied stage left, eating magic mushrooms, which made me nervous for a second. Momentum had taken over. Maybe it was the delicate drug combinations, but I think it was a core of camaraderie that hadn't been there before. Tucker, me, Raven, En Esch, Andrew, and Mary were all pretty tight. I felt sorry for the female bass player, but she was just rubbish. What can you do?

Boulder was mayhem. After soundcheck, Tucker had thrown a hapless interviewer's tape recorder into the hotel pool for asking one too many stupid questions. During the gig I was pulling out teenagers who were being crushed to death from the front of the stage. After the show, the party spiralled back to our motel, of course. The punch line to all of this is that we had to catch a flight to London in a few hours, so when that time came to leave, we were still in after-show mode; sun high in the sky as the bedroom doors opened and a zombie march of dishevelled Goth girls spilled into the motel parking lot, Aqua Net hair like a snapshot of a cyclone, piercings reddened against alabaster skin. Goodnight, ladies.

The airport was a nightmare. We had to check in all of our gear, which was a lot. William stood with me at the check in. Actually, he could barely stand. Every time he was told to put out a cigarette, he would light another one up, slurring to the security officer that we were smuggling handguns and heroin into Europe. "What are you gunna do about it, huh?" Eventually I led him off to the airport bar until we were ready to board.

I couldn't believe my good fortune upon boarding the aircraft, finding that Tucker had a window seat far enough away from me which meant he was no longer my problem. By the looks of things, he was the problem of the tiny, mortified-looking businesswoman who had a sheath of papers on her lap clearly intent on working for the duration of the trip. However, Tucker had very different plans for the two of them. A cocktail, maybe snuggle up for *City Slickers*, and then… who knows. He was a catch, having been up for days, never removing his leather jacket, not bathing, with white pancake make-up, poorly applied silver lipstick, and lank black hair in an impenetrable vortex around his skull. He looked like lap dog that had almost drowned in a vat of make-up.

"So are you going to London, my dear? We're all in a rock band, these are my friends," he indicated to us.

She just stared forward, clearly frozen in terror, not knowing what to do next.

"Tucker, go to sleep," I advised, to which he prized the recessed ashtray from his seat armrest and volleyed it at me, glancing the side of my skull. This was followed by the in-flight magazine and the safety instruction card, all of which hit except the card, which just sort of boomeranged back at him. I calmly looked at the businesswoman, who must have been on the lam from the law because she had not summoned a flight attendant yet.

"He's going to pass out any second, trust me—he's been up for days, I am so sorry," I advised. She looked at me blankly, and before we had become airborne Tucker's head was all the way back, mouth wide open, snoring like a drunken rhino. Peace restored, for a while.

London. We were, of course, playing that night. There was, of course, no hotel for a quick shower. Instead there was the club, a room in Camden, floor slick from years of melting Londoners. The day was that rare English barometric oddity rendering the atmosphere both freezing and clammy. A brace of Raven's friends appeared, they looked like refugees from Hawkwind's road crew (they probably were), and whisked him off. Mary, too, was whisked off. I decided I was too disgusting to inflict myself on any friends who I might have called. Would you want me showing up at your work after my last 48 hours? "No", you say flatly.

There is a vague promise of a delivery of speed. My brother and his wife were coming later. I hope they like jamming, I hope they like jamming…

The gig was sparsely attended; our names may have had the pistol-packing impact of a marshmallow being dropped in blancmange in the States, but here they meant nothing really, except for Mary, and perhaps Raven a little bit. The furore over the Cocks had long since been diverted to the Inspiral Carpets or some such. Plus, the fact that the only record available in Europe was horrible (*Gub!*), meant that the gloomy, cold club was dotted sparsely by a few tired looking "grebo" casualties and a couple of forlorn Goth-y, Killing Joke types.

We were all horribly jet-lagged and trying to make it kick start on the scant fuel of lager and prawn cocktail crisps, but it was not happening. I left the stage early and in the dressing room was introduced to a thuggish biker who looked like he should be a speed dealer. Oh! He is a speed dealer! A bit fucking late, aren't you? "Owroight, mate, yuuur …laaaaarvly stuff 'ere!" Fine, just gimme it, then. Of course, we were leaving for Europe any second, so I had to do it all really soon. Drug was purchased, horrible toilet was visited, drug was inhaled nasally, vomit was expelled orally, brother appeared unexpectedly.

The next day we were in Europe. Good grief, did we smoke a lot of hash and cigarettes! Bemused and bespectacled European scowlers mixed with crusty dreadlocked (look who's talking) "'Ow you say? Cybeehr pounks?" There were no hotels for almost all of Europe—we lived on the bus. However, the venues were all equipped with showers to varying degrees of hygiene and warmth, ranging from biohazard and freezing to soiled and lukewarm—surgically spotless and hot did not exist.

We ended up with one hotel, in Hamburg, thanks to a cancelled gig. Raven and I decided to spend the day sightseeing in the hotel bar. We didn't see very much except a bottle of strange looking Jägermeister. I will never know why I—no, WE—chose this to drink. It was a horrible mistake, and an irreversible one that would see me later standing in the middle of a few hundred earnest German headbangers watching the Ian Gillan Band at the venue Pigface would be playing at the next night. It was kind of like watching an old truck driver do "Smoke On the Water" with his kids as a backing band. I needed to leave, the mixture of cod-metal and thick syrupy alcoholic beverage was making me feel quite ill. I stumbled back to my room through the rain-slicked Hamburg streets, fading fast. I was just conscious enough when I reached my room to notice that somebody had nailed an inflatable woman to my room door. Uh… goodnight.

The next evening, the very same club that had, such a short time ago, been packed with brow-furrowed German hard-rock fans could not be emptier. The floor was dotted with a handful of the mildly curious. Sascha, he of KMFDM fame, showed up to relay just how unpopular we were, huffs all round. Pigface echoed vacuously off the club walls, the "jamming" part of the show died whimpering in a corner somewhere.

Oh, cheer up! Look! Tucker got up early specially to decorate the bus for us with coprophilia porn he bought on a stroll down Action Strasse earlier. Thoughtful, no?

Berlin was a more optimistic story. We were playing at The Loft, where the dressing room walls were covered in an incredibly vitriolic attack against Lenny Kravitz. Two people were there to see me from Dossier Records. Why? I strained my mind to remember but realised it was on the strength of a letter I sent to Damon Edge from the band Chrome about six years previously. I had forgotten about it, but they clearly had not. I could not tell if they wanted to put me in the studio to make a record with Damon, or haul me off to a members-only Berlin leather bar. Either way, I did not want to deal with these leather-duster coated, moustached, shaven-headed, grinning Gestapo boys, and I spent the entire evening (save when I was onstage) in a rib-tickling "Elmer Fudd and wabbit" hide-and-seek chase around The Loft. Every time I reached a quiet sanctuary, their grinning pop-eyed and shiny domes would spring from around a corner. After the show, the entire band was interviewed on film and I then grabbed Tucker and Andrew for protection and headed off into the streets of Berlin to escape.

At some point, Martin and I were required to fly back to London for a day of press to support the tour, the album—whatever this means. I would get a hotel room for the night, and, more importantly, it was possible that I might be able to disappear and have some fun in London. Usually, in these interviews, Martin would be pontificating so zealously about changing the face of rock music, that he wouldn't notice if the hotel was in flames around him, let alone, if a certain dreadlocked Scottish singer slipped out the side entrance to enjoy the temptations of London. And so, I was dozing softly during interview #2, aviator shades on in the hotel lobby; my motor functions so finely honed my head would react accordingly upon hearing the triggers "Al", "Jourgensen" (or, in Europe "Yoarginsin"), and increasingly "Trent", "Ogre", and "revolving line-up". Springing back to life when the "stop" button of the cassette player clicked, I excused myself, and walked out of the lobby into London and its possibilities. The sound of Martin's voice ricocheting around the busy WC2 streets, nattering on about no two gigs ever being the same, it's more performance art than music... drone... drone...

SHAZAM!!! Blink of the eyes and I was with two old friends from Edinburgh, all drunk and dancing to *Atlantic Crossing* by Rod Stewart in Martin Gore's apartment. Blink the eyes again, SHAZAM!! I was back at the hotel with our cute li'l press officer and the hapless tour manager, Jonathan, watching six weeks of rehab go down the toilet, or rather, up his nose, having carved him out a 24-inch line of amphetamine sulphate. All thigh-slapping fun as I giggled in the corner, devil! Well, we had to get rid of it somehow. We were flying to Vienna early the next morning.

SHAZAM!! Another blink of the eyes and we were running through Heathrow. I had a brutal hangover and we were late, late, late for our flight. Jonathan still had a gram of speed, when I spied with my little eye, something beginning with... REGGAE/POP-CROSSOVER SUPERSTAR MAXI PRIEST!! I tried to persuade Jonathan to sidle up to the dreadlocked chart-contender and slip the speed into his ample pockets whilst asking for directions. He didn't have the guts though, and I suppose, nor did I.

It was a public holiday in Vienna. We arrived at around 11 AM and I quickly learned two important facts. Public holiday means public holiday: nothing is open at all, the streets are absolutely deserted, and there is nothing to do. The other fact is that we were playing at 1.30 AM and the club opened at 11 PM, giving us a wait time of about fourteen hours. There were only about six crappy videos on the bus, all of which have been watched several times by now, ranging from *Predator* to *Mr Holland's Opus*. Plus I had almost finished my book, which was rubbish anyway. "This means nothing to meeeeee...."

By the time the club doors opened, what little food and drink we had on the bus was long gone, and certain band member's limbs were being considered for consumption. It is safe to say that everyone on the bus was insane and horny with a wolf's bloodlust. Tucker, Mary, and I hungrily walked in to patrol the club for possible female company. There was one pretty girl, accompanied of course by her monolithic boyfriend. Not that this should necessarily have posed a problem, but we soon learned that they are not staying for the show "anyvay". Pathetic. I actually had persuaded myself that the minute she saw me on the stage, half-heartedly croaking away, she would ditch Goliath and run away with me into the cold Austrian night. Well, croak I did, half-hearted it was too, into the murk of an empty club in the early hours of the morning—in other words, a complete waste of time all around.

Another cancelled gig meant a day off in Malmö. At least it was not a public holiday! However, it was prohibitively expensive. There was no hotel, so myself, Tucker, Mary, and Andrew were on the bus smoking hash, eventually electing to head out into the beautiful Malmö streets to find our new Swedish Model girlfriends. We were truly wretched at this point. No gig equals no shower—even dogs were crossing the street to avoid us.

Unfortunately for Malmö, we found a karaoke bar and proceeded to get drunk. No easy feat, as the beer, like everything else, was very, very expensive. Yet somehow we managed. Much later on, Tucker and I seemed to get separated from everyone, and we were hungry—hungry from spending any food money we may have had on beer, and from smoking hash all day. The streets were dark and austere, however there was a glimmer across the square; it was a confectioners. Really? A sweetie shop? Could it be? Or was it a figment of our stoned imaginations? No, it was indeed a sweetie shop, crammed to the gills with bottles and jars of every variety and colour of sweetie, reminding me of the sweetie shops in Edinburgh when I was young. We eagerly filled a bag with a selection and scraped together what coinage we had to pay. Payback is a bitch and in this case, all the sweetmeats we purchased were dusted with salt—it was not what we were expecting, to say the least. Actually they were inedible. Was it a practical joke? We were brutally disappointed.

The venue in Malmö boasted no booze and we had finished all of our hash. This was unacceptable—however, the house lighting guy, who looked like Rick Wakeman's halfwit brother, told us, "I am having a friend who is making some vodka, I am drinking some two days ago, and as yet I am not blind..." This was good enough for me and we gave him some local currency—knowing that, as he worked at the venue, he had to come back. Half an hour later he was back with a litre Coke bottle filled with the alleged moonshine. It was absolutely repulsive. He had probably just gone out and siphoned fuel from our bus, but it would do at a pinch. Rumour had it that Ogre was yellow. No one had seen him for days, which was not unusual. And as for turning yellow, I had yet to see Ogre in the daylight, maybe he had always been yellow, I dunno.

After the gig, and after slugging our hooch from the supermarket cola bottle with the finesse of connoisseurs, a number of us ambled over to a loft party we had been invited to. It was a refreshing, almost wholesome scene with kids in their early 20s dancing to things like R.E.M. and the B-52's. The huge Wakeman-esque lighting guy spied us and waddled over to us. "I would like you to watch THIS!" He pulled out a long thick needle and started to stick it through various points in his face. "This causes NO pain!" he gleefully exclaimed as the few women whose interest he had managed to pique quickly walked away. As if his trick was a signal, the lighting changed, the dancing kids cleared off the floor and the DJ put on that party record to hustle up the dance at any party, "Raping a Slave" by Swans. A couple of guys rolled out a huge black mat, and a couple of others wheeled over these large garbage bins and emptied the contents onto the mat: broken glass, we looked on in horror as everyone removed their shoes and took turns to walk across the mat, then roll, contort and generally thrash about for our entertainment. (Actually, we did not stay long enough to find out if this was for our entertainment, or if this was just something you did on your night out, like getting pizza or a kebab on the way home from the boozer.)

Ogre was really quite ill; he had to go to hospital, and we had to get injections in our bums as a result of his illness perhaps being contagious. Bah! We were back in London in the basement of a Thomas Cook with our trousers around our ankles while some quack with a syringe gleefully stuck us all. Ouchy! Ogre probably had hepatitis, quite possibly from a shrimp. Yep.

We were in London for a few days, booked into a studio with the intention of capturing the "live" sound of the band and the jams we had been developing into songs. Actually the jams they had been developing—I had not been participating particularly. I only know of a few vocalists who could jam well with a band, and his name is Damo Suzuki from Can. Jamming vocalists and poetry slammers? Run a mile! So, I did not actually see the studio. I remained in the lounge area where there was a bar and held court all weekend. A few of Raven's friends showed up, among them a girl who I had met at the last London show, who may have been a friend of Mary's, or perhaps of Raven's, I can't remember. Her name was Bella, and rather than focus on writing lyrics for the wall of noise that was happening in the studio, I focused my attentions on making her laugh and asserting my probably somewhat depleted charms. In hindsight, how could she resist a chain-smoking morose Scottish drunk who had not showered for days, and who was slumped on a sofa, acting like he was the second coming of Peter O'-fucking-Toole? (Later, in months to come, after a decent shower and a change of clothes, we would become close friends, but not now... noooo nooo nooo!)

A quick jump across the Channel to play at the Zenith in Paris opening for Siouxsie and the Banshees, where Tucker set the tone for the night when we walked on early in the evening to a hall scattered with les Goths who seemed to be as interested in us as we were in them. He told the crowd that, "Yes, we hate Siouxsie too!" I, of course, was mortified, and discreetly kicked him in the shin, vainly hoping that because these kids were so early, they didn't study their Anglais, and therefore did not know what he was saying. Siouxsie's crew knew what he said alright, and we high-tailed it out of there as soon as we were done with our stupid half-hour set.

During a last handful of shows in England, we picked up three hitchers in Portsmouth who apparently spent all of their time travelling to concerts. We took them to London and I spent the day wandering around Camden with them, playing the part of anarchist shoplifter for a day. It was my birthday in Birmingham, and to celebrate, after the show, we took turns hanging upside down from the bus skylight as it moved down the motorway, "wheeeeee!" We listened to the song "No More Tears" about 10,000 times—really.

A final show in London, we showed the motley dozen or so disenfranchised Killing Joke fans that we could really jam, man. Yeah, whatever...

Tucker and I stayed up all night at the Columbia, economically minded. We had one more day of press before we flew back to the States, and we had to smoke all our smoke and snort all our snort before boarding that plane! A pot of coffee in the Columbia dining room was quietly topped off with single malt. It was about 8 AM, and at 9 AM we were going to a TV studio to talk about ourselves. Tucker was in one of his extremely obnoxious moods, and I was in just the right mood to encourage him. Martin's job was to try and contain us. A car picked us up and Tucker ignored the protests of the driver as he lit up the pipe he had fashioned from a roll-on deodorant top and a ballpoint pen casing.

The presenter at the TV studio, who probably thought she was going to get Trent Reznor, looked at us with barely disguised horror as we stumbled in. Tucker took an immediate shine to her because she was a female. Actually, she was a very pretty Italian girl, and it's hard not to look back on the whole incident with absolute shame, but I bet the Gallagher Brothers were much worse than we were. We were told explicitly: NO SMOKING OF ANYTHING AT ALL. Tucker lit up his home-made pipe and a cigarette at the same time and started to try and seduce the poor woman, who was probably writing out her letter of resignation in her head as we slurred. Martin was trying—and you had to admire his determination—to present his familiar spiel about no two gigs being the same and how the integrity of Pigface is setting a template for the music of the future. However this kind of fell flat with Tucker chasing the petite presenter all over the studio and me necking a bottle of Bushmills and ignoring any questions fired my way.

I think we were eventually thrown out by security, but I don't remember, and I don't remember the rest of the day either. The next morning, we were at Heathrow again—destination: Florida, which would be nice after November in England.

As we boarded the plane, I reflected upon how no one in Europe gave a rat's ass about Pigface. It was time to leave. I hate being where I am not wanted.

# WHO AM I TRYING TO IMPRESS?

CHRIS CONNELLY

## International 2 Manchester

**MURDER INC.**

THURSDAY
JUNE 25
Doors Open 7.30pm

UNRESERVED

£5.00

No. 0003
To Be Given Up

## THE INTERNATIONAL 2

061-273 8834
210 Plymouth Grove, Manchester 13

# Murder Inc.
EX MEMBERS OF KILLING JOKE
Thursday 25th June 1992
Doors Open 7.30pm

UNRESERVED

£5.00 advance

No. 0003
Retain This Portion — Conditions Overleaf

**Above:** Ticket
to the one of
the five shows
that Murder Inc
played.

**Left:** Ad for
*Phenobarb*,
probably from
*Alternative Press*
magainze.

# phenobarb bambalam

THE NEW ALBUM FEATURING THE FIRST SINGLE "JULY"

## ON TOUR NOW!

JUNE: 3-KALAMAZOO, 4-DETROIT, 5-CLEVELAND, 6-TORONTO, 7-LONDON,
8-BUFFALO, 9-NEW YORK, 10-BOSTON, 12-WASHINGTON D.C., 17-DALLAS,
18-SAN ANTONIO, 23-SAN FRANCISCO
MORE DATES TO FOLLOW.

WAX TRAX!

FOR A CATALOGUE OF ALL WAX TRAX! RELEASES & MERCHANDISE, SEND A BUSINESS SIZE SASE TO:
WAX TRAX! RECORDS, 1659 N. DAMEN CHICAGO, IL 60647. TEL. 312-252-1000, FAX 312-252-1007

# 14

# LOCATE, SUBVERT & TERMINATE

A flight back to the US—to Florida, to be precise. We were mid-tour and all appeared "normal"—tour "normal" being a lot different than normal "normal". I felt quite awful. It wasn't just the constant physical abuse I administered daily—that could all be taken in stride really, I mean, most bands manage it alright—but the accumulated grime, filth, living on the bus, and the ice cold showers provided by most of the European venues had made me a little frail.

We were playing a few shows with Jim Foetus and his band, Scraping Foetus Off The Wheel, or just Foetus, I cannot remember which incarnation it was. What I do remember is that as soon as we hit the motel in Tampa, I unpacked and found a huge bag of mushrooms that I had smuggled over several international borders, quite unwittingly. Oops! The Foetus guys were an amalgam of various Swans, Unsane, and assorted NYC noisenicks who were all in the same motel as us and were ready to paaaarty! They were fantastic, kind of like the Skatenigs if they had read Henry Miller and enjoyed Beckett. After bonding over a few bottles of amyl nitrate, our gigs started to cross-pollinate; the Foetus all-stars came onstage to play, or simply stand onstage flagrantly inhaling amyl nitrate in front of our Florida trustees. After the first show I saw a tiny girl upend Jim Foetus—he smacked his head on the stone ground for no apparent reason—the poor guy didn't know what had happened and the little bitch took off howling with laughter.

I do not wish to be impolite about Jacksonville, but good lord, what a fucking dump! Jonathan, the hapless tour manager, was really starting to lose it; he had his head shaved into a Mohawk, which he dyed a shocking orange. He looked like a nightmarish fusion of Annie Lennox and William Hurt. To celebrate in his new look, William and I covered his bunk in junkie paraphernalia such as burnt teaspoons, cigarette filters, dirty cotton balls, and a little baggy filled with Coffeemate. We retreated guffawing to the back lounge to observe the thigh-slapping capers as Jonathan—still raw from rehab, remember—wailed into his bunk, "What kind of a sick fuck would DO THIS?? AWWWW GOD...!!" I think he knew very well what kind of a sick fuck did it, to be honest with you.

At a loose end, myself, William, and En Esch trawled the bleak streets of downtown Jacksonville, getting the usual looks that a dread-locked Scot, a 6'6" bald German guy with eye make-up, and the living embodiment of Johnny Thunders get in the South. We managed to find a "surplus" store, which was huge; it seemed to have a surplus of surplus. This was the last stop for everything that had no practical or social value before it became a landfill. (Which is probably where much of my back catalogue is languishing now...) William loved these kind of places and walked out proudly holding a cardboard box filled with rather horrifying little black inflatable baby dolls, the kind they are not really supposed to sell because they will either violently suffocate a toddler, or if not that, then the loosely adhered creepy little plastic eyes will certainly choke a child most heartily. Probably banned from every third world country they were shipped to, and shipped back to the malignant little factory somewhere here in Gator Country—now they were with William, what an odd and sinister circle. A merry old time was had by all as we inflated each one of them on the bus that afternoon, while everyone else was either out or napping. Later, whilst tripping, we enjoyed a toxic few hours microwaving them into interesting little deformities.

The venue was a disgusting dump—unlike the palaces we had been used to. This one was especially disgusting. We were informed that the Pixies and entourage destroyed it the night before and made a pointed effort to vomit on every single thing.

Who should appear at the show but our old friend Mike World, looking even more like a charred chia pet than ever. He endeared himself to all by stealing a disco ball and slapping his girlfriend openly in front of a ton of people. Later on he got his head kicked in by security, ha ha.

Momentum was gathering again. For all the mean things I have said about Pigface, it was apparent that—at this point in the band's career—people were staying and seemingly enjoying the shows. Millions of pretty Goths came up with gifts of cute jewellery every night—probably 'cos Ogre was gone and they had to give it to someone who sang and had black hair.

Atlanta was perhaps the pinnacle of this: a large and packed club, seas and seas of little vampires and vampirettes. William and I found some pharmaceutical morphine in pill form in some Goth's purse, she hissed at us to "help oursssselves" and we found oursssselves floating gracefully around a Piggly Wiggly supermarket after the show. We must have been really high because we arrived back at the bus hours later with two paper sacks filled to the brim with pomegranates. We stayed up all night listening to The Residents' *Commercial Album*, microwaving pomegranates, Bubblicious, bars of soap, and a bath sponge. Who said life on the road is not constructive?

The last quarter of the tour had been initiated and we all knew it. That scared feeling of having to go home was returning. Things turned from crazy to a lysergic kid's TV show—just like on previous tours, but now we knew how to really grab the reins and have the most fun. A sloppy set in New Orleans found Martin being woken before the set from a drunken blackout, claiming that we had already played—which became a moot point as fists were thrown in the crowd as soon as we started playing. This meant we could say we absolutely were "not going to play against such violence", and hit the sauce again, yippee! Night off!

Texas turned up a few things for the books: notably, a group of girls had been following us for a short while now, affectionately known as the "tripping strippers". They got on my nerves a lot, so in the interest of diplomacy, I steered well clear, wondering why the fuck they wanted to follow us. Weren't the Chili Peppers touring? Faith No More? Some other early nineties sensation? Tad?? And who should show up in Dallas, but Vogue!! I was excited to see her, but she was horribly drunk and acted like an asshole, eventually being thrown off the bus for crawling on all fours and screaming—it was all rather disturbing. This was actually the last time I ever saw her, apart from the occasional fashion rag, or the six-foot square, print ad leering at me tantalisingly in the Bloomingdales make-up department, or wherever. I think, or perhaps I assume, she eventually met a gentleman of money (no! really??) and settled down to a committed lifetime of looking at herself.

Glum disappointment in Dallas was paralleled by terror in Houston as a gorgeous, Greek college radio DJ I had "befriended" on the first Pigface tour showed up at soundcheck, looking daggers and wondering, "Where the fuck I got off returning NONE of her phone calls?" Her steely Alien-considers-Sigourney Weaver countenance told me that there was nothing I could do or say that was going to get me off the hook. I just stood there and listened until she ran out of steam, I had no argument. That was at soundcheck. By the time the show was over, she was putty in my hands. Ha!!

In San Antonio, Ogre's ex-girlfriend, Cyan, who you may remember from the *Mind* tour, showed up hoping to say hi to Ogre, only to find out he was recuperating in Calgary, or wherever he was from. After I got back from a long walk by myself, we reminisced and blethered all night.

Knoxville: uncharted territory for us, and our bus driver strongly cautioned us about not taking "that hillbilly acid", which naturally piqued our curiosity. Within an hour we had found some of "that hillbilly acid"—as had, apparently, the entire juvenile population of Knoxville, filling the three stories of the club we were playing in. I had a very strong perception that many of these people were related to one another, and were certainly on the wrong side of sane. Tucker and I couldn't find anywhere to go after the show that wasn't crawling with junior redneck psychos. Even the bus was packed with squealing freaks that seemed to be chanting, "Gooble gobble, we accept you…" Eventually we found that there was an empty apartment atop the club—well, relatively empty save for a comatose guy on the couch, and a lone female slow dancing to an AM radio station of doo-wop hits. Christ, could it be any more David Lynch? However, at least it was quiet, and Tucker and I flopped down to smoke and chat—that is, until the comatose guy awoke and walked to the window, opened it and started throwing empty beer bottles onto the people exiting the club three stories below. It took about three seconds for him to exit the room and about five for about six furious rednecks to burst into the apartment looking for blood. We thought we were done for, immediately going, "He went that-a-way," for all the world like a gothic Shaggy and Scooby. We must have looked too pathetic to have thrown bottles out of a third floor window (true), so they indeed went "that-a-way".

Somewhere along the way we had enlisted the services of a T-shirt vendor, a large bumbling 12-stepper who looked like Rodney Dangerfield. He was a strangely intrusive fellow who had an unhealthy interest in Ogre (who had re-joined the tour) and me, and I could never pinpoint whether he had financial or sexual designs on us (both, probably). What I did know is that he made me feel incredibly uncomfortable—one of those people who wouldn't let you leave or re-enter a room without hugging and kissing you, and telling you, "Hey, I love you man!" Bleeeeuch!! He would betray his true colours soon enough in a motel in Kansas City after a show, when he called my room and asked me to come by his. When I poked my head in the door he was sitting bug-eyed and drooling, a pretty girl sitting nearby, and a gram of coke out on the table. His dancing eyes and slobbering jowls said it all; he offered me a rolled up bill, and myself and the girl did a line. (He was a 12-stepper, remember—he didn't touch it, which made it all the more creepy.) Then I had the genius idea of splitting with the coke and the girl. It took but a few choice movements of my eyes and shoulders to communicate this much to her, the oblivious

T-shirt pervert was roaring away about how I should really duet with Elton John as he got up to use the bathroom. As soon as the door was closed the girl and I vanished like a wisp of smoke into the cold Kansas night.

Rochester paralleled Knoxville in terms of sheer bedlam, the only difference being that Tucker got slapped in the face by a girl he had designs on. "Fuck off you fucking creep!" Crack! Hilarious!! He retaliated to my laughter by ordering a container of cooked brains at a truck stop (these things are available) at about 5 AM and then leaving them on my pillow.

The tour climaxed at the Metro in Chicago a few days before Christmas. It was definitely the end of something, but I would not know until years later exactly what that was. Right now it felt like a beginning. Everyone had remained friends; talks were excitedly underway about future collaborations. The show was triumphant. I got even cooler jewellery from even cuter Goth girls! Ha ha!

Hugs goodbye to everyone (except pervo T-shirt guy, who I managed to avoid all evening—there's an art to it) and the next day I was on a plane to Scotland for the Christmas holidays.

A couple of weeks mooching around my old haunts in Edinburgh, going to raves and getting up to the same old hijinks (except now with ecstasy) with the Fini's, and I was on my way back to Chicago with a suitcase stuffed with *Viz* comics, Marmite, and Rose's Lime Marmalade.

A new Pigface album was cooking, half of which had been recorded a month or so previously in London. My contributions were few, not wishing to spread myself too thin. I duetted with the adorable Leslie Rankine (from Silverfish) on "Ten Ground and Down", and Martin found another song leftover from a year-old session called "Do No Wrong". A few weeks later, Martin, Tucker and myself, accompanied by Fluffy, drove up to Pachyderm to mix the album. This proved to be a disaster. I hate mixing, so I spent my time getting into trouble with Tucker and leaving Fluffy and Martin to mix. Fluffy had recently become engaged and his fiancée called every ten minutes to annoy/poke/prod/whine down the phone at Fluffy, who was doing a shitty job anyway. Eventually Martin fired him, and we told Martin where to go. The record was finished by Martin, along with the engineer at Pachyderm, their relationship being that of a simpering pupil determined to please the teacher—the engineer morphing into that simpering, cloying yes-man. Oh well, there was a swimming pool, there was booze, it was not like we were being paid… so Tucker and I just Brian Jones-ed it for the rest of the week.

A very small incarnation of Pigface played at the Metro—it was me, Tucker, Martin and Paul Barker—doing four or five songs at a benefit for my old friend, Cynthia Plastercaster.

As I wondered what to do next, the answer came in a phone call. It was Martin telling me that Murder Inc. had been asked to open for the Sisters of Mercy at the Birmingham NEC. A remix of the Sisters' song "This Corrosion" had worried the charts, and this was going to be the only gig they played in Europe, nay the world, that summer. After the band had assembled, we rehearsed a couple of times and it sounded perfectly presentable. There was only forty minutes of music to learn (*i.e.* the album) and each song—or most of the songs—were repetitive grooves (*i.e.* we could only come up with one part), so provided I could memorise the lyrics, we were in top form.

We had managed to get about four other gigs around the NEC gig, all of them in England, and then one immediately following England in New York at the Limelight. Funnily enough, we were not at the Columbia, but it did not take long before we had a full hotel lounge of friends, or rather, Raven had a full lounge of friends. Mary Byker came with his girlfriend, and everyone seemed to be having a fine time. However, later in the evening a commotion broke out between, of all people, Mary and Geordie.

"I love 'er" I love 'er," cried an indignant Mary whilst Geordie uttered laconically, "Mary, Oi think yer a cunt and I wanna fuck yer bird."

Hmmm, why don't you tell us what you are really feeling, Geordie?

The name we had for Geordie when he was drunk was Auntie Gladys, an aside from Raven onstage after observing the quick disappearance of a bottle of Stolichnaya. ("Oh dear, I think Auntie Gladys is coming to visit.") However, this situation was comical enough that most of us giggled into our hands silently.

The NEC gig was a disaster; Geordie's amp didn't work. The place was filled with thousands of Goths (from all over the world I presumed, or are there that many Goths in Birmingham?); black wedding dresses, fangs, cloaks, and made-up eyes stared impassively at us onstage while a technician tried to figure out the problem. Eventually, I decided to sing one of our songs *a cappella* whilst waiting. The drummers joined in, and when the amp was fixed, I think we got to play for ten minutes. Our consolation after the gig was that Raven, Geordie, and I went to the front desk of the hotel and Raven pretended to be a journalist who was reviewing the show, and who we knew was staying in the same hotel. The receptionist had no hesitation in providing us the key to his room, and upon entering, we emptied the contents of his mini bar into a Safeway bag and took it to my room to drink.

We had a chaotic day exiting the country. When we were almost at Heathrow, we found out that we were supposed to be at Gatwick—somehow we managed to make it. However, when we arrived at LaGuardia, we found out our equipment had not. So, heavily jetlagged, we had to spend several nail-biting hours waiting for the gear to show up on a following flight. The gig at the Limelight was the best of the five-date tour; it would prove to be the last date Murder Inc. ever played, the band collapsing with internal squabbles, I think. To be honest, I can't remember why Murder Inc. stopped trading, and at what point.

The odds were definitely stacked against me when I finally made the decision to go on my first solo tour in support of the unfortunately named *Phenobarb Bambalam* album. First of all, the album was supposed to be out, but it was not yet. Secondly, I was at loggerheads with Wax Trax!—not necessarily Jim or Dannie, but the insipid little pariahs that they had working for them. Thirdly, Ministry was going on the second *Lollapalooza* tour. And fourthly, 99% of the people who loved Ministry and the Cocks hated my solo records, and I still had these blinkers on that made me think I could convert them.

I had the makings of a good band: Chris Bruce, with whom I had become especially close; Tucker, of course; and Martin. The weak link was that I had made the dreadful mistake of asking along the female bass player who had been on the first leg of the last Pigface tour. Even though, as she kept reminding us, she was known as "Boston's premiere funk bass player"—that was kind of like saying you're the tallest palm tree on the North Pole—the woman lived very, very far away from funk. She also complicated matters by insisting on bringing two huge bass cabinets: one for her "clean" sound and one for her "dirty" sound. She looked like a backwoods dental receptionist and nobody could stand her, but it's always a good thing to have one member of a group that everyone can focus their hatred on.

So I cobbled together a set from my first album and the new one, along with a couple of cover versions. But, by the time rehearsals came around, there was still no album, so we were forced to cancel the tour, rescheduling it for a month later. During that time, we sat around and waited until, lo and behold, the album was not out again. The insects at the record company tried to placate me but I just went ahead and reassembled the band with a damn-you-all spirit, and hit the road.

The openers for the tour were the Final Cut, a likeable bunch of lads from Detroit who we got along with just fine. Tucker and I had contributed to their industrial-coat-tail-riding debut album, which was not a great thing, however, they satisfied the robot dancing quotient of our sparse audiences, I suppose.

This period still shines out loud and clear as the worst month of my career. The stress ran high. The audiences, for the most part, loathed what we were doing and it seemed that everyone else in the whole world was on Lollapa-fucking-looza… fuckers! The start of every evening was promising, with the usual smell of clove cigs wafting back to the dressing room (they are a Goth fave) and the rooms packed to the gills with bodies; me trying to ignore that they were all chomping at the bit for some jackhammer-in-the eye industrial exxxxxtreme action. Actually, their faces were a delight during the first song when I walked on stage to deliver a rather insipid Doors-esque version of "The Hawk, the Butcher, the Killer of Beauties", from my first album. Industrial jaw after industrial jaw dropped until, eventually, they just left. (I was actually passed some hate mail from the audience one night.) Every night was different, yet every night had its own little disaster. I stopped eating in a fit of complete pique, angry that I was trying to reinvent myself as a new kind of rock god and nobody cared. I took my shirt off and moved, trying to reduce the ladies in the house to jelly, but they didn't want to know.

Euphoric high points included a van break-in outside the club in Manhattan, followed by my leaving thousands of dollars in a bag in my hotel room. On one occasion Tucker stole money from my money belt and bought a case of whipped cream (the stuff in aerosol cans), just so he could inhale the nitrous oxide. (I thought this was really funny, and could scarcely blame him.)

On our way to El Paso, we broke down in the desert. We waited for hours for help with very little water, which was dangerous. However, we had some booze, some coke, and some acid, so if we died, we would leave interesting corpses for the forensic pathologists. Tucker and I did huge lines of coke and set off into the desert to find scorpions.

Eventually we made it to the show with seconds to spare. The gig was on the point of being cancelled as we literally screeched into the parking lot. Tucker hung out of the van window and yelled "Hey kids! Got any drugs?" as if we were not in bad enough shape. Martin refused to go onstage because there was not the regulation drum riser he required, so everyone could behold the man who once had music featured in the closing credits to Miami Vice. This was exacerbated by his refusal to play because he needed a crate of Newcastle Brown Ale—try finding that at 11 PM in El Paso. The runner (a runner is like an intern for a gig, someone with a car who will venture out and get things like strings, food, any emergency requirements), a pleasant girl called Tiffany, did not know what to do. I really don't think the poor thing was even old enough to buy alcohol, and she had this English lout on her case bellowing to anyone who'd listen that he was "not going to play tonight", like a punk rock Liz Taylor. Eventually the drummer from Final Cut played for us and did a great job.

After the show—which, ironically, was the best attended and best received on the tour—Martin and I got into a huge argument. Tucker was present, as was the eager-to-please Tiffany. Thankfully Martin eventually stormed off and I curled into a ball. We made up the next day. I apologised but only for the sake of the tour continuing. You do not tell your band you are not going to play minutes before stage time because of something like a drum riser.

It finally came to a sickening end. I arrived back in Chicago penniless, not on speaking terms with Wax Trax!, and with few prospects. I was on my own. I managed, although impoverished, to throw myself into a disgusting heroin daze for a while. I went to see Ministry at Lollapalooza, where Al acted like a prick and completely ignored me. I skulked off home, deflated. The next night, though, found me in fine spirits at Crash Palace with Miki and Emma from Lush—lustily singing along to *154* by Wire with them while inwardly wishing that Miki would confess her secret crush on me. It was all rather sweet.

Lollapalooza ended (I am glad I don't have to type that stupid word again), and Ministry were going to go on a more comprehensive tour that allowed them to play for more than the allotted forty minutes they had been given that summer. Paul called me up and asked if I would come out as a second vocalist. I was thrilled, having been sulking for a while, thinking that my old friends were too busy with their new fancy friends in Soundgarden and the loathsome Pearl Jam to care about little me.

I put on my Walkman, and started to learn the *Psalm 69* album. God, what a fucking pain that was. Every fucking song went "WOOF WOOF WOOF WOOF WOOF WOOF" except the slow one, "Scarecrow", which went "WOOF WOOF WOOF". I had to learn all of them, to be prepared for any set list whims that there might be; plus, I was supposed to be singing for Al at rehearsals—Al was otherwise disposed, probably sitting at home complaining. The band featured Paul's brother, Roland, on keyboards, as well as Bill and Mike—plus newcomer Louis Svitek on second guitar, who I would end up rooming with, and who I still hold in very high regard.

Rehearsals were as good as we could expect them to be, I suppose. The band sounded fantastic, but I had my work cut out for me trying to second-guess Al, who kept threatening to show up. The songs from the new album were really difficult. Singing them was like trying to jump through the rotor blades of a helicopter at full speed, and eventually I threw out my back and lost my voice. This became a moot point as Al decided to postpone the tour anyway, upon finally visiting a rehearsal and working his way around the room yelling, "UNACCEPTABLE! UNACCEPTABLE! UNACCEPTABLE!" to each member in turn. He told us we sounded horrible and that we were going to have to cancel two weeks' worth of dates in Europe. (We thought perhaps that he was just scared of leaving his drug connections and going on tour into unknown territory.) I was fine with staying another couple of weeks, but annoyed that we had to rehearse even more. It was incredibly boring.

Eventually, however, we were on our way, band and crew assembled. Sean Joyce and I nestled in a bar near the departure lounge in O'Hare. My money belt was stuffed with drugs; I had agreed to help Al mule his little pharmacopoeias across international borders. The night before, he had filled an empty Children's Tylenol bottle with capsules painstakingly filled with smack. He figured, who is going to suspect a child's aspirin being carried by a leather-clad guy with tattoos and shades on??? Well, gosh, no one!! After getting smashed in the airport bar, we got more smashed on the plane and I did all of Al's drugs during *Honey I Shrunk the Kids*. I guess I did not need to worry about customs at our final destination (Germany) because I was clean when I deplaned—high as a kite, but clean. We had to board a terrifying prop plane, which took us to Hamburg. It was just prior to this that I met our tour manager, who was skulking around German customs waiting for us. I was impressed that he was Scottish, from Fife no less. He would be a constant source of coke and late night ramblings on this tour.

We had a full day's rehearsal in Hamburg at an empty club—the same one Pigface had played at and where I saw poor old Ian Gillan! I had a full service hangover; every part of my body was bathing in its own particular post-toxic hell. The rehearsal was horrible, and I was horrible; my throat was still raw, and I still had shooting pains up my spine and neck. Wretched, truly wretched.

My role onstage was somewhat marginalised. One of the tools I brought with me was that I basically knew the set in case Al's voice gave out—which I think was a thinly veiled euphemism for if he couldn't find the right drugs, which was not easy for him (or our tour manager, for that matter). There were many after-hours excursions through unknown cities. Sometimes I tagged along but, being a very recreational user, this got boring very quickly and I would generally end up doing coke and drinking or smoking weed with whoever was up. Throughout this European leg of the tour, Al made a few train journeys by himself to Amsterdam or wherever to get what he needed and head back with minutes to spare before the gig. He almost blew it in Nottingham when we were one-and-a-half hours late going onstage and the crowd was worked into an absolute frenzy, angrily chanting "YOU FAT BASTARD, YOU FAT BASTARD".

Louis maintained that, "Naw, man, that means they like you!"

I looked at him, "No, Louis, it means they are going to cave our skulls in right about now."

I was getting ready to do the unmentionable: go out there and pretend to be Al, making the crew promise to pump enough dry ice onto the stage to hide my face. I had the dreadlocks and the peaked "Blakey"-style bus conductor hat Al favoured, and then he showed up! Bent double from withdrawal cramps and sweating ice, but hey! Here he is!

After the show we retired to the hotel bar while our tour manager was booted out to try and find some methadone, which he did with help from one of Madchester's most famous sons, no less!

Other highlights included Sean Joyce having his ankle crushed, in part due to the clumsy hands of a careless German roadie who let a huge piece of rock gear on wheels slide down on him from a truck loading ramp. He was last seen stuffing his backpack with German-strength Grolsch to take back to Chicago. *Auf Weidersehn*, Sean.

Back in the USA, Ministry were about as big as they ever were—that is to say, they never got any bigger than the *Psalm 69* tour. We were in huge venues, the bands Helmet and Sepultura opening. The huge arenas blended into one, with some stand-out nights, notably: meeting up with the Foetus entourage after our New York show and going to after-hours drinking clubs; a duet with Chris Cornell during "So What" in Seattle; a mad, knife-wielding stalker in New Orleans… wait, what? Oh, it's not that unusual, and she was not my stalker, thank you very much.

I was in our hotel lobby on a Sunday morning, about to leave to find coffee, when I was approached by an incredibly beautiful woman. I can't think why she thought I may have been in Ministry and zeroed in on me like a heat seeking missile. (Hmm, yes, I wonder, Chris—perhaps it was the leather trousers and jacket, the black dreadlocks and the mirrored aviator shades?) She told me she was a friend of Mikey's and was waiting for him. I asked if she wanted to go for a walk whilst I found coffee, and while we walked, I realised that she was a complete psychopath. When we got back to the hotel I told her I was going to get something from my room and I would be right back. Of course I went up to Mikey's room where he was sitting with Al.

"Man," Mikey was dejected, "all I fuckin' did was go over to her apartment after meetin' her in a bar and she started actin' all crazy 'n' shit, and then she pulls out this fuckin' knife and says she'll cut her own throat if I try to leave…"

Always with the ideal solution to a crisis, Al ordered a tray of Hurricanes from room service, "Yeah, and just keep 'em comin'!" he gleefully barked down the phone. Later at the gig, she was stopped by security with a butcher knife in her purse. Me, Al, and Mikey were wasted—not a very nice drink, Hurricanes, to be sure.

Christmas at the Mondrian in L.A.: a couple of days off where I could spend time with the recently relocated Chris Bruce, then a couple of ludicrous hotel room parties and a couple of shows at the Universal Amphitheatre (where I stared at Al in pride as he refused backstage admittance to Gene Simmons).

Then we were off to our final gig in Hawaii, where we had a week off. We hardly had to work because the military shut off the power to our outdoors show, which meant that we couldn't really go outside because the radio was telling people that we were just assholes and cut our set short because we were lazy. Not that I really cared—I hated Hawaii and sat in my hotel room playing guitar. I was looking forward to returning to the mainland, having given up my apartment and with nebulous plans of regrouping the band later. In a week? A month? No one knew for sure, but Al kept alluding to some "big ideas" he may or may not have had.

It had been a remarkable year in terms of my career. I had gone out and frightened a tiny audience away with my solo tour, and yet months later played in front of the largest crowds I would ever see. Where the solo tour had kicked my self-esteem to the curb, beyond humbling, and turned me into an anorexic burbling freak, the turnaround of the *Psalm 69* tour had inflated my ego by way of travelling in a large rock band and (probably) doing too much coke. I am quite sure I was horrible and I thought I was soooo great. However, the following year, and subsequent times afterwards, I would be brought back down to earth many, many times with resounding thumps.

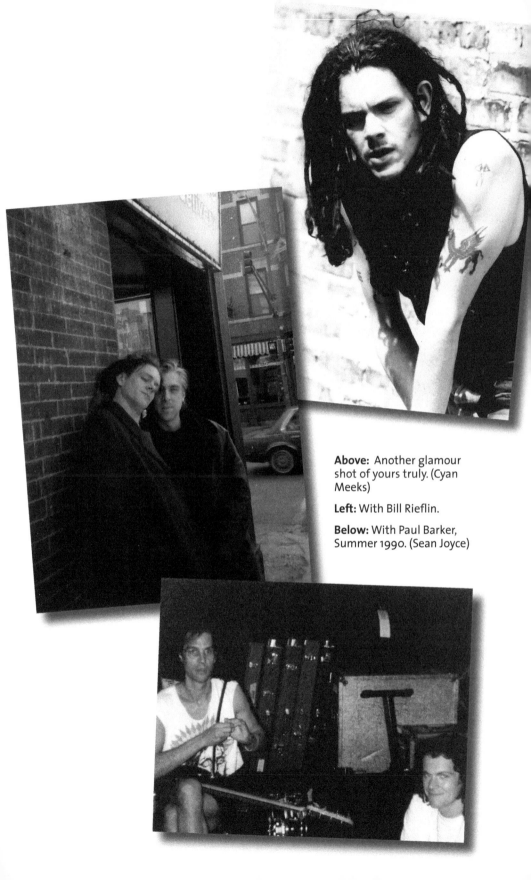

**Above:** Another glamour shot of yours truly. (Cyan Meeks)

**Left:** With Bill Rieflin.

**Below:** With Paul Barker, Summer 1990. (Sean Joyce)

# 15

## CONCRETE, BULLETPROOF, INVISIBLE & FRIED

So, exactly what was the big idea? Well the big idea was to pour ourselves into Trax as soon as we had scrubbed off the grease from the *Psalm 69* tour, apply a few dabs of studio rouge, and build a new Revolting Cocks record, our first for Sire. And our last, need you ask. Actually, it would be the last Revolting Cocks album proper, despite a couple of feeble attempts to revive the band over the next decade—resulting in a 2006 album in name alone, steered by Al, unable to coax any of the rest of us back into his little adventure playground of poor decisions.

Well, in true Cocks' fashion, we convened in Chicago without any material whatsoever, not being the sit-down-with-a-guitar kind of band—or the band kind of band, if you really think about it. We were piloting a concept, a lowbrow concept, but a concept nonetheless. No material was plenty of material, okay?

Al and Paul sat me down and spoke like a mum and dad about to announce a divorce to an eight-year-old. "Okay, so Al and I think it would be a great idea if me, you, Bill, and Roland did one side of the record, and Al did the other." I started screaming and begged for a pony—no, not really. Al chimed in, "Yeah, and MY side's gonna KICK your side's fuckin' ASS!" I suppose I was sceptical only in as much as I did kind of want the band to be a unit, but working with Paul and Bill was always highly entertaining—so, great, why not?

Before we set foot in the studio, we set up in the spare room of Paul's apartment: myself, Paul, Roland, and Bill. We each had a sampler connected to either a VCR or to a laserdisc player, our M.O. was to go to any video rental establishment when they opened at ten in the morning and rent twenty or more films from which to stockpile vocal and sound samples. I cannot think what we must have looked like, waiting outside for the stores to open every morning, four guys in leather jackets, running in and grabbing a hodgepodge of movies spanning from *Uncle Buck* to *Caravaggio*. The task itself could be tedious, but I actually enjoyed it: working a loose 9-5 day, pouring espresso down our throats, and dining almost exclusively on bananas. Samples were stacked, clipped, looped, and ditched. I spent ages trying to get a perfect sample of a top British dignitary saying "titty" several score times in a row: "titty-titty-titty-titty". Yes, well, with these guys it was always the incredible collision of technology, toilet humour, and dada. It was kind of like Benny Hill and the Terminator rubbing shoulders with Kurt Schwitters. Eventually we had plenty of disks amassed with samples, and we shifted operations to Trax, where we would be occasionally augmented by Mikey and/or Louis.

I was staying at Tucker's, who was actually on tour with Pigface at the time. His generous girlfriend, Nicole, was only too happy to have me stay on their couch for as long as I liked. There were a couple of tiresome setbacks in the studio—mainly to do with the Fairlight III—so I rolled my eyes and either went record shopping, drinking, or on the hunt for pharmaceutical fun during these long hours. The sessions themselves were relaxed and very creative, yielding what I consider to be some of the best songs in the Cocks' catalogue. It felt more like an album because we were focusing on an album, and not on a few different projects without any clear view as to an end point.

At first I was struggling a bit with lyrics, desperately trying to write what may be construed as a typical Cocks' lyric, where there existed no typical Cocks' lyrics. Fortunately, Paul had no problem telling me in a matter-of-fact fashion that the way I was approaching needed to be rethought, (*i.e.* what I was writing was kind of bad). Ultimately the six tracks we worked on as a unit of four give as true an essence of the Cocks as you are ever going to hear—the humour, the focus, and the driving, pummelling grooves. In other words, an extension, in a way, of the original Cocks single "No Devotion"/"Attack Ships"—long tracks that shifted little, maintained a pace covered in layer-upon-layer of interlocking loops, anchored by Paul's bass and Bill's drums.

"Sergio" is my personal favourite. We actually came up with a fifteen-minute mix, and I edited together a two-minute radio version, but the six-and-a-half minute version that made into onto the album is the definitive version. Unfortunately, the first (and best) vocal I did was slightly flat. I argued the point with Bill; he thought it was great, and even if it was flat, it was worth keeping. But there was no way I was going to live with a flat vocal for the rest of my life, so I did it again, and it sounded fine to me, in key. This was in the days before things like pitch correction devices. It was a toss-up between performance and technical prowess. I think I managed to get a bit of both on the final version.

"Mr Lucky", borrowed heavily from the Ohio Players' "Fopp", boasted a brass section and a whiny, smarmy vocal detailing the hapless exploits of a hustler, whose every endeavour resolves itself in a good, stiff, kicking. There is a subtle Lou Reed reference in the outro.

"The Rockabye" is based on a rhythm I programmed, influenced by "In a Silent Way" by Miles Davis; busy hi-hat and sparse snare offbeats. Here Paul carries the tune with a fantastic repetitive bass figure, stretching out over seven minutes. It's the nightmare cousin of glam rock, frozen in time; a mechanical vocal delivery flanked by glitter band guitars.

"Butcher Flower's Woman", an oblique tribute to Francis Bacon, abandoning the Cocks' groove formula for a few minutes, almost dives into Birthday Party territory circa "Dead Joe" or "Hamlet". I crammed a lot of samples from the movie *Fire Walk With Me,* mostly electrical and ambient sounds that give it a nasty crackle throughout.

I think "Da Ya Think I'm Sexy" is a great single. I hear that the "band", such as it is these days, still plays it live. But here it was Paul, Roland, Bill and I, eschewing the Cocks' formula altogether—abandoning all electronics, we set up an organ in the live room (Bill played it), a simple drum kit (again, Bill, of course), Paul distorted his bass, and Roland went for a Roland Kirk effect with the sax. I originally sang the whole song with a kind of Jake Burns/Steve Ignorant gravelly throttle, like it is in the choruses, but Paul suggested I sing it in a voice rich with indifference, ennui, and camp. Searching for a character to emulate, I chose Buffalo Bill or Jame Gumb from *Silence of the Lambs* to be my inspiration here— remaining deadpan, impassive and aloof throughout, until near the end, when you can hear me lose it and I burst out laughing. Paul and Bill were speaking to me the whole time I was singing through my headphones, quoting from the movie—"It puts the lotion in the basket or it gets the hose", "Was she a great big fat person?"—eagerly trying to break my concentration. Unfortunately Al eventually put synthetic horns on the track, which kind of ruined it. His contributions to the rest of the album were patchy—at best, okay.

Al at this point? Not really a well man. A lot of heavy usage of drugs, he was a spectral presence, and rumours abounded of unnamed Chicago rock stars being carted off from Al's place in ambulances after overdosing. He and his wife were again separated, his pad was the centre of malicious intake. It was no secret that Bill was staying there part of the time, which helped keep Al kind of clean—Bill being the grounding factor, and certainly not a drug user—but still Al's contributions to the album were frustrating.

"Crackin' Up" had already been recorded, having been developed originally by Al and Michael Balch from a loop they snatched from "Yo! MTV Raps". Over this, Al stole the riff from A Certain Ratio's "Shack Up" (originally recorded by Banbarra, so technically he nicked it off them), added a dash of "Crack Attack" by Big Stick, and then asked me to impersonate Lydon. (Again!! God, get a room, you pair!) Add to this Al's, er... rapping, and you have it. I suppose it's a fine enough Cocks' song, but it was all pretty much done-and-dusted in early 1990—I had already tried to sing over this track just after Mike Balch had come to live in Chicago—and we were now in 1993. I spent a weekend at Trax with

Al working on material. He was smoking crack the entire time, it was horrible. The first track he played me was, by his admittance, another Keith LeBlanc refugee, either a disused Tackhead track, or an outtake from his *Major Malfunction* album. Whatever it was, it dated from the mid-80s, and boy, did it sound that way!

"Yeah, I think I traded this with Leblanc for a gram of speed!" Al said with a chuckle, "that New York poodle!" All is fair in love and war I suppose.

I sat on the couch at the back of Trax "A" room, bored out of my mind while Al "twirled up a mix". I was beginning to recognise an ugly and Sisyphean pattern emerging: Al presses play, Al smokes crack, Al gets high, Al mixes whilst riding the high—a few minutes later, Al changes everything because what he mixes when he is high sounds dreadful when he is not high (which has historically worked adequately in rock music, giving us some of our favourite drug damaged classics, which we love because of their flaws, naming no names). But this was all happening within the six or seven minutes of the track. When he was high it sounded like 1985 trapped in some huge underground cavern, but five minutes later when he came down it sounded like 1985 had been run over by a bus.

Either way, I knew this was going absolutely nowhere, and I knew better than to mention it. Talking to people when high like this never resolves itself like a movie, where they quickly have an orchestra-swelling epiphany and hug you, howling, "I've been a fool, such a fool!" No. Al just kept chasing his leather-studded tail, babbling, occasionally announcing that Nash Kato from (90s one-hit wonders) Urge Overkill was coming down to contribute a vocal to the album, "Nash is a hoot, man! You're gonna fucking love him!!" I sincerely doubted that I would, and I suspected that he was possibly one of the Chicago rock dignitaries that may have woken up surrounded by paramedics *chez Jourgensen*. I sincerely doubted that he would be popping in to contribute a vocal. He was probably cowering in a corner somewhere clinging to his Urge Teddy Bear, whimpering.

I was, needless to say, wholly uninspired to sing, and really just wanted to go out and play. It was like being kept behind after class to write an essay, the fun was absent. My vocal is a passable amalgam informed by other lyrics, either used or unused, a runt brother to "Something Wonderful" from *Beers, Steers and Queers*. However, nothing had prepared me for the other track that Al had been working on. This time it was contemporary; he had actually been busy with it over the previous week or so. The plain fact is that you cannot fit a square peg into a round hole, and I couldn't do the title track, "Linger Ficken' Good". It was as if the Stray Cats had stolen all of Yello's equipment, a yawning 10-minute black hole of finger snappin', hand jivin', pig mucous. Al told me to write down as many metaphors for masturbation as I could think of, and get out there and sing them onto the track. I should have just told him to call Phildo, what had I to lose? Most of the time Al thought I was a killjoy anyway, but I had been so excited about this album that I didn't want to endanger the release, or the subsequent tour, so I did it, yuck! Was he was making me do it on purpose? Making me atone for not being the unhinged Scottish football hooligan he had wanted me to be? This was the end of the line for me. I would never collaborate with Al Jourgensen on music again. Not that I was resolute in this at that time, but I had a strong inkling. Thankfully, I did such a piss-poor job, I don't think I am on the title track at all, which turned out to be way beyond embarrassing. Clearly filler, taking up a half of Al's side, his saving grace was the track "Gila Copter", with vocals by Timothy Leary. Not that it was particularly good, but it was not embarrassing, and it gave interviewers something else to talk about.

A few months later, with the album mixed, Al and Paul had moved to Texas as they had threatened to, and I was ready to go on tour again. First of all, though, Paul and I were sent on a press junket to Europe for a week, our European record company being far more sympathetic than Sire in the US.

They were even marketing "Da Ya Think I'm Sexy" in a K-Y Jelly-filled bubble-pack sleeve on clear vinyl—with the full cooperation of the manufacturers of K-Y, I may add. (On a whim, whilst recording the vocal, I changed the lyric from "I'm sorry baby but I'm out of milk and cawfee" to "I'm sorry baby but I'm out of K-Y Jelly".) They had approached the company with the idea that the song was a fun and novel approach to safe sex with condoms and lubricant. Sensible fun! Yeah, right… I was happy to go along with this, though. I loved the packaging design, and I knew it would piss Al off.

After a transatlantic flight surrounded by hundreds of chirping and screeching boy scouts, we arrived at Heathrow at around 7 AM. We had a solid week of interviews: London, Paris, Cologne, and Amsterdam. I had called ahead to our A&R rep to make sure there was easy access to amphetamines at each of our ports of call. The rep was possibly the only A&R rep I have ever worked with who was not a two-faced, lying asshole; in fact she was enthusiastic, fun, honest, tolerant, loved drugs and drink, and was gorgeous. She was going to chaperone us good-naturedly through our week-long press tour. At that time in the UK, you could not turn without running into something Suede-related, it was like T-Rex-mania again. I felt mildly threatened because I thought Suede were a lot more exciting than us, but I did not voice this view; I just pretended that I thought they were crap to save face.

After a quick shower, it was down to the bar for a breakfast of lager and cigs. Speed was on the way, so there was no need to worry about jetlag. Jetlag is for complete sissies, certainly not the Revolting Cocks. The journalists started to arrive about eleven, some we spoke to together, some on our own. A lot of the questions were the same, so Paul and I started to get bored pretty quickly (I think by about 11.45 AM). So it was at this point we started to make up incredible lies to amuse ourselves as the day wore on. Eventually we were out speeding and clubbing around London with little miss cutie-pie A&R and her femme-fatale androgenous boyfriend, with unfeasibly huge hoop earrings. It was lovely to be back in London, I thought, throwing up my curry in the club bathroom.

In Paris, Paul and I decided to pretend we both had ailments of the leg, making every movement excruciating-looking for the baffled journalists and photographers. It did not however, impede their confounding existentialism, in both the incredibly infuriating questions they asked ("So what exactly are you asking in 'Da Ya Think I'm Sexy?' And exactly who are you asking? Are you turning Rod Stewart into a malignant figure? An evil martyr?"), or the ludicrous poses they asked us to fashion in their photographs ("Perhaps eef wan uv you liess oan zee floor, and zee uzzer ess standing above like zee crucifeex?"). They clearly didn't give a crap about our gangrenous appendages, and as soon as we could, we limped off in a huff to the supermarket on the corner to purchase a few gallons of cheap *vin rouge*. That night we were taken to a party on a boat by the singer from France's premier industrial/metal band, Treponem Pal. He became annoyed at me when I wouldn't take acid with him. I heard a French rapper start to do his thing at the end of the deck, and as there were no slinky French models to be seen anywhere on this *bateau d'ugly mugs*, I jumped ship and took a taxi back to my hotel, lolling around the bar for a couple before trickling into my room.

In Cologne, I found myself standing in the Museum Ludwig confronted with a huge Hermann Nitsch painting, the one where he cut himself open and rolled down a strip of canvas about six feet high by a mile long. This was just the tonic for the hangover I still had from Paris. I turned around to a huge bank of televisions splattering that fast edit, over-sensory art that was so popular in the late 80s/early 90s—so popular, that is, with everyone but me. I can overload my own senses very well without your help, Mattheus, or whatever the fuck your name is, thank you very much.

The German press round was the same as the French one, but with an added layer of gravity, making it a gruelling seven hours of lying through our teeth, but being extra cautious to give drastically different lies to the Germans than those we gave to the French. Eventually we shooed the last of them out, grunting and huffing their way from the hotel to give us time to lager 'n' lather before hitting a few nightspots.

Finally, Amsterdam; we were spending two and a half days here, joined by A&R cutie's hoopy boy again. It was a Saturday afternoon, so

Paul and I went out to do a bit of shopping. By the time we got back to the hotel, the local distributor of our products in Benelux had dropped off his own weight in crystal meth to bolster me through a Saturday night in Amsterdam. We had dinner and went to the famous Milkweg, where I hid in a corner and snorted dessert until about four in the morning… I was not feeling so clever the next day. Well, I may as well speak for myself: I felt hideous, and we had a lot of press to do. However, it was just holding court in the hotel bar with a constantly replenishing glass of Grolsch and a Silk Cut that never went out. I could handle it, and this pattern continued for the next day in the same bar, same chair, until we had to split to fly back to London, leaving a huge amount of speed languishing in a bin by the elevators. Sad, but if I had done it, I probably would have perforated my blood, and who wants perforated blood?

Back in London, the record company took us out for a meal, and we called it a night. Paul had an early flight, but I was staying to do one more day of press before heading back to the States, where I would meet up with Paul and the rest of the Cocks to make a video for "Da Ya Think I'm Sexy?" My day of press was the most annoying; I was now sick of talking about the record, and this crop of English journos… who probably were not "A" list like the ones when we first arrived… were just knuckleheads writing for mostly knuckleheaded metal magazines. I managed to blah blah my way through it, meeting up in my hotel bar with Mary Byker, and then later Miki Berenyi, where I instructed them to order everything possible on the menu. The record company would be footing the bill.

It's a big jump physically and mentally from the bustling streets of London to the death rattle glare of Texas, but, there I was; a day later at a Westin Hotel in the middle of nowhere (nearest town: Waco), to shoot the "Da Ya Think I'm Sexy?" video. The director was an old friend of Mikey's, Tom Rainone, who had a lot of film credits under his belt— mostly horror, mostly special effects. He is a very sick puppy, but a very likeable sick puppy. The night before we all arrived, he had stayed up all night drinking with Mikey, ending the evening at 11 AM in the morning by careering off the road and crashing into his neighbour's front yard lawn furniture. Tom still lived with his mother, so this was the cause of much shame. He had a collection of Henry Lee Lucas paintings, and a couple of John Wayne Gacy's, of which he was particularly proud. His family also owned a disused airstrip, littered with warplanes and other aircraft, and covered in guns, guns, guns—I have never seen so many guns. One of his relatives gave me a ride and he had a grocery bag full of guns, which his four-year-old daughter was rifling (ha! rifling!!) through, calling out the names of the guns. ("That's right sweetheart, LUGER," said daddy.)

The airstrip was where we would be shooting the bulk of the video, which was to be a horror-short, with a celebrity cast of extras, strippers and B-movie actors, including: Ed Neal, famous for his role in the movie *The Texas Chainsaw Massacre* as the hitcher; and Jewell Sheppard, famous for her many roles including *Hollywood Hot Tubs*. There were others, many starlets from much gore. I ran into Jewell Sheppard as I was checking-in upon arrival, but I did not know who she was, and she did not know who I was, but we developed a rapport almost instantly, and I soon learned that she would be my "love interest" in the video, before she turned into a serpent-tongued witch at the end. She was fantastic—I had a pal for the week, and a sexually charged undercurrent to go along with it! Ta-da!!!

The shooting schedule was intense. Every day a new crop of made-up freaks showed up at our little Dante's Inferno; a huge air-hangar littered with bombers and tanks—augmented now with fossilised grandparents—giant serpents' heads, enough skulls and bones to make Auschwitz look like a Kentucky Fried Chicken dumpster, and oh, did I mention, strippers, strippers, strippers…. Although gruelling, it was really good fun, and I got a taste of what it was like to work under direction, which I enjoyed. We were also joined by Paul Elledge and his producer Leasha, who were going to take photographs of the week. He had done the sleeve to *Psalm 69*, and would go on to do many other Ministry covers, videos, and graphics. (He would also end up officiating my wedding in 2004!). I don't think I spoke to Al the whole week, enjoying the company of Paul and

Bill, and spending an unhealthy amount of time with my "love interest". Eventually, we had to make out on camera, as I unzipped her dress to reveal the lizard tongued harpy. It was fun to make out for a few seconds, even if it was fake making out. You know, hooray for Hollywood, and all that.

Guns, guns, guns, strippers, strippers, strippers. Other highlights included Paul Barker on a bucking bronco machine that was a missile instead of a horse—I bet he couldn't sit down for days after that. There was also a tense evening where I had to sprint across the floor avoiding an upside-down trapeze artist brandishing a lit flame-thrower. I had just about had my fill of tits jiggling and weapons being brandished. Texans, as you may know, love this kind of thing—a lot. The video was fantastic when Tom finally finished it and we were all thrilled. But they were not so thrilled at Sire, our record company; scuppering our plans for a follow up video for "Mr Lucky" featuring TELLY SAVALAS!! It never happened, in fact, the record never really happened in the US; while in the UK, "Sexy" even scraped the bottom reaches of the charts. I held my breath and waited for a call from *Top of the Pops*, but that, like so many things in my life, never came. (Awwwwwwwww!)

Instead, we managed to get Sire to bankroll one more video, this time for "Crackin' Up"—and this time no tits and blood, you kids, understand? We want a clean, dancey, happy video they can show on MTV and VH1. Okay, okay... So poor Tom was unceremoniously dumped, and we had a Japanese director on board. We were shooting in L.A., so Jewell came out to the airport to collect me; I had the afternoon to kill before shooting so we went to see *Mrs Doubtfire*. The video was shot using a blue screen, the studio was all blue screen—you couldn't walk anywhere that was not either blue or screen, there was nothing blue screener in the world, I tell you. So as you might imagine, the video is the Cocks cavorting around over giant spirals and things—kind of like something Deee-Lite would do, but with ugly rockers instead of prissy NYC DJs. It was perfectly inoffensive I suppose. Al, at the time, was friends with Johnny Depp, being involved in his short lived "P" band, and could barely talk about anything else except that "Mr D" might come by to visit—the subtext being that he was Al's friend and no one else got to talk to him. They were both very busy celebs and couldn't possibly talk to us. Of course "Mr D" never arrived, but Timothy Leary showed up for a cameo in the video. I think this was at the time where it was mandatory to have Timothy Leary in your video, he came with the cameras and film stock.

It was coming to the end of the year, and we were going on tour to support *Linger Ficken' Good*. I was really excited to tour, and to try out these songs live. Plus, I was just bored out of my mind in general and need to blow off some steam with a long tour.

I received a phone call, I can't remember who from—it certainly was not Al—telling me that there would be no tour. Al didn't want to. *Linger Ficken' Good*, having been sabotaged by Al's lukewarm creative input and his eventual disinterest in the whole project, sank without a trace.

The postscript to this was Paul and Bill remixing "Crackin' Up" for the single release, only to have their creativity usurped by Al when he asked to "tweak" the mix a little before they finished. I think he spent two weeks undoing what Paul and Bill had done, turning the already bland song into something so horribly embarrassing. I couldn't wait to disown my legacy.

I never recorded or collaborated with Al again, and although I maintained a close friendship with Paul, meetings with Al were very few and far between. His attitude towards me ranged from mild camaraderie to cold disdain, as I would occasionally visit studio sessions and the odd Ministry gig. Gaps between the records increased and the rumours of Al's drug use became as pathetic as they were incredible. Everyone just got on with their lives, I suppose.

# CONNECT THE GODDAMN DOTS

**Left:** Tucker and me, up to our old antics, 1994.

**Below:** The Damage Manual.

**Bottom:** The world's quietest band on blue vinyl.

TVT 8710-0

songs for **swingin'** junkies

Chris **Connelly &** William **Tucker**

WAX TRAX!     TVT RECORDS

side a. heartburn
side b. the hawk,
        the butcher,
        a killer of beauties

# AFTERMATH

## POSTSCRIPT 1: AUSTIN, 1994

I was on the road with Tucker as "the world's quietest band"—he played guitar, I sang. This was about a year after *Linger Ficken' Good* had been released.

We played at Emo's in Austin, and Al came to the show along with Mikey. He, Mikey, and Paul had all moved down to Austin. Paul was living with his family close to the city centre, whereas Al was living about an hour outside of town in what may as well have been Southfork Ranch, a sprawling, palatial, rock star dream house. Somewhere between a ranch and a hotel, it had been used in the 70s to "entertain" corporate clients—hookers, golf, the usual stuff businessmen seem to enjoy. Now it belonged to Al and it was kind of the fulfilment of all of his rock star aspirations. It was horrible—it was like *The Shining* with electric guitars—I hated it.

After Tucker and I played, he invited us back and we jumped into his sports car, Al tearing through the streets of Austin with an eight ball of coke down his boot. Eventually, we were stopped by a cop, and with some incredible sleight-of-hand moves, Al got us unstopped by the cop and we were on our merry way.

The living room(s), bedroom(s), tennis court(s), and golf course(s) seemed to sprawl on forever, reminding me of Hugh Hefner's pad in *Star 80*, except there seemed to be guns lying all around the place.

Tucker and I sat and listened while Al boasted away about how he was gonna do this, how he was gonna buy that, while we did a bunch of coke and drank. I realized that this was a person whom I did not know, and whose prime directive at that moment was to hammer home how successful he was and to steamroller over anything I might have to say.

I woke up on the porch in the baking morning sun, which—unbeknownst to me when I had curled up for the night—had been very recently painted; I was covered in two-inch green stripes. Feeling wretched, Tucker and I managed to hitch a ride back to Austin.

It would be less than a year before the DEA burst through the door and apprehended everyone in the compound, bringing Al's palace of industrial rock to an end. Redrum! Redrum!

## POSTSCRIPT 2: TUCKER, 1999

It's a fair assumption to say that Tucker and I drifted apart slowly. We both went our separate ways musically over time, but remained friends, occasionally collaborating. The last time we appeared together was at a New Year's party for the almost defunct Wax Trax! at a loft in Chicago. Along with Paul Barker, we formed a one-off band called Gloryhole, playing glam-rock nuggets such as "Hello, Hurray", "Action", "Honaloochie Boogie", and "Rock 'n' Roll Suicide". It was a nice way to wind things down, although we weren't aware that we were winding anything down.

Tucker was always one of these people who I took for granted would be around forever, having been through so much together, and having been such excellent and dastardly complements to each other over the years. Tucker was unwell—he had been unwell for a long time, and had undergone exploratory surgeries with apparently no tangible diagnosis in sight. Through this time, Frank had been with him, sitting with him in waiting rooms for hours on end. I always thought that doctors dismissed Tucker as a drug addict on the hunt for painkillers, when in fact he was in agony around the clock.

One summer morning I was at work when I received a telephone call from a panicked friend telling me that Tucker was dead. I worked near his apartment so I left and ran the five or six blocks to where he lived. There was already a gathering of shocked friends with the distraught roommate who had found him.

Tucker had taken his own life because he was in far too much pain, physical pain that could not and would not be controlled. He was one of the best people I have ever known: a shockingly irreverent sense of humour, coupled with compassion, love, mischief, and an incredible musical know-how. He will always be missed.

A week later I got a summons from Al to get together and talk about what happened. Al, myself, and Paul drove to a bar, Al at the wheel of his SUV, one-hand steering, the other smoking a crack pipe, and forever digging into a huge gym bag to hunt for some other narcotic distraction. When we got to the bar, I asked what they wanted to drink. Al looked at me square in the face and said, "A Coke, Chris. I stopped drinking." Good for you, Al.

As soon as we sat down he asked me, "So what's the skinny?" I had barely begun to explain what had led up to Tucker taking his own life when Al said, "Man, I gotta get out of here, I'll catch up with you guys later."

I shrugged and wondered why he had bothered.

# POSTSCRIPT 3: DAMAGE MANUAL

About a year after Tucker's passing, I got a phone call from Martin at work. I had not been a part of any Pigface or related projects for about eight years, having tired of Martin's creative business practices—and also just sick in general of the genre I used to be a part of. I had continued to make increasingly melodic and introspective albums with musicians like Chris Bruce, who weren't interested in jackhammering the listener with sonic terrorism whilst singing like Fozzy Bear on crystal meth.

However, Martin had been working with Jah Wobble and Geordie Walker, from Public Image Ltd. and Killing Joke, respectively. I had enjoyed working with Geordie before and I had a lot of respect for Jah

Wobble, so I agreed to listen to what they were doing. In a few weeks I had written lyrics and recorded them at a studio in Chicago. I had done my bit and was now ready to tour and work with a new band.

It was not to be. I have never known such incredible power struggles and ended up trying to be a mediator between the other three. A first tour was aborted after a week in England with almost nightly fights— even before we played the first show. Wobble refused to show up for key rehearsals. There was an incredible fight in Southport in the dressing room after soundcheck (whilst I played pool with one of the crew), which pretty much drove the last nail into the coffin. Wobble was gone. A few months later we played a week of dates in the U.S. with Charles Levi on bass. This too, ground to a screeching halt. The death throes lasted until 2004, when we tried to put together a line-up with just me, Martin, Charles, and a few others. This too, choked on its own vomit—although the swan song album, *Limited Edition*, has its moments.

A 2001 tour with Pigface made me realise that I had come to dislike touring. It was just a series of episodes where you tried to find a clean bathroom and something to eat that wouldn't poison you. Audiences dwindled; I felt as bored as they probably did. I tried it one more time, mainly because Thrill Kill Kult were on the same bill and it was enticing to be on the road with Frank for a month. However, apart from our record-buying excursions, I was bored; sitting for hours a day watching *Tom and Jerry* and *Law & Order* on satellite TV in the bus (this was one major step forward: satellite TV).

Although I occasionally contribute to Pigface records, unfortunately it's for the few hundred bucks I get. The music is not exciting to me. As I have detailed earlier in the book, I changed gears musically. In the eyes of the audience that I had, this has proven to be a very difficult path to follow. However, I continue because I have to move forward and explore new ways of writing music. Even if I never release another record, I am always working on the next one.

# POSTSCRIPT 4: LUBBOCK, TEXAS, 2003

I was standing alone, onstage with my guitar, singing my songs; facing a tiny crowd comprised of three overweight teenage death metal bands, who opened for me, and their portly entourage. It was difficult for me to focus on my playing whilst marveling at these gormless, slack-jawed salad-dodgers; the only thing separating them from the thousands of cattle that inhabited this part of the USA was the fact that the cattle did not wear "Marilyn Manson" T-shirts.

There was no reason for me to be there. The fatties hated me as passionately as I hated the fatties; however, and perhaps lucky for me, this hatred remained tacit for the most part. Perhaps there was a threat that, at any given moment, someone like Ministry would sneak onstage and bulldoze the barn with some high octane DEATH ROCK. (I have become an expert over the years at reading the faces in an audience, not because I am any kind of rock 'n' roll anthropologist, but because the audiences are small enough that I can make these assumptions during the course of a set.) My only bitter satisfaction was that I would walk offstage without giving them anything they wanted.

I hated this tour. It was winter and freezing cold. We were sleeping in Walmart parking lots, using Walmart bathrooms. The band I was traveling with, bless them, were suspicious of almost any food that did not come from McDonalds, so I either didn't eat or satisfied myself with chocolate parfaits, being too polite to say anything. I had a sinus infection and I was miserable.

Okay! My crown has toppled! It had been a slow and steady decline over a decade to get to this point. As I stood on the stage I resolved to never do this again. I stopped playing and communicated my feelings to the crowd.

"You know what? You can all fuck off, ya fat bastards!"

It was about as eloquent as I could be.

# POSTSCRIPT 5: THE LAST TIME

The last time I performed with Ministry was at the Vic in Chicago. It was April of 2003 and I was asked to come up and sing "So What". The band sounded fantastic and it was great to be up there again. Al was in a great mood and danced about like a clown while I belted out the lyrics like it was 1990. This was just prior to Paul's decision to leave the band, and just after Al's decision to quit doing drugs. I was pleased to see him clean, humour intact, and in such buoyant spirits.

A while later, as I have mentioned before, I was asked to re-join the Cocks for an album and tour. Now that Paul had left—Bill quit years ago—there was no one from the original line-up left, and I was too scared to go by myself to Al's live-in studio somewhere in the middle of nowhere (nearest town, El Paso). I decided to not go and we have not spoken since.

The Cocks' album came out and I found it horrible. The tired histrionics of Jello Biafra and Gibby Haynes—along with Phildo, still keeping it real—plus a whole slew of misogynist jokes which made me sigh with relief that I had opted out. When the tour subsequently came through Chicago, I was too busy washing my hair or something.

# POST-POSTSCRIPT: THE MONKEY'S PAW?

April 2011

After a few false starts, there is to be a massive three-night celebration of the Wax Trax! label at Cabaret Metro. This will prove to bring much closure to many people, including myself—a celebration of Jim's and Dannie's lives and legacy, two beautiful people who are no longer here, who gave me everything.

Should we reform the Cocks? It's all for a very worthy cause, why not? Okay, we are NOT inviting Al. At least, I am not. Paul certainly isn't. The simple reason being, when you boil it down, he hates our guts, as he has made perfectly clear. No one wants to deal with him or his insane amount of Al-baggage, or his deluded and truly awe-inspiring sense of self-worth, and, well… we don't really need him. This is something we learned a long time ago when we were making *Linger Ficken' Good*, whilst he was on a six-month crack binge. He had long since run out of steam.

And what of the Cocks in 2011? Well, for a start, we weren't allowed to call ourselves the Cocks. The law offices of Petulant, Sulky, Infantile & Associates, attorneys to the Jourgensen concern, had made that perfectly clear. So myself, Paul Barker, Luc Van Acker, Duane Buford, Jamie Duffy, and Dan Brill were the "Cocks" cover band, We were to play twice, a Saturday night and a Sunday night, along with former members of KMFDM—who also were not allowed to call themselves that, as Sascha was having DAS TANTRUM somewhere in Germany about not being invited. No one wanted to deal with him either. Although he did, along with Al, post (another) manifesto on his site and the Ministry site affirming his and Als' solidarity—they actually hate each other's guts, always have—and WOE BETIDE ANYONE who even BREATHES their hallowed NAMES or their hallowed BAND NAMES anywhere near anything, anytime. One could imagine the inside of their situation room: the 50+ year-old sagging cyberpunks, dreadlocked and mohawked satanic Mr Potato Heads, as they huddled around computer screens typing out instructions to the five or six industrial lap dogs that had not yet been euthanized by time. Again, no one really cared what they thought, and the show went ahead with everyone enjoying themselves and having a great time.

Front 242 played twice, and boy was I wrong about poor old Richard 23. He is actually a lovely guy who kept everyone backstage in stitches with his capers. Luc was his usual self, and noises were even made about doing another Cocks record, and playing more shows, but ultimately, I think that was that. We all have our own very busy lives, and I don't think anyone wishes to look back.

Recently, Paul, Bill, and I—along with (but separately from) Al— did a long probing interview about the making of *The Mind is a Terrible Thing to Taste*. Again, Al shrieked to the high heavens about how we, and especially I, did nothing on that album, how I was a talentless poseur, and how he is working out five hours a day, has quit drugs… blah, blah… quit drinking… blah, blah… AGAIN, nobody cares. An asshole is an asshole, whether addicted to drugs or not. It's good to know his jaw muscles are unscathed…

And, so on it goes…

# ABBREVIATED DISCOGRAPHY

**Albums with the Revolting Cocks**

*Revolting Cocks: Live! You Goddamned Son of a Bitch!* (1988)

*Beers, Steers and Queers* (1990)

*Linger Ficken' Good... and Other Barnyard Oddities* (1993)

**Albums with Ministry**

*The Land of Rape and Honey* (1988)

*The Mind is a Terrible Thing to Taste* (1989)

*Psalm 69* (1992)

**Albums with Pigface**

*Gub* (1991)

*Welcome to Mexico... Asshole* (1991)

*Fook* (1992)

*Easy Listening... for Difficult Fuckheads* (2003)

**Solo Albums**

*Whiplash Boychild* (1991)

*Phenobarb Bambalam* (1992)

*Shipwreck* (1994)

*The Ultimate Seaside Companion* (as The Bells) (1997)

*Blonde Exodus* (as Chris Connelly and The Bells) (2001)

*Private Education* (2002)

*Night of Your Life* (2004)

*The Episodes* (2007)

*Forgiveness & Exile* (2008)

*Pentland Firth Howl* (2009)

*How This Ends* (2010)

*Artificial Madness* (2011)

Excerpted from *www.chrisconnelly.com/discography/*

Lightning Source UK Ltd.
Milton Keynes UK
UKHW051504220822
407634UK00002B/7